The Great Books Reading & Discussion Program

THIRD SERIES · VOLUME ONE

D1160822

The Great Books Foundation
A Nonprofit Educational Corporation

Designed by Don Walkoe Design, Chicago

Handmade marbled paper, photographed on cover,
courtesy of Skycraft Designs, Gresham, Oregon.

9 8 7 6 5 4 3

Published and distributed by

The Great Books Foundation
A Nonprofit Educational Corporation
35 East Wacker Drive, Suite 2300
Chicago, Illinois 60601-2298

Acknowledgments

"Habits and Will" from *Human Nature and Conduct* in Volume 14 of *The Middle Works, 1899–1924* by John Dewey, edited by Jo Ann Boydston. Reprinted by permission of the publisher, Center for Dewey Studies, Southern Illinois University at Carbondale.

"History of the Peloponnesian War" from *History of the Peloponnesian War* by Thucydides, translated by Rex Warner. Copyright 1954 by Rex Warner. Reprinted by permission of the publisher, Penguin Books, Ltd.

"What is War?" from *On War* by Karl von Clausewitz, translated by O. J. Matthijs Jolles. Copyright 1943 by Random House, Inc. Reprinted by permission of the publisher.

"Uncle Vanya" from *Chekhov: The Major Plays*, translated by Ann Dunnigan. Copyright 1964 by Ann Dunnigan. Reprinted by permission of the publisher, The New American Library, Inc.

"On Evil" from *The Guide of the Perplexed*, Vol. II, Part III, by Moses Maimonides, translated by Shlomo Pines. Copyright 1963 by The University of Chicago. Reprinted by permission of the publisher, The University of Chicago Press.

"The Iliad" from *The Iliad* by Homer, translated by Robert Fitzgerald. Copyright 1974 by Robert Fitzgerald. Reprinted by permission of the publisher, Doubleday & Company, Inc.

"Principles of Government" from *The Spirit of the Laws* by Baron de Montesquieu, translated by Thomas Nugent. Copyright 1949 by Hafner Publishing Company. Reprinted by permission of the publisher, Macmillan Publishing Company, Inc.

"The Canterbury Tales" from *The Canterbury Tales* by Geoffrey Chaucer, translated by Nevill Coghill. Copyright 1952 by Nevill Coghill. Reprinted by permission of the publisher, Penguin Books, Ltd.

"Agamemnon" from *The Oresteia* by Aeschylus, translated by Robert Fagles. Copyright 1977 by Robert Fagles. Reprinted by permission of the publisher, Viking Penguin Inc.

"The Prince" from *The Prince, A Bilingual Edition* by Niccolò Machiavelli, translated and edited by Mark Musa. Copyright 1964 by St. Martin's Press, Inc. Reprinted by permission of the publisher, St. Martin's Press, Inc.

"The Death of Ivan Ilych" from *The Death of Ivan Ilych and Other Stories* by Leo Tolstoy, translated by Louise and Aylmer Maude. Reprinted by permission of the publisher, Oxford University Press, Inc.

A source note appears, together with biographical information about the author, opposite the opening page of each work in this series. Footnotes by the author are not bracketed; footnotes by GBF or a translator are [bracketed].

CONTENTS

*

JOHN DEWEY was born in Vermont in 1859. His father was a grocer, but Dewey was descended from a long line of New England farmers. Dewey attended the University of Vermont and received his Doctor of Philosophy degree in 1884 from Johns Hopkins University. He taught philosophy at the University of Minnesota and the University of Michigan before accepting a position in 1894 as professor of philosophy and chairman of the department of philosophy, psychology, and pedagogy at the recently founded University of Chicago. At Chicago, Dewey established an experimental school for about a hundred students aged four to fifteen that was useful as a laboratory for his educational theories. This work won him national recognition, but in 1904 Dewey resigned from Chicago because of disagreements with the president of the university.
He went to Columbia University as professor of philosophy, teaching there until 1930. Dewey was a prolific writer on philosophy, education, and psychology until his death in 1952. His works include *How We Think* (1910), *Democracy and Education* (1916), and *Human Nature and Conduct* (1922).

From *Human Nature and Conduct*, in *The Middle Works, 1899–1924*, edited by Jo Ann Boydston. Publisher: Southern Illinois University Press, 1978. Volume 14, pages 21–32.

Habits and Will

It is a significant fact that in order to appreciate the peculiar place of habit in activity we have to betake ourselves to bad habits, foolish idling, gambling, addiction to liquor and drugs. When we think of such habits, the union of habit with desire and with propulsive power is forced upon us. When we think of habits in terms of walking, playing a musical instrument, typewriting, we are much given to thinking of habits as technical abilities existing apart from our likings and as lacking in urgent impulsion. We think of them as passive tools waiting to be called into action from without. A bad habit suggests an inherent tendency to action and also a hold, command over us. It makes us do things we are ashamed of, things which we tell ourselves we prefer not to do. It overrides our formal resolutions, our conscious decisions. When we are honest with ourselves we acknowledge that a habit has this power because it is so intimately a part of ourselves. It has a hold upon us because we are the habit.

Our self-love, our refusal to face facts, combined perhaps with a sense of a possible better although unrealized self, leads us to eject the habit from the thought of ourselves and conceive it as an evil power which has somehow overcome us. We feed our conceit by recalling that the habit was not deliberately formed; we never intended to become idlers or gamblers or roués. And how can anything be deeply ourselves which developed accidentally, without set intention? These traits of a bad habit are precisely the things which are most instructive about all habits and about ourselves. They teach us that all habits are affections, that all have projectile power, and that a predisposition formed by a number of specific acts is an immensely more intimate and fundamental part of ourselves than are vague, general, conscious choices. All habits are demands for certain kinds of activity; and they constitute the self. In any intelligible sense of the word will, they *are* will. They form our effective desires and they furnish us with our working capacities. They rule our thoughts, determining which shall appear and be strong and which shall pass from light into obscurity.

We may think of habits as means, waiting, like tools in a box, to be used by conscious resolve. But they are something more than that. They are active means, means that project themselves, energetic and dominating ways of acting. We need to distinguish between materials, tools and means proper. Nails and boards are not strictly speaking means of a box. They are only materials for making it. Even the saw and hammer are means only when they are employed in some actual making. Otherwise they are tools, or potential means. They are actual means only when brought in conjunction with eye, arm, and hand in some specific operation. And eye, arm, and hand are, correspondingly, means proper only when they are in active operation. And whenever they are in action they are cooperating with external materials and energies. Without support from beyond themselves the eye stares blankly and the hand moves fumblingly. They are means only when they enter into organization with things which independently accomplish definite results. These organizations are habits.

This fact cuts two ways. Except in a contingent sense, with an "if," neither external materials nor bodily and mental organs are in themselves means. They have to be employed in coordinated conjunction with one another to be actual means, or habits. This statement may seem like the formulation in technical language of a commonplace. But belief in magic has played a large part in human history. And the essence of all hocus-pocus is the supposition that results can be accomplished without the joint adaptation to each other of human powers and physical conditions. A desire for rain may induce men to wave willow branches and to sprinkle water. The reaction is natural and innocent. But men then go on to believe that their act has immediate power to bring rain without the cooperation of intermediate conditions of nature. This is magic; while it may be natural or spontaneous, it is not innocent. It obstructs intelligent study of operative conditions and wastes human desire and effort in futilities.

Belief in magic did not cease when the coarser forms of superstitious practice ceased. The principle of magic is found whenever it is hoped to get results without intelligent control of means; and also when it is supposed that means can exist and yet remain inert and inoperative. In morals and politics such expectations still prevail, and insofar the most important phases of human action are still affected by magic. We think that by feeling strongly enough about something, by wishing hard enough, we can get a desirable result, such as virtuous execution of a good resolve, or peace among nations, or good will in industry. We slur over the necessity of the cooperative action of objective conditions, and the fact that this cooperation is assured only by persistent and close study. Or, on the other hand, we fancy we can get these results by external machinery, by tools or potential means, without a corresponding functioning of human desires and capacities. Often times these two false and contradictory beliefs are combined in the same person. The man who feels that *his* virtues are his own personal accomplishments is likely to be also the one who thinks that by passing laws he can throw the fear of God into others and make them virtuous by edict and prohibitory mandate.

Recently a friend remarked to me that there was one superstition current among even cultivated persons. They suppose that if one is told what to do, if the right *end* is pointed to them, all that is required in order to bring about the right act is will or wish on the part of the one who is to act. He used as an illustration the matter of physical posture; the assumption is that if a man is told to stand up straight, all that is further needed is wish and effort on his part, and the deed is done. He pointed out that this belief is on a par with primitive magic in its neglect of attention to the means which are involved in reaching an end. And he went on to say that the prevalence of this belief, starting with false notions about the control of the body and extending to control of mind and character, is the greatest bar to intelligent social progress. It bars the way because it makes us neglect intelligent inquiry to discover the means which will produce a desired result, and intelligent invention to procure the means. In short, it leaves out the importance of intelligently controlled habit.

We may cite his illustration of the real nature of a physical aim or order and its execution in its contrast with the current false notion. A man who has a bad habitual posture tells himself, or is told, to stand up straight. If he is interested and responds, he braces himself, goes through certain movements, and it is assumed that the desired result is substantially attained; and that the position is retained at least as long as the man keeps the idea or order in his mind. Consider the assumptions which are here made. It is implied that the means or effective conditions of the realization of a purpose exist independently of established habit and even that they may be set in motion in opposition to habit. It is assumed that means are there, so that the failure to stand erect is wholly a matter of failure of purpose and desire. It needs paralysis or a broken leg or some other equally gross phenomenon to make us appreciate the importance of objective conditions.

Now in fact a man who *can* stand properly does so, and only a man who can, does. In the former case, fiats of will are unnecessary, and in the latter useless. A man who does not stand properly forms a habit of standing improperly, a positive, force-ful habit. The common implication that his mistake is merely negative, that he is simply failing to do the right thing, and that the failure can be made good by an order of will is absurd. One might as well suppose that the man who is a slave of whiskey-drinking is merely one who fails to drink water. Conditions have been formed for producing a bad result, and the bad result will occur as long as those conditions exist. They can no more be dismissed by a direct effort of will than the conditions which create drought can be dispelled by whistling for wind. It is as reasonable to expect a fire to go out when it is ordered to stop burning as to suppose that a man can stand straight in consequence of a direct action of thought and desire. The fire can be put out only by changing objective conditions; it is the same with rectification of bad posture.

Of course something happens when a man acts upon his idea of standing straight. For a little while, he stands differently, but only a different kind of badly. He then takes the unaccustomed feeling which accompanies his unusual stand as evidence that he is now standing right. But there are many ways of standing badly, and he has simply shifted his usual way to a compensatory bad way at some opposite extreme. When we realize this fact, we are likely to suppose that it exists because control of the *body* is physical and hence is external to mind and will. Transfer the command inside character and mind, and it is fancied that an idea of an end and the desire to realize it will take immediate effect. After we get to the point of recognizing that habits must intervene between wish and execution in the case of bodily acts, we still cherish the illusion that they can be dispensed with in the case of mental and moral acts. Thus the net result is to make us sharpen the distinction between non-moral and moral activities, and to lead us to confine the latter strictly within a private, immaterial realm. But in fact, formation of ideas as well as their execution depends upon habit. *If* we could form a correct idea without a correct habit, then possibly we could carry it out irrespective of habit. But a wish gets definite form only in connection with an idea, and an idea gets shape and consistency only when it has a habit back of it. Only when a man can already perform an act of standing straight does he know what it is like to have a right posture and only then can he summon the idea required for proper execution. The act must come before the thought, and a habit before an ability to evoke the thought at will. Ordinary psychology reverses the actual state of affairs.

Ideas, thoughts of ends, are not spontaneously generated. There is no immaculate conception of meanings or purposes. Reason pure of all influence from prior habit is a fiction. But pure sensations out of which ideas can be framed apart from habit are equally fictitious. The sensations and ideas which are the "stuff" of thought and purpose are alike affected by habits manifested in the acts which give rise to sensations and meanings. The dependence of thought, or the more intellectual factor in our conceptions, upon prior experience is usually admitted. But those who attack the notion of thought pure from the influence of experience, usually identify experience with sensations impressed upon an empty mind. They therefore replace the theory of unmixed thoughts with that of pure unmixed sensations as the stuff of all conceptions, purposes, and beliefs. But distinct and independent sensory qualities, far from being original elements, are the products of a highly skilled analysis which disposes of immense technical scientific resources. To be able to single out a definitive sensory element in any field is evidence of a high degree of previous training, that is, of well-formed habits. A moderate amount of observation of a child will suffice to reveal that even such gross discriminations as black, white, red, green, are the result of some years of active dealings with things in the course of which habits have been set up. It is not such a simple matter to have a clear-cut sensation. The latter is a sign of training, skill, habit.

Admission that the idea of, say, standing erect is dependent upon sensory materials is, therefore, equivalent to recognition that it is dependent upon the habitual attitudes which govern concrete sensory materials. The medium of habit filters all the material that reaches our perception and thought. The filter is not, however, chemically pure. It is a reagent which adds new qualities and rearranges what is received. Our ideas truly depend upon experience, but so do our sensations. And the experience upon which they both depend is the operation of habits—originally of instincts. Thus our purposes and commands regarding action (whether physical or moral) come to us through the refracting medium of bodily and moral habits. Inability to think aright is sufficiently striking to have caught the attention of moralists. But a false psychology has led them to interpret it as due to a necessary conflict of flesh and spirit, not as an indication that our ideas are as dependent, to say the least, upon our habits as are our acts upon our conscious thoughts and purposes.

Only the man who can maintain a correct posture has the stuff out of which to form that idea of standing erect which can be the starting point of a right act. Only the man whose habits are already good can know what the good is. Immediate, seemingly instinctive, feeling of the direction and end of various lines of behavior is in reality the feeling of habits working below direct consciousness. The psychology of illusions of perception is full of illustrations of the distortion introduced by habit into observation of objects. The same fact accounts for the intuitive element in judgments of action, an element which is valuable or the reverse in accord with the quality of dominant habits. For, as Aristotle remarked, the untutored moral perceptions of a good man are usually trustworthy, those of a bad character, not. (But he should have added that the influence of social custom as well as personal habit has to be taken into account in estimating who is the good man and the good judge.)

What is true of the dependence of execution of an idea upon habit is true, then, of the formation and quality of the idea.

Suppose that by a happy chance a right concrete idea or purpose—concrete, not simply correct in words—has been hit upon: What happens when one with an incorrect habit tries to act in accord with it? Clearly the idea can be carried into execution only with a mechanism already there. If this is defective or perverted, the best intention in the world will yield bad results. In the case of no other engine does one suppose that a defective machine will turn out good goods simply because it is invited to. Everywhere else we recognize that the design and structure of the agency employed tell directly upon the work done. Given a bad habit and the "will" or mental direction to get a good result, and the actual happening is a reverse or looking-glass manifestation of the usual fault—a compensatory twist in the opposite direction. Refusal to recognize this fact only leads to a separation of mind from body, and to supposing that mental or "psychical" mechanisms are different in kind from those of bodily operations and independent of them. So deep seated is this notion that even so "scientific" a theory as modern psychoanalysis thinks that mental habits can be straightened out by some kind of purely psychical manipulation without reference to the distortions of sensation and perception which are due to bad bodily sets. The other side of the error is found in the notion of "scientific" nerve physiologists that it is only necessary to locate a particular diseased cell or local lesion, independent of the whole complex of organic habits, in order to rectify conduct.

Means are means; they are intermediates, middle terms. To grasp this fact is to have done with the ordinary dualism of means and ends. The "end" is merely a series of acts viewed at a remote stage; and a means is merely the series viewed at an earlier one. The distinction of means and end arises in surveying the *course* of a proposed *line* of action, a connected series in time. The "end" is the last act thought of; the means are the acts to be performed prior to it in time. To *reach* an end we must take our mind off from it and attend to the act which is next to be performed. We must make that the end. The only exception to this statement is in cases where customary habit determines the course of the series. Then all that is wanted is a cue to set it off. But when the proposed end involves any deviation from usual action, or any rectification of it—as in the case of standing straight—then the main thing is to find some act which is different from the usual one. The discovery and performance of this unaccustomed act is the "end" to which we must devote all attention. Otherwise we shall simply do the old thing over again, no matter what is our conscious command. The only way of accomplishing this discovery is through a flank movement. We must stop even thinking of standing up straight. To think of it is fatal, for it commits us to the operation of an established habit of standing wrong. We must find an act within our power which is disconnected from any thought about standing. We must start to do another thing which on one side inhibits our falling into the customary bad position and on the other side is the beginning of a series of acts which may lead into the correct posture. The hard-drinker who keeps thinking of not drinking is doing what he can to initiate the acts which lead to drinking. He is starting with the stimulus to his habit. To succeed he must find some positive interest or line of action which will inhibit the drinking series and which by instituting another course of action will bring him to his desired end. In short, the man's true aim is to discover some course of action, having nothing to do with the habit of drink or standing erect, which will take him where he wants to go. The discovery of this other series is at once his means and his end. Until one takes intermediate acts seriously enough to treat them as ends, one wastes one's time in any effort at change of habits. Of the intermediate acts, the most important is the *next* one. The first or earliest means is the most important *end* to discover.

Means and ends are two names for the same reality. The terms denote not a division in reality but a distinction in judgment. Without understanding this fact we cannot understand the nature of habits nor can we pass beyond the usual separation of the moral and non-moral in conduct. "End" is a name for a series of acts taken collectively—like the term army. "Means" is a name for the same series taken distributively—like this soldier, that officer. To think of the end signifies to extend and enlarge our view of the act to be performed. It means to look at the next act in perspective, not permitting it to occupy the entire field of vision. To bear the end in mind signifies that we should not stop thinking about our *next* act until we form some reasonably clear idea of the *course* of action to which it commits us. To attain a remote end means on the other hand to treat the end as a series of means. To say that an end is remote or distant, to say in fact that it is an end at all, is equivalent to saying that obstacles intervene between us and it. If, however, it remains a distant end, it becomes a *mere* end, that is a dream. As soon as we have projected it, we must begin to work backward in thought. We must change *what* is to be done into a *how*, the means whereby. The end thus reappears as a series of "what nexts," and the what next of chief importance is the one nearest the present state of the one acting. Only as the end is converted into means is it definitely conceived, or intellectually defined, to say nothing of being executable. Just as end, it is vague, cloudy, impressionistic. We do not *know* what we are really after until a *course* of action is mentally worked out. Aladdin with his lamp could dispense with translating ends into means, but no one else can do so.

Now the thing which is closest to us, the means within our power, is a habit. Some habit impeded by circumstances is the source of the projection of the end. It is also the primary means in its realization. The habit is propulsive and moves anyway toward some end, or result, whether it is projected as an end-in-view or not. The man who can walk does walk; the man who can talk does converse—if only with himself. How is this statement to be reconciled with the fact that we are not always walking and talking; that our habits seem so often to be latent, inoperative? Such inactivity holds only of *overt*, visibly obvious operation. In actuality each habit operates all the time of waking life; though like a member of a crew taking his turn at the wheel, its operation becomes the dominantly characteristic trait of an act only occasionally or rarely.

The habit of walking is expressed in what a man sees when he keeps still, even in dreams. The recognition of distances and directions of things from his place at rest is the obvious proof of this statement. The habit of locomotion is latent in the sense that it is covered up, counteracted, by a habit of seeing which is definitely at the fore. But counteraction is not suppression. Locomotion is a potential energy, not in any metaphysical sense, but in the physical sense in which potential energy as well as kinetic has to be taken account of in any scientific description. Everything that a man who has the habit of locomotion does and thinks, he does and thinks differently on that account. This fact is recognized in current psychology, but is falsified into an association of sensations. Were it not for the continued operation of all habits in every act, no such thing as character could exist. There would be simply a bundle, an untied bundle at that, of isolated acts. Character is the interpenetration of habits. If each habit existed in an insulated compartment and operated without affecting or being affected by others, character would not exist. That is, conduct would lack unity being only a juxtaposition of disconnected reactions to separated situations. But since environments overlap, since situations are continuous and those remote from one another contain like elements, a continuous modification of habits by one another is constantly going on. A man may give himself away in a look or a gesture. Character can be read through the medium of individual acts.

Of course interpenetration is never total. It is most marked in what we call strong characters. Integration is an achievement rather than a datum. A weak, unstable, vacillating character is one in which different habits alternate with one another rather than embody one another. The strength, solidity of a habit is not its own possession but is due to reinforcement by the force of other habits which it absorbs into itself. Routine specialization always works against interpenetration. Men with "pigeon-hole" minds are not infrequent. Their diverse standards and methods of judgment for scientific, religious, political matters testify to isolated compartmental habits of action. Character that is unable to undergo successfully the strain of thought and effort required to bring competing tendencies into a unity, builds up barriers between different systems of likes and dislikes. The emotional stress incident to conflict is avoided not by readjustment but by effort at confinement. Yet the exception proves the rule. Such persons are successful in keeping different ways of reacting apart from one another in consciousness rather than in action. Their character is marked by stigmata resulting from this division.

The mutual modification of habits by one another enables us to define the nature of the moral situation. It is not necessary nor advisable to be always considering the interaction of habits with one another, that is to say, the effect of a particular habit upon character—which is a name for the total interaction. Such consideration distracts attention from the problem of building up an effective habit. A man who is learning French, or chess-playing or engineering has his hands full with his particular occupation. He would be confused and hampered by constant inquiry into its effect upon character. He would resemble the centipede who by trying to think of the movement of each leg in relation to all the others was rendered unable to travel. At any given time, certain habits must be taken for granted as a matter of course. Their operation is not a matter of moral judg- ment. They are treated as technical, recreational, professional, hygienic or economic or esthetic rather than moral. To lug in morals, or ulterior effect on character at every point, is to cultivate moral valetudinarianism or priggish posing. Nevertheless any act, even that one which passes ordinarily as trivial, may entail such consequences for habit and character as upon occasion to require judgment from the standpoint of the whole body of conduct. It then comes under moral scrutiny. To know when to leave acts without distinctive moral judgment and when to subject them to it is itself a large factor in morality. The serious matter is that this relatively pragmatic, or intellectual, distinction between the moral and non-moral, has been solidified into a fixed and absolute distinction, so that some acts are popularly regarded as forever within and others forever without the moral domain. From this fatal error recognition of the relations of one habit to others preserves us. For it makes us see that character is the name given to the working interaction of habits, and that the cumulative effect of insensible modifications worked by a particular habit in the body of preferences may at any moment require attention.

The word habit may seem twisted somewhat from its customary use when employed as we have been using it. But we need a word to express that kind of human activity which is influenced by prior activity and in that sense acquired; which contains within itself a certain ordering or systematization of minor elements of action; which is projective, dynamic in quality, ready for overt manifestation; and which is operative in some subdued subordinate form even when not obviously dominating activity. Habit even in its ordinary usage comes nearer to denoting these facts than any other word. If the facts are recognized we may also use the words attitude and disposition. But unless we have first made clear to ourselves the facts which have been set forth under the name of habit, these words are more likely to be misleading than is the word habit. For the latter conveys explicitly the sense of operativeness, actuality. Attitude and, as ordinarily used, disposition suggest something latent, potential, something which requires a positive stimulus outside themselves to become active. If we perceive that they denote positive forms of action which are released merely through removal of some counteracting "inhibitory" tendency, and then become overt, we may employ them instead of the word habit to denote subdued, non-patent forms of the latter.

In this case, we must bear in mind that the word disposition means predisposition, readiness to act overtly in a specific fashion whenever opportunity is presented, this opportunity consisting in removal of the pressure due to the dominance of some overt habit; and that attitude means some special case of a predisposition, the disposition waiting as it were to spring through an opened door. While it is admitted that the word habit has been used in a somewhat broader sense than is usual, we must protest against the tendency in psychological literature to limit its meaning to repetition. This usage is much less in accord with popular usage than is the wider way in which we have used the word. It assumes from the start the identity of habit with routine. Repetition is in no sense the essence of habit. Tendency to repeat acts is an incident of many habits but not of all. A man with the habit of giving way to anger may show his habit by a murderous attack upon someone who has offended. His act is nonetheless due to habit because it occurs only once in his life. The essence of habit is an acquired predisposition to *ways* or modes of response, not to particular acts except as, under special conditions, these express a way of behaving. Habit means special sensitiveness or accessibility to certain classes of stimuli, standing predilections and aversions, rather than bare recurrence of specific acts. It means will.

JOHN STUART MILL, who claimed that his life was "uneventful," was born in 1806 in London, England. The son of a philosopher and reformer, Mill was faulted by his stern and domineering father for his "general slackness of mind," but he had learned Greek by the age of three, Latin at eight, logic at twelve, and political economy at thirteen. "The education which my father gave me," Mill noted, "was in itself much more fitted for training me to know than to do." As a young man, Mill went to work for his father at the British East India Company, where he remained for thirty-six years, writing works of philosophy and political economy meanwhile. When he was twenty, Mill experienced an emotional and intellectual crisis probably caused by overwork and his father's persistent meddling. He despaired of reason and read poetry for comfort. But Mill recovered: "I was no longer hopeless: I was not a stock or a stone." He met his future wife in 1830, but couldn't marry her until twenty years later, when her husband died. Their courtship was considered scandalous; Mill lost the esteem of many friends and his family. He served as a member of the House of Commons from 1865 to 1868 and died in Avignon, France, in 1873.

A selection from *On Liberty*, edited by Gertrude Himmelfarb. Publisher: Penguin Books, 1974. Portions of Chapters I, II, and III.

On Liberty

The subject of this Essay is not the so-called Liberty of the Will, so unfortunately opposed to the misnamed doctrine of Philosophical Necessity; but Civil, or Social Liberty: the nature and limits of the power which can be legitimately exercised by society over the individual. A question seldom stated, and hardly ever discussed, in general terms, but which profoundly influences the practical controversies of the age by its latent presence, and is likely soon to make itself recognised as the vital question of the future. It is so far from being new, that, in a certain sense, it has divided mankind, almost from the remotest ages; but in the stage of progress into which the more civilised portions of the species have now entered, it presents itself under new conditions, and requires a different and more fundamental treatment. . . .

The object of this Essay is to assert one very simple principle, as entitled to govern absolutely the dealings of society with the individual in the way of compulsion and control, whether the means used be physical force in the form of legal penalties, or the moral coercion of public opinion. That principle is, that the sole end for which mankind are warranted, individually or collectively, in interfering with the liberty of action of any of their number, is self-protection. That the only purpose for which power can be rightfully exercised over any member of a civilised community, against his will, is to prevent harm to others. His own good, either physical or moral, is not a sufficient warrant.

He cannot rightfully be compelled to do or forbear because it will be better for him to do so, because it will make him happier, because, in the opinions of others, to do so would be wise, or even right. These are good reasons for remonstrating with him, or reasoning with him, or persuading him, or entreating him, but not for compelling him, or visiting him with any evil in case he do otherwise. To justify that, the conduct from which it is desired to deter him must be calculated to produce evil to someone else. The only part of the conduct of anyone, for which he is amenable to society, is that which concerns others. In the part which merely concerns himself, his independence is, of right, absolute. Over himself, over his own body and mind, the individual is sovereign.

It is, perhaps, hardly necessary to say that this doctrine is meant to apply only to human beings in the maturity of their faculties. We are not speaking of children, or of young persons below the age which the law may fix as that of manhood or womanhood. Those who are still in a state to require being taken care of by others, must be protected against their own actions as well as against external injury. For the same reason, we may leave out of consideration those backward states of society in which the race itself may be considered as in its nonage. The early difficulties in the way of spontaneous progress are so great, that there is seldom any choice of means for overcoming them; and a ruler full of the spirit of improvement is warranted in the use of any expedients that will attain an end, perhaps otherwise unattainable. Despotism is a legitimate mode of government in dealing with barbarians, provided the end be their improvement, and the means justified by actually effecting that end. Liberty, as a principle, has no application to any state of things anterior to the time when mankind have become capable of being improved by free and equal discussion. Until then, there is nothing for them but implicit obedience to an Akbar or a Charlemagne, if they are so fortunate as to find one. But as soon as mankind have attained the capacity of being guided to their own improvement by conviction or persuasion (a period long since reached in all nations with whom we need here concern ourselves), compulsion, either in the direct form or in that of pains and penalties for non-compliance, is no longer admissible as a means to their own good, and justifiable only for the security of others.

It is proper to state that I forego any advantage which could be derived to my argument from the idea of abstract right, as a thing independent of utility.[1] I regard utility as the ultimate appeal on all ethical questions; but it must be utility in the largest sense, grounded on the permanent interests of man as a progressive being. Those interests, I contend, authorise the subjection of individual spontaneity to external control, only in respect to those actions of each, which concern the interest of other people. If anyone does an act hurtful to others, there is a *prima facie* case for punishing him, by law, or, where legal penalties are not safely applicable, by general disapprobation. There are also many positive acts for the benefit of others, which he may rightfully be compelled to perform; such as to give evidence in a court of justice; to bear his fair share in the common defence, or in any other joint work necessary to the interest of the society of which he enjoys the protection; and to perform certain acts of individual beneficence, such as saving a fellow-creature's life, or interposing to protect the defenceless against ill-usage, things which whenever it is obviously a man's duty to do, he may rightfully be made responsible to society for not doing. A person may cause evil to others not only by his actions but by his inaction, and in either case he is justly accountable to them for the injury. The latter case, it is true, requires a much more cautious exercise of compulsion than the former. To make anyone answerable for doing evil to others is the rule; to

---

[1] [By the utility of something, Mill means its ability to produce happiness.]

make him answerable for not preventing evil is, comparatively speaking, the exception. Yet there are many cases clear enough and grave enough to justify that exception. In all things which regard the external relations of the individual, he is *de jure* amenable to those whose interests are concerned, and, if need be, to society as their protector. There are often good reasons for not holding him to the responsibility; but these reasons must arise from the special expediencies of the case: either because it is a kind of case in which he is on the whole likely to act better, when left to his own discretion, than when controlled in any way in which society have it in their power to control him; or because the attempt to exercise control would produce other evils, greater than those which it would prevent. When such reasons as these preclude the enforcement of responsibility, the conscience of the agent himself should step into the vacant judgment seat, and protect those interests of others which have no external protection; judging himself all the more rigidly, because the case does not admit of his being made accountable to the judgment of his fellow-creatures.

But there is a sphere of action in which society, as distinguished from the individual, has, if any, only an indirect interest; comprehending all that portion of a person's life and conduct which affects only himself, or if it also affects others, only with their free, voluntary, and undeceived consent and participation. When I say only himself, I mean directly, and in the first instance; for whatever affects himself, may affect others through himself; and the objection which may be grounded on this contingency, will receive consideration in the sequel. This, then, is the appropriate region of human liberty. It comprises, first, the inward domain of consciousness; demanding liberty of conscience in the most comprehensive sense; liberty of thought and feeling; absolute freedom of opinion and sentiment on all subjects, practical or speculative, scientific, moral, or theological. The liberty of expressing and publishing opinions may seem to fall under a different principle, since it belongs to that part of the conduct of an individual which concerns other people; but, being almost of as much importance as the liberty of thought itself, and resting in great part on the same reasons, is practically inseparable from it. Secondly, the principle requires liberty of tastes and pursuits; of framing the plan of our life to suit our own character; of doing as we like, subject to such consequences as may follow: without impediment from our fellow-creatures, so long as what we do does not harm them, even though they should think our conduct foolish, perverse, or wrong. Thirdly, from this liberty of each individual, follows the liberty, within the same limits, of combination among individuals; freedom to unite, for any purpose not involving harm to others: the persons combining being supposed to be of full age, and not forced or deceived.

No society in which these liberties are not, on the whole, respected, is free, whatever may be its form of government; and none is completely free in which they do not exist absolute and unqualified. The only freedom which deserves the name, is that of pursuing our own good in our own way, so long as we do not attempt to deprive others of theirs, or impede their efforts to obtain it. Each is the proper guardian of his own health, whether bodily, *or* mental and spiritual. Mankind are greater gainers by suffering each other to live as seems good to themselves, than by compelling each to live as seems good to the rest. . . .

It will be convenient for the argument, if, instead of at once entering upon the general thesis, we confine ourselves in the first instance to a single branch of it, on which the principle here stated is, if not fully, yet to a certain point, recognised by the current opinions. This one branch is the Liberty of Thought: from which it is impossible to separate the cognate liberty of speaking and of writing. Although these liberties, to some considerable amount, form part of the political morality of all countries which profess religious toleration and free institutions, the grounds, both philosophical and practical, on which they rest, are perhaps not so familiar to the general mind, nor so thoroughly appreciated by many even of the leaders of opinion, as might have been expected. Those grounds, when rightly understood, are of much wider application than to only one division of the subject, and a thorough consideration of this part of the question will be found the best introduction to the remainder. Those to whom nothing which I am about to say will be new, may therefore, I hope, excuse me, if on a subject which for now three centuries has been so often discussed, I venture on one discussion more.

Of the Liberty of Thought and Discussion

The time, it is to be hoped, is gone by, when any defence would be necessary of the "liberty of the press" as one of the securities against corrupt or tyrannical government. No argument, we may suppose, can now be needed, against permitting a legislature or an executive, not identified in interest with the people, to prescribe opinions to them, and determine what doctrines or what arguments they shall be allowed to hear. This aspect of the question, besides, has been so often and so triumphantly enforced by preceding writers, that it needs not be specially insisted on in this place. Though the law of England, on the subject of the press, is as servile to this day as it was in the time of the Tudors, there is little danger of its being actually put in force against political discussion, except during some temporary panic, when fear of insurrection drives ministers and judges from their propriety; and, speaking generally, it is not, in constitutional countries, to be apprehended, that the government, whether completely responsible to the people or not, will often attempt to control the expression of opinion, except when in doing so it makes itself the organ of the general intolerance of the public. Let us suppose, therefore, that the government is entirely at one with the people, and never thinks of exerting any power of coercion unless in agreement with what it conceives to be their voice. But I deny the right of the people to exercise such coercion, either by themselves or by their government. The power itself is illegitimate. The best government has no more title to it than the worst. It is as noxious, or more noxious, when exerted in accordance with public opinion, than when in opposition to it.

If all mankind minus one were of one opinion, and only one person were of the contrary opinion, mankind would be no more justified in silencing that one person, than he, if he had the power, would be justified in silencing mankind. Were an opinion a personal possession of no value except to the owner; if to be obstructed in the enjoyment of it were simply a private injury, it would make some difference whether the injury was inflicted only on a few persons or on many. But the peculiar evil of silencing the expression of an opinion is, that it is robbing the human race; posterity as well as the existing generation; those who dissent from the opinion, still more than those who hold it. If the opinion is right, they are deprived of the opportunity of exchanging error for truth: if wrong, they lose, what is almost as great a benefit, the clearer perception and livelier impression of truth, produced by its collision with error.

It is necessary to consider separately these two hypotheses, each of which has a distinct branch of the argument corresponding to it. We can never be sure that the opinion we are endeavouring to stifle is a false opinion; and if we were sure, stifling it would be an evil still.

First: the opinion which it is attempted to suppress by authority may possibly be true. Those who desire to suppress it, of course deny its truth; but they are not infallible. They have no authority to decide the question for all mankind, and exclude every other person from the means of judging. To refuse a hearing to an opinion, because they are sure that it is false, is to assume that *their* certainty is the same thing as *absolute* certainty. All silencing of discussion is an assumption of infallibility. Its condemnation may be allowed to rest on this common argument, not the worse for being common.

Unfortunately for the good sense of mankind, the fact of their fallibility is far from carrying the weight in their practical judgment which is always allowed to it in theory; for while everyone well knows himself to be fallible, few think it necessary to take any precautions against their own fallibility, or admit the supposition that any opinion, of which they feel very certain, may be one of the examples of the error to which they acknowledge themselves to be liable. Absolute princes, or others who are accustomed to unlimited deference, usually feel this complete confidence in their own opinions on nearly all subjects. People more happily situated, who sometimes hear their opinions disputed, and are not wholly unused to be set right when they are wrong, place the same unbounded reliance only on such of their opinions as are shared by all who surround them, or to whom they habitually defer; for in proportion to a man's want of confidence in his own solitary judgment, does he usually repose, with implicit trust, on the infallibility of "the world" in general. And the world, to each individual, means the part of it with which he comes in contact; his party, his sect, his church, his class of society; the man may be called, by comparison, almost liberal and large-minded to whom it means anything so comprehensive as his own country or his own age. Nor is his faith in this collective authority at all shaken by his being aware that other ages, countries, sects, churches, classes, and parties have thought, and even now think, the exact reverse. He devolves upon his own world the responsibility of being in the right against the dissentient worlds of other people; and it never troubles him that mere accident has decided which of these numerous worlds is the object of his reliance, and that the same causes which make him a Churchman in London, would have made him a Buddhist or a Confucian in Peking. Yet it is as evident in itself, as any amount of argument can make it, that ages are no more infallible than individuals; every age having held many opinions which subsequent ages have deemed not only false but absurd; and it is as certain that many opinions now general will be rejected by future ages, as it is that many, once general, are rejected by the present.

The objection likely to be made to this argument would probably take some such form as the following. There is no greater assumption of infallibility in forbidding the propagation of error, than in any other thing which is done by public authority on its own judgment and responsibility. Judgment is given to men that they may use it. Because it may be used erroneously, are men to be told that they ought not to use it at all? To prohibit what they think pernicious, is not claiming exemption from error, but fulfilling the duty incumbent on them, although fallible, of acting on their conscientious conviction. If we were never to act on our opinions, because those opinions may be wrong, we should leave all our interest uncared for, and all our duties unperformed. An objection which applies to all conduct can be no valid objection to any conduct in particular. It is the duty of governments, and of individuals, to form the truest opinions they can; to form them carefully, and never impose them upon others unless they are quite sure of being right. But when they are sure (such reasoners may say), it is not conscientiousness but cowardice to shrink from acting on their opinions, and allow doctrines which they honestly think dangerous to the welfare of mankind, either in this life or in another, to be scattered abroad without restraint, because other people, in less enlightened times, have persecuted opinions now believed to be true. Let us take care, it may be said, not to make the same mistake: but governments and nations have made mistakes in other things, which are not denied to be fit subjects for the exercise of authority: they have laid on bad taxes, made unjust wars. Ought we therefore to lay on no taxes, and, under whatever provocation, make no wars? Men, and governments, must act to the best of their ability. There is no such thing as absolute certainty, but there is assurance sufficient for the purposes of human life. We may, and must, assume our opinion to be true for the guidance of our own conduct: and it is assuming no more when we forbid bad men to pervert society by the propagation of opinions which we regard as false and pernicious.

I answer, that it is assuming very much more. There is the greatest difference between presuming an opinion to be true, because, with every opportunity for contesting it, it has not been refuted, and assuming its truth for the purpose of not permitting its refutation. Complete liberty of contradicting and disproving our opinion is the very condition which justifies us in assuming its truth for purposes of action; and on no other terms can a being with human faculties have any rational assurance of being right.

When we consider the history of opinion, or the ordinary conduct of human life, to what is it to be ascribed that the one and the other are no worse than they are? Not certainly to the inherent force of the human understanding; for, on any matter not self-evident, there are ninety-nine persons totally incapable of judging of it for one who is capable; and the capacity of the hundredth person is only comparative; for the majority of the eminent men of every past generation held many opinions now known to be erroneous, and did or approved numerous things which no one will now justify. Why is it, then, that there is on the whole a preponderance among mankind of rational opinions and rational conduct? If there really is this preponderance—which there must be unless human affairs are, and have always been, in an almost desperate state—it is owing to a quality of the human mind, the source of everything respectable in man either as an intellectual or as a moral being, namely, that his errors are corrigible. He is capable of rectifying his mistakes, by discussion and experience. Not by experience alone. There must be discussion, to show how experience is to be interpreted. Wrong opinions and practices gradually yield to fact and argument; but facts and arguments, to produce any effect on the mind, must be brought before it. Very few facts are able to tell their own story, without comments to bring out their meaning. The whole strength and value, then, of human judgment, depending on the one property, that it can be set right when it is wrong, reliance can be placed on it only when the means of setting it right are kept constantly at hand. In the case of any person whose judgment is really deserving of confidence, how has it become so? Because he has kept his mind open to criticism of his opinions and conduct. Because it has been his practice to listen to all that could be said against him; to profit by as much of it as was just, and expound to himself, and upon occasion to others, the fallacy of what was fallacious. Because he has felt, that the only way in which a human being can make some approach to knowing the whole of a subject, is by hearing what can be said about it by persons of every variety of opinion, and studying all modes in which it can be looked at by every character of mind. No wise man ever acquired his wisdom in any mode but this; nor is it in the nature of human intellect to become wise in any other manner. The steady habit of correcting and completing his own opinion by collating it with those of others, so far from causing doubt and hesitation in carrying it into practice, is the only stable foundation for a just reliance on it: for, being cognisant of all that can, at least obviously, be said against him, and having taken up his position against all gainsayers—knowing that he has sought for objections and difficulties, instead of avoiding them, and has shut out no light which can be thrown upon the subject from any quarter—he has a right to think his judgment better than that of any person, or any multitude, who have not gone through a similar process. . . .

In the present age—which has been described as "destitute of faith, but terrified at scepticism"—in which people feel sure, not so much that their opinions are true, as that they should not know what to do without them—the claims of an opinion to be protected from public attack are rested not so much on its truth, as on its importance to society. There are, it is alleged, certain beliefs so useful, not to say indispensable, to well-being that it is as much the duty of governments to uphold those beliefs, as to protect any other of the interests of society. In a case of such necessity, and so directly in the line of their duty, something less than infallibility may, it is maintained, warrant, and even bind, governments to act on their own opinion, confirmed by the general opinion, of mankind. It is also often argued, and still oftener thought, that none but bad men would desire to weaken these salutary beliefs; and there can be nothing wrong, it is thought, in restraining bad men, and prohibiting what only such men would wish to practise. This mode of thinking makes the justification of restraints on discussion not a question of the truth of doctrines, but of their usefulness; and flatters itself by that means to escape the responsibility of claiming to be an infallible judge of opinions. But those who thus satisfy themselves, do not perceive that the assumption of infallibility is merely shifted from one point to another. The usefulness of an opinion is itself a matter of opinion: as disputable, as open to discussion, and requiring discussion as much as the opinion itself. There is the same need of an infallible judge of opinions to decide an opinion to be noxious, as to decide it to be false, unless the opinion condemned has full opportunity of defending itself. And it will not do to say that the heretic may be allowed to maintain the utility or harmlessness of his opinion, though forbidden to maintain its truth. The truth of an opinion is part of its utility. If we would know whether or not it is desirable that a proposition should be believed, is it possible to exclude the consideration of whether or not it is true? In the opinion, not of bad men, but of the best men, no belief which is contrary to truth can be really useful: and can you prevent such men from urging that plea, when they are charged with culpability for denying some doctrine which they are told is useful, but which they believe to be false? Those who are on the side of received opinions never fail to take all possible advantage of this plea; you do not find *them* handling the question of utility as if it could be completely abstracted from that of truth: on the contrary, it is, above all, because their doctrine is "the truth," that the knowledge or the belief of it is held to be so indispensable. There can be no fair discussion of the question of usefulness when an argument so vital may be employed on one side, but not on the other. And in point of fact, when law or public feeling do not permit the truth of an opinion to be disputed, they are just as little tolerant of a denial or its usefulness. The utmost they allow is an extenuation of its absolute necessity, or of the positive guilt of rejecting it. . . .

Let us now pass to the second division of the argument, and dismissing the supposition that any of the received opinions may be false, let us assume them to be true, and examine into the worth of the manner in which they are likely to be held, when their truth is not freely and openly canvassed. However unwillingly a person who has a strong opinion may admit the possibility that his opinion may be false, he ought to be moved by the consideration that, however true it may be, if it is not fully, frequently, and fearlessly discussed, it will be held as a dead dogma, not a living truth.

There is a class of persons (happily not quite so numerous as formerly) who think it enough if a person assents undoubtingly to what they think true, though he has no knowledge whatever of the grounds of the opinion, and could not make a tenable defence of it against the most superficial objections. Such persons, if they can once get their creed taught from authority, naturally think that no good, and some harm, comes of its being allowed to be questioned. Where their influence prevails, they make it nearly impossible for the received opinion to be rejected wisely and considerately, though it may still be rejected rashly and ignorantly; for to shut out discussion entirely is seldom possible, and when it once gets in, beliefs not grounded on conviction are apt to give way before the slightest semblance of an argument. Waiving, however, this possibility—assuming that the true opinion abides in the mind, but abides as a prejudice, a belief independent of, and proof against, argument—this is not the way in which truth ought to be held by a rational being. This is not knowing the truth. Truth, thus held, is but one superstition the more, accidently clinging to the words which enunciate a truth.

If the intellect and judgment of mankind ought to be cultivated, a thing which Protestants at least do not deny, on what can these faculties be more appropriately exercised by anyone, than on the things which concern him so much that it is considered necessary for him to hold opinions on them? If the cultivation of the understanding consists in one thing more than in another, it is surely in learning the grounds of one's own opinions. Whatever people believe, on subjects on which it is of the first importance to believe rightly, they ought to be able to defend against at least the common objections. But, someone may say, "Let them be *taught* the grounds of their opinions. It does not follow that opinions must be merely parroted because they are never heard controverted. Persons who learn geometry do not simply commit the theorems to memory, but understand and learn likewise the demonstrations; and it would be absurd to say that they remain ignorant of the grounds of geometrical truths, because they never hear anyone deny, and attempt to disprove them." Undoubtedly: and such teaching suffices on a subject like mathematics, where there is nothing at all to be said on the wrong side of the question. The peculiarity of the evidence of mathematical truths is that all the argument is on one side. There are no objections, and no answers to objections. But on every subject on which difference of opinion is possible, the truth depends on a balance to be struck between two sets of conflicting reasons. Even in natural philosophy, there is always some other explanation possible of the same facts; some geocentric theory instead of heliocentric, some phlogiston instead of oxygen; and it has to be shown why that other theory cannot be the true one: and until this is shown, and until we know how it is shown, we do not understand the grounds of our opinion. But when we turn to subjects infinitely more complicated, to morals, religion, politics, social relations, and the business of life, three-fourths of the arguments for every disputed opinion consist in dispelling the appearances which favour some opinion different from it. The greatest orator, save one, of antiquity, has left it on record that he always studied his adversary's case with as great, if not still greater, intensity than even his own: What Cicero practised as the means of forensic success requires to be imitated by all who study any subject in order to arrive at the truth. He who knows only his own side of the case, knows little of that. His reasons may be good, and no one may have been able to refute them. But if he is equally unable to refute the reasons on the opposite side; if he does not so much as know what they are, he has no ground for preferring either opinion. The rational position for him would be suspension of judgment, and unless he contents himself with that, he is either led by authority, or adopts, like the generality of the world, the side to which he feels most inclination. Nor is it enough that he should hear the arguments of adversaries from his own teachers, presented as they state them, and accompanied by what they offer as refutations. That is not the way to do justice to the arguments, or bring them into real contact with his own mind. He must be able to hear them from persons who actually believe them; who defend them in earnest, and do their very utmost for them. He must know them in their most plausible and persuasive form; he must feel the whole force of the difficulty which the true view of the subject has to encounter and dispose of; else he will never really possess himself of the portion of truth which meets and removes that difficulty. Ninetynine in a hundred of what are called educated men are in this condition; even of those who can argue fluently for their opinions. Their conclusion may be true, but it might be false for anything they know: they have never thrown themselves into the mental position of those who think differently from them, and considered what such persons may have to say; and consequently they do not, in any proper sense of the word, know the doctrine which they themselves profess. They do not know those parts of it which explain and justify the remainder; the considerations which show that a fact which seemingly conflicts with another is reconcilable with it, or that, of two apparently strong reasons, one and not the other ought to be preferred. All that part of the truth which turns the scale, and decides the judgment of a completely informed mind, they are strangers to; nor is it ever really known, but to those who have attended equally and impartially to both sides, and endeavoured to see the reasons of both in the strongest light. So essential is this discipline to a real understanding of moral and human subjects, that if opponents of all important truths do not exist, it is indispensable to imagine them, and supply them with the strongest arguments which the most skilful devil's advocate can conjure up.

To abate the force of these considerations, an enemy of free discussion may be supposed to say, that there is no necessity for mankind in general to know and understand all that can be said against or for their opinions by philosophers and theologians. That it is not needful for common men to be able to expose all the misstatements or fallacies of an ingenious opponent. That it is enough if there is always somebody capable of answering them, so that nothing likely to mislead uninstructed persons remains unrefuted. That simple minds, having been taught the obvious grounds of the truths inculcated on them, may trust to authority for the rest, and being aware that they have neither knowledge nor talent to resolve every difficulty which can be raised, may repose in the assurance that all those which have been raised have been or can be answered, by those who are specially trained to the task.

Conceding to this view of the subject the utmost that can be claimed for it by those most easily satisfied with the amount of understanding of truth which ought to accompany the belief of it; even so, the argument for free discussion is no way weakened. For even this doctrine acknowledges that mankind ought to have a rational assurance that all objections have been satisfactorily answered; and how are they to be answered if that which requires to be answered is not spoken? Or how can the answer be known to be satisfactory, if the objectors have no opportunity of showing that it is unsatisfactory? If not the public, at least the philosophers and theologians who are to resolve the difficulties, must make themselves familiar with those difficulties in their most puzzling form; and this cannot be accomplished unless they are freely stated, and placed in the most advantageous light which they admit of. . . .

If, however, the mischievous operation of the absence of free discussion, when the received opinions are true, were confined to leaving men ignorant of the grounds of those opinions, it might be thought that this, if an intellectual, is no moral evil, and does not affect the worth of the opinions, regarded in their influence on the character. The fact, however, is, that not only the grounds of the opinion are forgotten in the absence of discussion, but too often the meaning of the opinion itself. The words which convey it cease to suggest ideas, or suggest only a small portion of those they were originally employed to communicate. Instead of a vivid conception and a living belief, there remain only a few phrases retained by rote; or, if any part, the shell and husk only of the meaning is retained, the finer essence being lost. The great chapter in human history which this fact occupies and fills, cannot be too earnestly studied and meditated on.

It is illustrated in the experience of almost all ethical doctrines and religious creeds. They are all full of meaning and vitality to those who originate them, and to the direct disciples of the originators. Their meaning continues to be felt in undiminished strength and is perhaps brought out into even fuller consciousness, so long as the struggle lasts to give the doctrine or creed an ascendancy over other creeds. At last it either prevails, and becomes the general opinion, or its progress stops; it keeps possession of the ground it has gained, but ceases to spread further. When either of these results has become apparent, controversy on the subject flags, and gradually dies away. The doctrine has taken its place, if not as a received opinion, as one of the admitted sects or divisions of opinion: those who hold it have generally inherited, not adopted it; and conversion from one of these doctrines to another, being now an exceptional fact, occupies little place in the thoughts of their professors. Instead of being, as at first, constantly on the alert either to defend themselves against the world, or to bring the world over to them, they have subsided into acquiescence, and neither listen, when they can help it, to arguments against their creed, nor trouble dissentients (if there be such) with arguments in its favour. From this time may usually be dated the decline in the living power of the doctrine. We often hear the teachers of all creeds lamenting the difficulty of keeping up in the minds of believers a lively apprehension of the truth which they nominally recognise, so that it may penetrate the feelings, and acquire a real mastery over the conduct. No such difficulty is complained of while the creed is still fighting for its existence: even the weaker combatants then know and feel what they are fighting for, and the difference between it and other doctrines; and in that period of every creed's existence, not a few persons may be found, who have realised its fundamental principles in all the forms of thought, have weighed and considered them in all their important bearings, and have experienced the full effect on the character which belief in that creed ought to produce in a mind thoroughly imbued with it. But when it has come to be a hereditary creed, and to be received passively, not actively— when the mind is no longer compelled, in the same degree as at first, to exercise its vital powers on the questions which its belief presents to it, there is a progressive tendency to forget all of the belief except the formularies, or to give it a dull and torpid assent, as if accepting it on trust dispensed with the necessity of realising it in consciousness, or testing it by personal experience, until it almost ceases to connect itself at all with the inner life of the human being. Then are seen the cases, so frequent in this age of the world as almost to form the majority, in which the creed remains as it were outside the mind, incrusting and petrifying it against all other influences addressed to the higher parts of our nature; manifesting its power by not suffering any fresh and living conviction to get in, but itself doing nothing for the mind or heart, except standing sentinel over them to keep them vacant. . . .

It still remains to speak of one of the principal causes which make diversity of opinion advantageous, and will continue to do so until mankind shall have entered a stage of intellectual advancement which at present seems at an incalculable distance. We have hitherto considered only two possibilities: that the received opinion may be false, and some other opinion, consequently, true; or that, the received opinion being true, a conflict with the opposite error is essential to a clear apprehension and deep feeling of its truth. But there is a commoner case than either of these; when the conflicting doctrines, instead of being one true and the other false, share the truth between them; and the nonconforming opinion is needed to supply the remainder of the truth, of which the received doctrine embodies only a part. Popular opinions, on subjects not palpable to sense, are often true, but seldom or never the whole truth. They are a part of the truth; sometimes a greater, sometimes a smaller part, but exaggerated, distorted, and disjointed from the truths by which they ought to be accompanied and limited. Heretical opinions, on the other hand, are generally some of these suppressed and neglected truths, bursting the bonds which kept them down, and either seeking reconciliation with the truth contained in the common opinion, or fronting it as enemies, and setting themselves up, with similar exclusiveness, as the whole truth. The latter case is hitherto the most frequent, as, in the human mind, one-sidedness has always been the rule, and many-sidedness the exception. Hence, even in revolutions of opinion, one part of the truth usually sets while another rises. Even progress, which ought to superadd, for the most part only substitutes one partial and incomplete truth for another; improvement consisting chiefly in this, that the new fragment of truth is more wanted, more adapted to the needs of the time, than that which it displaces. Such being the partial character of prevailing opinions, even when resting on a true foundation, every opinion which embodies somewhat of the portion of truth which the common opinion omits, ought to be considered precious, with whatever amount of error and confusion that truth may be blended. No sober judge of human affairs will feel bound to be indignant because those who force on our notice truths which we should otherwise have overlooked, overlook some of those which we see. Rather, he will think that so long as popular truth is one-sided, it is more desirable than otherwise that unpopular truth should have one-sided assertors too; such being usually the most energetic, and the most likely to compel reluctant attention to the fragment of wisdom which they proclaim as if it were the whole. . . .

OF INDIVIDUALITY AS ONE OF THE ELEMENTS OF WELL-BEING

Such being the reasons which make it imperative that human beings should be free to form opinions, and to express their opinions without reserve; and such the baneful consequences to the intellectual, and through that to the moral nature of man, unless this liberty is either conceded, or asserted in spite of prohibition; let us next examine whether the same reasons do not require that men should be free to act upon their opinions—to carry these out in their lives, without hindrance, either physical or moral, from their fellow-men, so long as it is at their own risk and peril. This last proviso is of course indispensable. No one pretends that actions should be as free as opinions. On the contrary, even opinions lose their immunity when the circumstances in which they are expressed are such as to constitute their expression a positive instigation to some mischievous act. An opinion that corn-dealers are starvers of the poor, or that private property is robbery, ought to be unmolested when simply circulated through the press, but may justly incur punishment when delivered orally to an excited mob assembled before the house of a corn-dealer, or when handed about among the same mob in the form of a placard. Acts, of whatever kind, which, without justifiable cause, do harm to others, may be, and in the more important cases absolutely require to be, controlled by the unfavourable sentiments, and, when needful, by the active interference of mankind. The liberty of the individual must be thus far limited; he must not make himself a nuisance to other people. But if he refrains from molesting others in what concerns them, and merely acts according to his own inclination and judgment in things which concern himself, the same reasons which show that opinion should be free, prove also that he should be allowed, without molestation, to carry his opinions into practice at his own cost. That mankind are not infallible; that their truths, for the most part, are only half-truths; that unity of opinion, unless resulting from the fullest and freest comparison of opposite opinions, is not desirable, and diversity not an evil, but a good, until mankind are much more capable than at present of recognising all sides of the truth, are principles applicable to men's modes of action, not less than to their opinions. As it is useful that while mankind are imperfect there should be different opinions, so it is that there should be different experiments of living; that free scope should be given to varieties of character, short of injury to others; and that the worth of different modes of life should be proved practically, when anyone thinks fit to try them. It is desirable, in short, that in things which do not primarily concern others, individuality should assert itself. Where, not the person's own character, but the traditions or customs of other people are the rule of conduct, there is wanting one of the principal ingredients of human happiness, and quite the chief ingredient of individual and social progress.

In maintaining this principle, the greatest difficulty to be encountered does not lie in the appreciation of means towards an acknowledged end, but in the indifference of persons in general to the end itself. If it were felt that the free development of individuality is one of the leading essentials of well-being; that it is not only a co-ordinate element with all that is designated by the terms civilisation, instruction, education, culture, but is itself a necessary part and condition of all those things; there would be no danger that liberty should be undervalued, and the adjustment of the boundaries between it and social control would present no extraordinary difficulty. But the evil is, that individual spontaneity is hardly recognised by the common modes of thinking as having any intrinsic worth, or deserving any regard on its own account. The majority, being satisfied with the ways of mankind as they now are (for it is they who make them what they are), cannot comprehend why those ways should not be good enough for everybody; and what is more, spontaneity forms no part of the ideal of the majority of moral and social reformers, but is rather looked on with jealousy, as a troublesome and perhaps rebellious obstruction to the general acceptance of what these reformers, in their own judgment, think would be best for mankind. Few persons, out of Germany, even comprehend the meaning of the doctrine which Wilhelm von Humboldt, so eminent both as a *savant* and as a politician, made the text of a treatise—that "the end of man, or that which is prescribed by the eternal or immutable dictates of reason, and not suggested by vague and transient desires, is the highest and most harmonious development of his powers to a complete and consistent whole"; that, therefore, the object "towards which every human being must ceaselessly direct his efforts, and on which especially those who design to influence their fellow-men must ever keep their eyes, is the individuality of power and development"; that for this there are two requisites, "freedom, and variety of situations"; and that from the union of these arise "individual vigour and manifold diversity," which combine themselves in "originality."

Little, however, as people are accustomed to a doctrine like that of von Humboldt, and surprising as it may be to them to find so high a value attached to individuality, the question, one must nevertheless think, can only be one of degree. No one's idea of excellence in conduct is that people should do absolutely nothing but copy one another. No one would assert that people ought not to put into their mode of life, and into the conduct of their concerns, any impress whatever of their own judgment, or of their own individual character. On the other hand, it would be absurd to pretend that people ought to live as if nothing whatever had been known in the world before they came into it; as if experience had as yet done nothing towards showing that one mode of existence, or of conduct, is preferable to another. Nobody denies that people should be so taught and trained in youth as to know and benefit by the ascertained results of human experience. But it is the privilege and proper condition of a human being, arrived at the maturity of his faculties, to use and interpret experience in his own way. It is for him to find out what part of recorded experience is properly applicable to his own circumstances and character. The traditions and customs of other people are, to a certain extent, evidence of what their experience has taught *them;* presumptive evidence, and as such, have a claim to his deference: but, in the first place, their experience may be too narrow; or they may not have interpreted it rightly. Secondly, their interpretation of experience may be correct, but unsuitable to him. Customs are made for customary circumstances and customary characters; and his circumstances or his character may be uncustomary. Thirdly, though the customs be both good as customs, and suitable to him, yet to conform to custom, merely as custom, does not educate or develop in him any of the qualities which are the distinctive endowment of a human being. The human faculties of perception, judgment, discriminative feeling, mental activity, and even moral preference, are exercised only in making a choice. He who does anything because it is the custom makes no choice. He gains no practice either in discerning or in desiring what is best. The mental and moral, like the muscular powers, are improved only by being used. The faculties are called into no exercise by doing a thing merely because others do it, no more than by believing a thing only because others believe it. If the grounds of an opinion are not conclusive to the person's own reason, his reason cannot be strengthened, but is likely to be weakened, by his adopting it: and if the inducements to an act are not such as are consentaneous to his own feelings and character (where affection, or the rights of others, are not concerned) it is so much

done towards rendering his feelings and character inert and torpid, instead of active and energetic.

He who lets the world, or his own portion of it, choose his
plan of life for him, has no need of any other faculty than the
ape-like one of imitation. He who chooses his plan for himself,
employs all his faculties. He must use observation to see, reasoning and judgment to foresee, activity to gather materials for
decision, discrimination to decide, and when he has decided,
firmness and self-control to hold to his deliberate decision. And
these qualities he requires and exercises exactly in proportion as
the part of his conduct which he determines according to his
own judgment and feelings is a large one. It is possible that he
might be guided in some good path, and kept out of harm's
way, without any of these things. But what will be his comparative worth as a human being? It really is of importance, not
only what men do, but also what manner of men they are that
do it. Among the works of man, which human life is rightly
employed in perfecting and beautifying, the first in importance
surely is man himself. Supposing it were possible to get houses
built, corn grown, battles fought, causes tried, and even churches
erected and prayers said, by machinery—by automatons in human form—it would be a considerable loss to exchange for these
automatons even the men and women who at present inhabit
the more civilised parts of the world, and who assuredly are but
starved specimens of what nature can and will produce. Human
nature is not a machine to be built after a model, and set to
do exactly the work prescribed for it, but a tree, which requires
to grow and develop itself on all sides, according to the tendency
of the inward forces which make it a living thing. . . .

It is not by wearing down to uniformity all that is individual in themselves, but by cultivating it, and calling it forth,
within the limits imposed by the rights and interests of others,
that human beings become a noble and beautiful object of
contemplation; and as the works partake the character of those

who do them, by the same process human life also becomes rich, diversified, and animating, furnishing more abundant aliment to high thoughts and elevating feelings, and strengthening the tie which binds every individual to the race, by making the race infinitely better worth belonging to. In proportion to the development to his individuality, each person becomes more valuable to himself, and is therefore capable of being more valuable to others. There is a greater fulness of life about his own existence, and when there is more life in the units there is more in the mass which is composed of them. As much compression as is necessary to prevent the stronger specimens of human nature from encroaching on the rights of others cannot be dispensed with; but for this there is ample compensation even in the point of view of human development. The means of development which the individual loses by being prevented from gratifying his inclinations to the injury of others, are chiefly obtained at the expense of the development of other people. And even to himself there is a full equivalent in the better development of the social part of his nature, rendered possible by the restraint put upon the selfish part. To be held to rigid rules of justice for the sake of others, develops the feelings and capacities which have the good of others for their object. But to be restrained in things not affecting their good, by their mere displeasure, develops nothing valuable, except such force of character as may unfold itself in resisting the restraint. If acquiesced in, it dulls and blunts the whole nature. To give any fair play to the nature of each, it is essential that different persons should be allowed to lead different lives. In proportion as this latitude has been exercised in any age, has that age been noteworthy to posterity. Even despotism does not produce its worst effects, so long as individuality exists under it; and whatever crushes individuality is despotism, by whatever name it may be called, and whether it professes to be enforcing the will of God or the injunctions of men.

WILLIAM SHAKESPEARE's birth date is uncertain, but he was baptized in 1564 in Stratford-on-Avon, England. Many of the details of Shakespeare's life are unknown or contested. His father was a shopkeeper and glover who was a prominent local citizen, serving Stratford as a burgess, an alderman, and as bailiff. William Shakespeare was educated only at the local grammar school, where he studied Latin and most likely read the plays of Terence and Plautus. He married in 1582 and had three children. It is unclear when and how Shakespeare went to London and began working in the theater, but by 1594 he had joined the Lord Chamberlain's Company of players as an actor, a playwright, and a shareholder. *The Comedy of Errors,* probably first performed in 1591, was one of Shakespeare's earliest plays; his latest dates to 1613. *Hamlet* was first performed sometime between 1600 and 1601. Shakespeare enjoyed some degree of prosperity, purchasing one of the largest homes in Stratford in 1597 and acquiring 107 acres of farmland in 1602. Shakespeare's plays were published in his lifetime, but none with his approval. He died in 1616.

From *The Tragedy of Hamlet, King of Denmark,* edited by Jack Randall Crawford. Publisher: Yale University Press, 1943.

Hamlet

CHARACTERS

CLAUDIUS, King of Denmark
HAMLET, Son to the late, and Nephew to the
    present King
FORTINBRAS, Prince of Norway
HORATIO, Friend to Hamlet
POLONIUS, Lord Chamberlain
LAERTES, his Son

VOLTIMAND	GUILDENSTERN	⎫
CORNELIUS	OSRIC	⎬ Courtiers
ROSENCRANTZ	A Gentleman	⎭

A Priest
MARCELLUS and BERNARDO, Officers
FRANCISCO, a Soldier
REYNALDO, Servant to Polonius
A Captain
English Ambassadors
Players · Two Clowns · Grave-diggers
GERTRUDE, Queen of Denmark and Mother to Hamlet
OPHELIA, Daughter to Polonius
Lords, Ladies, Officers, Soldiers, Sailor, Messenger,
    and Attendants
Ghost of Hamlet's Father

SCENE: *Denmark*

ACT I

SCENE ONE—*Elsinore. A Platform of the Castle.*

Enter BERNARDO *and* FRANCISCO, *two Sentinels.*

BERNARDO: Who's there?
FRANCISCO: Nay, answer me; stand, and unfold yourself.
BERNARDO: Long live the king!
FRANCISCO: Bernardo?
BERNARDO: He.
FRANCISCO: You come most carefully upon your hour.
BERNARDO: 'Tis now struck twelve; get thee to bed, Francisco.
FRANCISCO: For this relief much thanks; 'tis bitter cold,
And I am sick at heart.
BERNARDO: Have you had quiet guard?
FRANCISCO: Not a mouse stirring.
BERNARDO: Well, good-night.
If you do meet Horatio and Marcellus,
The rivals[1] of my watch, bid them make haste.

Enter HORATIO *and* MARCELLUS.

FRANCISCO: I think I hear them. Stand, ho! Who's there?
HORATIO: Friends to this ground.
MARCELLUS: And liegemen to the Dane.
FRANCISCO: Give you good-night.
MARCELLUS: O! farewell, honest soldier:
Who hath reliev'd you?
FRANCISCO: Bernardo has my place.
Give you good-night.   *Exit* FRANCISCO.
MARCELLUS: Holla! Bernardo!
BERNARDO: Say,
What! is Horatio there?
HORATIO: A piece of him.

---

[1] [*rivals:* partners.]

BERNARDO: Welcome, Horatio; welcome, good Marcellus.
MARCELLUS: What! has this thing appear'd again to-night?
BERNARDO: I have seen nothing.
MARCELLUS: Horatio says 'tis but our fantasy,
  And will not let belief take hold of him
  Touching this dreaded sight twice seen of us:
  Therefore I have entreated him along
  With us to watch the minutes of this night;
  That if again this apparition come,
  He may approve our eyes and speak to it.
HORATIO: Tush, tush! 'twill not appear.
BERNARDO: Sit down awhile,
  And let us once again assail your ears,
  That are so fortified against our story,
  What we two nights have seen.
HORATIO: Well, sit we down,
  And let us hear Bernardo speak of this.
BERNARDO: Last night of all,
  When yond same star that's westward from the pole
  Had made his course to illume that part of heaven
  Where now it burns, Marcellus and myself,
  The bell then beating one,—

Enter the GHOST.

MARCELLUS: Peace! break thee off; look, where it comes again!
BERNARDO: In the same figure, like the king that's dead.
MARCELLUS: Thou art a scholar; speak to it, Horatio.
BERNARDO: Looks it not like the king? mark it, Horatio.
HORATIO: Most like: it harrows me with fear and wonder.
BERNARDO: It would be spoke to.
MARCELLUS: Question it, Horatio.
HORATIO: What art thou that usurp'st this time of night,
  Together with that fair and warlike form
  In which the majesty of buried Denmark
  Did sometimes march? by heaven I charge thee, speak!

MARCELLUS: It is offended.

BERNARDO: See! it stalks away.

HORATIO: Stay! speak, speak! I charge thee, speak!

Exit the GHOST.

MARCELLUS: 'Tis gone, and will not answer.

BERNARDO: How now, Horatio! you tremble and look pale:
Is not this something more than fantasy?
What think you on 't?

HORATIO: Before my God, I might not this believe
Without the sensible and true avouch
Of mine own eyes.

MARCELLUS: Is it not like the king?

HORATIO: As thou art to thyself:
Such was the very armour he had on
When he the ambitious Norway combated;
So frown'd he once, when, in an angry parle,
He smote the sledded Polacks on the ice.
'Tis strange.

MARCELLUS: Thus twice before, and jump at this dead hour,
With martial stalk hath he gone by our watch.

HORATIO: In what particular thought to work I know not;
But in the gross and scope of my opinion,
This bodes some strange eruption to our state.

MARCELLUS: Good now, sit down, and tell me, he that knows,
Why this same strict and most observant watch
So nightly toils the subject of the land;
And why such daily cast of brazen cannon,
And foreign mart for implements of war;
Why such impress of shipwrights, whose sore task
Does not divide the Sunday from the week;
What might be toward, that this sweaty haste
Doth make the night joint-labourer with the day:
Who is 't that can inform me?

HORATIO: That can I;
At least, the whisper goes so. Our last king,

Whose image even but now appear'd to us,
Was, as you know, by Fortinbras of Norway,
Thereto prick'd on by a most emulate pride,
Dar'd to the combat; in which our valiant Hamlet—
For so this side of our known world esteem'd him—
Did slay this Fortinbras; who, by a seal'd compact,
Well ratified by law and heraldry,
Did forfeit with his life all those his lands
Which he stood seiz'd of, to the conqueror;
Against the which, a moiety competent[2]
Was gaged by our king; which had return'd
To the inheritance of Fortinbras,
Had he been vanquisher; as, by the same covenant,
And carriage of the article design'd,
His fell to Hamlet. Now, sir, young Fortinbras,
Of unimproved mettle hot and full,
Hath in the skirts of Norway here and there
Shark'd up a list of lawless resolutes,
For food and diet, to some enterprise
That hath a stomach in 't; which is no other—
As it doth well appear unto our state—
But to recover of us, by strong hand
And terms compulsative, those foresaid lands
So by his father lost. And this, I take it,
Is the main motive of our preparations,
The source of this our watch and the chief head
Of this post-haste and romage in the land.
BERNARDO: I think it be no other but e'en so;
    Well may it sort that this portentous figure
    Comes armed through our watch, so like the king
    That was and is the question of these wars.
HORATIO: A mote it is to trouble the mind's eye.
    In the most high and palmy state of Rome,
    A little ere the mightiest Julius fell,

---

[2] [*moiety competent:* equal amount.]

The graves stood tenantless and the sheeted dead
Did squeak and gibber in the Roman streets;
As stars with trains of fire and dews of blood,
Disasters in the sun; and the moist star
Upon whose influence Neptune's empire stands
Was sick almost to doomsday with eclipse;
And even the like precurse of fierce events,
As harbingers preceding still the fates
And prologue to the omen coming on,
Have heaven and earth together demonstrated
Unto our climatures and countrymen.

Enter GHOST *again.*

But, soft! behold! lo! where it comes again.
I'll cross it, though it blast me. Stay, illusion!
If thou hast any sound, or use of voice,
                                    It spreads his arms.
Speak to me:
If there be any good thing to be done,
That may to thee do ease and grace to me,
Speak to me:
If thou art privy to thy country's fate,
Which happily foreknowing may avoid,
O! speak;
Or if thou hast uphoarded in thy life
Extorted treasure in the womb of earth,
For which, they say, you spirits oft walk in death,
                                    The cock crows.
Speak of it: stay, and speak! Stop it, Marcellus.
MARCELLUS: Shall I strike at it with my partisan?
HORATIO: Do, if it will not stand.
BERNARDO: 'Tis here!
HORATIO: 'Tis here!
                                    Exit GHOST.

MARCELLUS: 'Tis gone!
  We do it wrong, being so majestical,
  To offer it the show of violence;
  For it is, as the air, invulnerable,
  And our vain blows malicious mockery.
BERNARDO: It was about to speak when the cock crew.
HORATIO: And then it started like a guilty thing
  Upon a fearful summons. I have heard,
  The cock, that is the trumpet to the morn,
  Doth with his lofty and shrill-sounding throat
  Awake the god of day; and at his warning,
  Whether in sea or fire, in earth or air,
  The extravagant and erring spirit hies
  To his confine; and of the truth herein
  This present object made probation.
MARCELLUS: It faded on the crowing of the cock.
  Some say that ever 'gainst that season comes
  Wherein our Saviour's birth is celebrated,
  The bird of dawning singeth all night long;
  And then, they say, no spirit can walk abroad;
  The nights are wholesome; then no planets strike,
  No fairy takes, nor witch hath power to charm,
  So hallow'd and so gracious is the time.
HORATIO: So have I heard and do in part believe it.
  But, look, the morn in russet mantle clad,
  Walks o'er the dew of yon high eastern hill;
  Break we our watch up; and by my advice
  Let us impart what we have seen to-night
  Unto young Hamlet; for, upon my life,
  This spirit, dumb to us, will speak to him.
  Do you consent we shall acquaint him with it,
  As needful in our loves, fitting our duty?
MARCELLUS: Let's do 't, I pray; and I this morning know
  Where we shall find him most conveniently.   *Exeunt.*

SCENE TWO—*A Room of State in the Castle.*

Flourish. **Enter** CLAUDIUS, KING OF DENMARK, GERTRUDE
THE QUEEN, COUNCILORS, POLONIUS *and his son* LAERTES,
HAMLET, *cum aliis* [*including* VOLTIMAND *and* CORNELIUS].

KING: Though yet of Hamlet our dear brother's death
    The memory be green, and that it us befitted
    To bear our hearts in grief and our whole kingdom
    To be contracted in one brow of woe,
    Yet so far hath discretion fought with nature
    That we with wisest sorrow think on him,
    Together with remembrance of ourselves.
    Therefore our sometime sister, now our queen,
    The imperial jointress of this warlike state,
    Have we, as 'twere with a defeated joy,
    With one auspicious and one dropping eye,
    With mirth in funeral and with dirge in marriage,
    In equal scale weighing delight and dole,
    Taken to wife: nor have we herein barr'd
    Your better wisdoms, which have freely gone
    With this affair along: for all, our thanks.
    Now follows, that you know, young Fortinbras,
    Holding a weak supposal of our worth,
    Or thinking by our late dear brother's death
    Our state to be disjoint and out of frame,
    Colleagued with the dream of his advantage,
    He hath not fail'd to pester us with message,
    Importing the surrender of those lands
    Lost by his father, with all bands of law,
    To our most valiant brother. So much for him.
    Now for ourself and for this time of meeting.
    Thus much the business is: we have here writ
    To Norway, uncle of young Fortinbras,
    Who, impotent and bed-rid, scarcely hears
    Of this his nephew's purpose, to suppress
    His further gait herein; in that the levies,

The lists and full proportions, are all made
Out of his subject; and we here dispatch
You, good Cornelius, and you, Voltimand,
For bearers of this greeting to old Norway,
Giving to you no further personal power
To business with the king more than the scope
Of these delated articles allow.
Farewell and let your haste commend your duty.

CORNELIUS, VOLTIMAND: In that and all things will we show
   our duty.

KING: We doubt it nothing: heartily farewell.

                    Exeunt VOLTIMAND *and* CORNELIUS.

And now, Laertes, what's the news with you?
You told us of some suit; what is't, Laertes?
You cannot speak of reason to the Dane,
And lose your voice; what wouldst thou beg, Laertes,
That shall not be my offer, not thy asking?
The head is not more native to the heart,
The hand more instrumental to the mouth,
Than is the throne of Denmark to thy father.
What wouldst thou have, Laertes?

LAERTES: Dread my lord,
Your leave and favour to return to France;
From whence though willingly I came to Denmark,
To show my duty in your coronation,
Yet now, I must confess, that duty done,
My thoughts and wishes bend again toward France
And bow them to your gracious leave and pardon.

KING: Have you your father's leave? What says Polonius?

POLONIUS: He hath, my lord, wrung from me my slow leave
   By laboursome petition, and at last
   Upon his will I seal'd my hard consent:
   I do beseech you, give him leave to go.

KING: Take thy fair hour, Laertes; time be thine,
   And thy best graces spend it at thy will.
   But now, my cousin Hamlet, and my son, —

HAMLET [*aside*]: A little more than kin, and less than kind.

KING: How is it that the clouds still hang on you?

HAMLET: Not so, my lord; I am too much i' the sun.

QUEEN: Good Hamlet, cast thy nighted colour off,
And let thine eye look like a friend on Denmark.
Do not for ever with thy vailed lids
Seek for thy noble father in the dust:
Thou know'st 'tis common; all that lives must die,
Passing through nature to eternity.

HAMLET: Ay, madam, it is common.

QUEEN: If it be,
Why seems it so particular with thee?

HAMLET: Seems, madam! Nay, it is; I know not "seems."
'Tis not alone my inky cloak, good mother,
Nor customary suits of solemn black,
Nor windy suspiration of forc'd breath,
No, nor the fruitful river in the eye,
Nor the dejected haviour of the visage,
Together with all forms, moods, shows of grief,
That can denote me truly; these indeed seem,
For they are actions that a man might play:
But I have that within which passeth show;
These but the trappings and the suits of woe.

KING: 'Tis sweet and commendable in your nature, Hamlet,
To give these mourning duties to your father:
But, you must know, your father lost a father;
That father lost, lost his; and the survivor bound
In filial obligation for some term
To do obsequious sorrow; but to persever
In obstinate condolement is a course
Of impious stubbornness; 'tis unmanly grief:
It shows a will most incorrect to heaven,
A heart unfortified, a mind impatient,
An understanding simple and unschool'd:
For what we know must be and is as common
As any the most vulgar thing to sense,

Why should we in our peevish opposition
Take it to heart? Fie! 'tis a fault to heaven,
A fault against the dead, a fault to nature,
To reason most absurd, whose common theme
Is death of fathers, and who still hath cried,
From the first corse till he that died to-day,
"This must be so." We pray you, throw to earth
This unprevailing woe, and think of us
As of a father; for let the world take note,
You are the most immediate to our throne;
And with no less nobility of love
Than that which dearest father bears his son
Do I impart toward you. For your intent
In going back to school in Wittenberg,
It is most retrograde to our desire;
And we beseech you, bend you to remain
Here, in the cheer and comfort of our eye,
Our chiefest courtier, cousin, and our son.
QUEEN: Let not thy mother lose her prayers, Hamlet:
I pray thee, stay with us; go not to Wittenberg.
HAMLET: I shall in all my best obey you, madam.
KING: Why, 'tis a loving and a fair reply:
Be as ourself in Denmark. Madam, come;
This gentle and unforc'd accord of Hamlet
Sits smiling to my heart; in grace whereof,
No jocund health that Denmark drinks to-day,
But the great cannon to the clouds shall tell,
And the king's rouse the heavens shall bruit again,[3]
Re-speaking earthly thunder. Come away.

Exeunt [*all except* HAMLET].

HAMLET: O! that this too too solid flesh would melt,
Thaw and resolve itself into a dew;
Or that the Everlasting had not fix'd

---

[3] [*rouse:* draught of liquor; *bruit again:* echo loudly.]

His canon 'gainst self-slaughter! O God! O God!
How weary, stale, flat, and unprofitable
Seem to me all the uses of this world.
Fie on 't! O fie! 'tis an unweeded garden,
That grows to seed; things rank and gross in nature
Possess it merely. That it should come to this!
But two months dead: nay, not so much, not two:
So excellent a king; that was, to this,
Hyperion to a satyr; so loving to my mother
That he might not beteem the winds of heaven
Visit her face too roughly. Heaven and earth!
Must I remember? why, she would hang on him,
As if increase of appetite had grown
By what it fed on; and yet, within a month,
Let me not think on 't: Frailty, thy name is woman!
A little month; or ere those shoes were old
With which she follow'd my poor father's body,
Like Niobe, all tears; why she, even she,—
O God! a beast, that wants discourse of reason,
Would have mourn'd longer,—married with mine uncle,
My father's brother, but no more like my father
Than I to Hercules: within a month,
Ere yet the salt of most unrighteous tears
Had left the flushing in her galled eyes,
She married. O! most wicked speed, to post
With such dexterity to incestuous sheets.
It is not nor it cannot come to good;
But break, my heart, for I must hold my tongue!

Enter HORATIO, BERNARDO, *and* MARCELLUS.

HORATIO: Hail to your lordship!
HAMLET: I am glad to see you well.
  Horatio,—or I do forget myself.
HORATIO: The same, my lord, and your poor servant ever.

HAMLET: Sir, my good friend; I'll change that name with you.
And what make you from Wittenberg, Horatio?
Marcellus?

MARCELLUS: My good lord,—

HAMLET: I am very glad to see you. [*To* BERNARDO.] Good
even, sir.
But what, in faith, make you from Wittenberg?

HORATIO: A truant disposition, good my lord.

HAMLET: I would not hear your enemy say so,
Nor shall you do mine ear that violence,
To make it truster of your own report
Against yourself; I know you are no truant.
But what is your affair in Elsinore?
We'll teach you to drink deep ere you depart.

HORATIO: My lord, I came to see your father's funeral.

HAMLET: I pray thee, do not mock me, fellow-student;
I think it was to see my mother's wedding.

HORATIO: Indeed, my lord, it follow'd hard upon.

HAMLET: Thrift, thrift, Horatio! the funeral bak'd meats
Did coldly furnish forth the marriage tables.
Would I had met my dearest foe in heaven
Ere I had ever seen that day, Horatio!
My father, methinks I see my father.

HORATIO: O! where, my lord?

HAMLET: In my mind's eye, Horatio.

HORATIO: I saw him once; he was a goodly king.

HAMLET: He was a man, take him for all in all,
I shall not look upon his like again.

HORATIO: My lord, I think I saw him yesternight.

HAMLET: Saw? Who?

HORATIO: My lord, the king your father.

HAMLET: The king, my father?

HORATIO: Season your admiration for a while
With an attent ear, till I may deliver,

Upon the witness of these gentlemen,
This marvel to you.

HAMLET: For God's love, let me hear.

HORATIO: Two nights together had these gentlemen,
Marcellus and Bernardo, on their watch,
In the dead vast and middle of the night,
Been thus encounter'd: a figure like your father,
Arm'd at all points exactly, cap-a-pe,[4]
Appears before them, and with solemn march
Goes slow and stately by them: thrice he walk'd
By their oppress'd and fear-surprised eyes,
Within his truncheon's length; whilst they, distill'd
Almost to jelly with the act of fear,
Stand dumb and speak not to him. This to me
In dreadful secrecy impart they did,
And I with them the third night kept the watch;
Where, as they had deliver'd, both in time,
Form of the thing, each word made true and good,
The apparition comes. I knew your father;
These hands are not more like.

HAMLET: But where was this?

MARCELLUS: My lord, upon the platform where we watch'd.

HAMLET: Did you not speak to it?

HORATIO: My lord, I did;
But answer made it none; yet once methought
It lifted up its head and did address
Itself to motion, like as it would speak;
But even then the morning cock crew loud,
And at the sound it shrunk in haste away
And vanish'd from our sight.

HAMLET: 'Tis very strange.

HORATIO: As I do live, my honour'd lord, 'tis true;
And we did think it writ down in our duty
To let you know of it.

---

[4] [cap-a-pe: from head to foot.]

HAMLET: Indeed, indeed, sirs, but this troubles me.
Hold you the watch to-night?
MARCELLUS, BERNARDO: We do, my lord.
HAMLET: Arm'd, say you?
MARCELLUS, BERNARDO: Arm'd, my lord.
HAMLET: From top to toe?
MARCELLUS, BERNARDO: My lord, from head to foot.
HAMLET: Then saw you not his face?
HORATIO: O yes! my lord; he wore his beaver up.
HAMLET: What! look'd he frowningly?
HORATIO: A countenance more in sorrow than in anger.
HAMLET: Pale or red?
HORATIO: Nay, very pale.
HAMLET: And fix'd his eyes upon you?
HORATIO: Most constantly.
HAMLET: I would I had been there.
HORATIO: It would have much amaz'd you.
HAMLET: Very like, very like. Stay'd it long?
HORATIO: While one with moderate haste might tell a hundred.
MARCELLUS, BERNARDO: Longer, longer.
HORATIO: Not when I saw it.
HAMLET: His beard was grizzled, no?
HORATIO: It was, as I have seen it in his life,
A sable silver'd.
HAMLET: I will watch to-night;
Perchance 'twill walk again.
HORATIO: I warrant it will.
HAMLET: If it assume my noble father's person,
I'll speak to it, though hell itself should gape
And bid me hold my peace. I pray you all,
If you have hitherto conceal'd this sight,
Let it be tenable in your silence still;
And whatsoever else shall hap to-night,
Give it an understanding, but no tongue:
I will requite your loves. So, fare you well.

Upon the platform, 'twixt eleven and twelve,
I'll visit you.
ALL: Our duty to your honour.
HAMLET: Your loves, as mine to you. Farewell.
                        Exeunt [*all but* HAMLET].
My father's spirit in arms! all is not well;
I doubt some foul play: would the night were come!
Till then sit still, my soul: foul deeds will rise,
Though all the earth o'erwhelm them, to men's eyes. *Exit.*

SCENE THREE—POLONIUS' *Apartment in the Castle.*

Enter LAERTES *and* OPHELIA.

LAERTES: My necessaries are embark'd; farewell:
    And, sister, as the winds give benefit
    And convoy is assistant, do not sleep,
    But let me hear from you.
OPHELIA: Do you doubt that?
LAERTES: For Hamlet, and the trifling of his favour,
    Hold it a fashion and a toy in blood,
    A violet in the youth of primy nature,
    Forward, not permanent, sweet, not lasting,
    The perfume and suppliance of a minute;
    No more.
OPHELIA: No more but so?
LAERTES: Think it no more:
    For nature, crescent, does not grow alone
    In thews and bulk; but, as this temple waxes,
    The inward service of the mind and soul
    Grows wide withal. Perhaps he loves you now,
    And now no soil nor cautel doth besmirch
    The virtue of his will; but you must fear,
    His greatness weigh'd, his will is not his own,
    For he himself is subject to his birth;
    He may not, as unvalu'd persons do,

Carve for himself, for on his choice depends
The safety and the health of the whole state;
And therefore must his choice be circumscrib'd
Unto the voice and yielding of that bod
Whereof he is the head. Then if he says he loves you,
It fits your wisdom so far to believe it
As he in his particular act and place
May give his saying deed; which is no further
Than the main voice of Denmark goes withal.
Then weigh what loss your honour may sustain,
If with too credent ear you list his songs,
Or lose your heart, or your chaste treasure open
To his unmaster'd importunity.
Fear it, Ophelia, fear it, my dear sister;
And keep you in the rear of your affection,
Out of the shot and danger of desire.
The chariest maid is prodigal enough
If she unmask her beauty to the moon;
Virtue herself 'scapes not calumnious strokes;
The canker galls the infants of the spring
Too oft before their buttons be disclos'd,
And in the morn and liquid dew of youth
Contagious blastments are most imminent.
Be wary then; best safety lies in fear:
Youth to itself rebels, though none else near.

OPHELIA: I shall th' effect of this good lesson keep,
   As watchman to my heart. But, good my brother,
   Do not, as some ungracious pastors do,
   Show me the steep and thorny way to heaven,
   Whiles, like a puff'd and reckless libertine,
   Himself the primrose path of dalliance treads,
   And recks not his own rede.

LAERTES: O! fear me not.

Enter POLONIUS.

   I stay too long; but here my father comes.

A double blessing is a double grace;
Occasion smiles upon a second leave.
POLONIUS: Yet here, Laertes! aboard, aboard, for shame!
The wind sits in the shoulder of your sail,
And you are stay'd for. There, my blessing with thee!
And these few precepts in thy memory
Look thou character. Give thy thoughts no tongue,
Nor any unproportion'd thought his act.
Be thou familiar, but by no means vulgar;
The friends thou hast, and their adoption tried,
Grapple them to thy soul with hoops of steel;
But do not dull thy palm with entertainment
Of each new-hatch'd, unfledg'd comrade. Beware
Of entrance to a quarrel, but, being in,
Bear 't that th' opposed may beware of thee.
Give every man thine ear, but few thy voice;
Take each man's censure, but reserve thy judgment.
Costly thy habit as thy purse can buy,
But not express'd in fancy; rich, not gaudy;
For the apparel oft proclaims the man,
And they in France of the best rank and station
Are most select and generous, chief in that.
Neither a borrower, nor a lender be;
For loan oft loses both itself and friend,
And borrowing dulls the edge of husbandry.
This above all: to thine own self be true,
And it must follow, as the night the day,
Thou canst not then be false to any man.
Farewell; my blessing season this in thee!
LAERTES: Most humbly do I take my leave, my lord.
POLONIUS: The time invites you; go, your servants tend.
LAERTES: Farewell, Ophelia; and remember well
What I have said to you.
OPHELIA: 'Tis in my memory lock'd,
And you yourself shall keep the key of it.

LAERTES: Farewell.   *Exit* LAERTES.

POLONIUS: What is 't, Ophelia, he hath said to you?

OPHELIA: So please you, something touching the Lord Hamlet.

POLONIUS: Marry, well bethought:
'Tis told me, he hath very oft of late
Given private time to you; and you yourself
Have of your audience been most free and bounteous.
If it be so,—as so 'tis put on me,
And that in way of caution,—I must tell you,
You do not understand yourself so clearly
As it behoves my daughter and your honour.
What is between you? give me up the truth.

OPHELIA: He hath, my lord, of late made many tenders
Of his affection to me.

POLONIUS: Affection! pooh! you speak like a green girl,
Unsifted in such perilous circumstance.
Do you believe his tenders, as you call them?

OPHELIA: I do not know, my lord, what I should think.

POLONIUS: Marry, I'll teach you: think yourself a baby,
That you have ta'en these tenders for true pay,
Which are not sterling. Tender yourself more dearly;
Or,—not to crack the wind of the poor phrase,
Roaming it thus,—you'll tender me a fool.[5]

OPHELIA: My lord, he hath importun'd me with love
In honourable fashion.

POLONIUS: Ay, fashion you may call it: go to, go to.

OPHELIA: And hath given countenance to his speech, my lord,
With almost all the holy vows of heaven.

POLONIUS: Ay, springes to catch woodcocks. I do know,
When the blood burns, how prodigal the soul
Lends the tongue vows: these blazes, daughter,
Giving more light than heat, extinct in both,
Even in their promise, as it is a-making,

---

[5] [*tender me a fool:* give me a grandchild. "Fool" was an affectionate term
for child.]

You must not take for fire. From this time
Be somewhat scanter of your maiden presence;
Set your entreatments at a higher rate
Than a command to parley. For Lord Hamlet,
Believe so much in him, that he is young,
And with a larger tether may he walk
Than may be given you: in few, Ophelia,
Do not believe his vows, for they are brokers,
Not of that dye which their investments show,
But mere implorators of unholy suits,
Breathing like sanctified and pious bonds,
The better to beguile. This is for all:
I would not, in plain terms, from this time forth,
Have you so slander any moment's leisure,
As to give words or talk with the Lord Hamlet.
Look to 't, I charge you; come your ways.
OPHELIA: I shall obey, my lord.   *Exeunt.*

SCENE FOUR—*A Platform of the Castle.*

Enter HAMLET, HORATIO, *and* MARCELLUS.

HAMLET: The air bites shrewdly; it is very cold.
HORATIO: It is a nipping and an eager air.
HAMLET: What hour now?
HORATIO: I think it lacks of twelve.
MARCELLUS: No, it is struck.
HORATIO: Indeed? I heard it not: then it draws near the season
Wherein the spirit held his wont to walk.

> *A flourish of trumpets, and two pieces*
> *[of ordnance]*[6] *go off.*

What does this mean, my lord?

---

[6] [*ordnance:* cannon.]

HAMLET: The king doth wake to-night and takes his rouse,
Keeps wassail, and the swaggering up-spring reels;
And, as he drains his draughts of Rhenish down,
The kettle-drum and trumpet thus bray out
The triumph of his pledge.
HORATIO: Is it a custom?
HAMLET: Ay, marry, is 't:
But to my mind,—though I am native here
And to the manner born,—it is a custom
More honour'd in the breach than the observance.
This heavy-headed revel east and west
Makes us traduc'd and tax'd of other nations;
They clepe us drunkards, and with swinish phrase
Soil our addition; and indeed it takes
From our achievements, though perform'd at height,
The pith and marrow of our attribute.
So, oft it chances in particular men,
That for some vicious mole of nature in them,
As, in their birth,—wherein they are not guilty,
Since nature cannot choose his origin,—
By the o'ergrowth of some complexion,
Oft breaking down the pales and forts of reason,
Or by some habit that too much o'er-leavens
The form of plausive manners; that these men,
Carrying, I say, the stamp of one defect,
Being nature's livery, or fortune's star,
Their virtues else, be they as pure as grace,
As infinite as man may undergo,
Shall in the general censure take corruption
From that particular fault: the dram of eale[7]
Doth all the noble substance of a doubt,
To his own scandal.

Enter GHOST.

---

[7] [*eale:* evil (?).]

HORATIO: Look, my lord, it comes.

HAMLET: Angels and ministers of grace defend us!
Be thou a spirit of health or goblin damn'd,
Bring with thee airs from heaven or blasts from hell,
Be thy intents wicked or charitable,
Thou com'st in such a questionable shape
That I will speak to thee: I'll call thee Hamlet,
King, father, royal Dane; O! answer me:
Let me not burst in ignorance; but tell
Why thy canoniz'd bones, hearsed in death,
Have burst their cerements; why the sepulchre,
Wherein we saw thee quietly inurn'd,
Hath op'd his ponderous and marble jaws,
To cast thee up again. What may this mean,
That thou, dead corse, again in complete steel
Revisit'st thus the glimpses of the moon,
Making night hideous; and we fools of nature
So horridly to shake our disposition
With thoughts beyond the reaches of our souls?
Say, why is this? wherefore? what should we do?

GHOST beckons HAMLET.

HORATIO: It beckons you to go away with it,
As if it some impartment did desire
To you alone.

MARCELLUS: Look, with what courteous action
It waves you to a more removed ground:
But do not go with it.

HORATIO: No, by no means.

HAMLET: It will not speak; then, will I follow it.

HORATIO: Do not, my lord.

HAMLET: Why, what should be the fear?
I do not set my life at a pin's fee;
And for my soul, what can it do to that,
Being a thing immortal as itself?
It waves me forth again; I'll follow it.

HORATIO: What if it tempt you toward the flood, my lord,
  Or to the dreadful summit of the cliff
  That beetles o'er his base into the sea,
  And there assume some other horrible form,
  Which might deprive your sovereignty of reason
  And draw you into madness? think of it;
  The very place puts toys of desperation,
  Without more motive, into every brain
  That looks so many fathoms to the sea
  And hears it roar beneath.
HAMLET: It wafts me still. Go on, I'll follow thee.
MARCELLUS: You shall not go, my lord.
HAMLET: Hold off your hands!
HORATIO: Be rul'd; you shall not go.
HAMLET: My fate cries out,
  And makes each petty artery in this body
  As hardy as the Nemean lion's nerve.
  Still am I call'd. Unhand me, gentlemen,
                          [*Breaking from them.*]
  By heaven! I'll make a ghost of him that lets me:
  I say, away! Go on, I'll follow thee.
                          Exeunt GHOST *and* HAMLET.

HORATIO: He waxes desperate with imagination.
MARCELLUS: Let's follow; 'tis not fit thus to obey him.
HORATIO: Have after. To what issue will this come?
MARCELLUS: Something is rotten in the state of Denmark.
HORATIO: Heaven will direct it.
MARCELLUS: Nay, let's follow him.
                          Exeunt.

SCENE FIVE—*A more remote Part of the Platform.*

Enter GHOST *and* HAMLET.

HAMLET: Whither wilt thou lead me? speak; I'll go no further.
GHOST: Mark me.

HAMLET: I will.
GHOST: My hour is almost come,
  When I to sulphurous and tormenting flames
  Must render up myself.
HAMLET: Alas! poor ghost.
GHOST: Pity me not, but lend thy serious hearing
  To what I shall unfold.
HAMLET: Speak; I am bound to hear.
GHOST: So art thou to revenge, when thou shalt hear.
HAMLET: What?
GHOST: I am thy father's spirit;
  Doom'd for a certain term to walk the night,
  And for the day confin'd to fast in fires,
  Till the foul crimes done in my days of nature
  Are burnt and purg'd away. But that I am forbid
  To tell the secrets of my prison-house,
  I could a tale unfold whose lightest word
  Would harrow up thy soul, freeze thy young blood,
  Make thy two eyes, like stars, start from their spheres,
  Thy knotted and combined locks to part,
  And each particular hair to stand an end,
  Like quills upon the fretful porpentine:
  But this eternal blazon must not be
  To ears of flesh and blood. List, list, O list!
  If thou didst ever thy dear father love—
HAMLET: O God!
GHOST: Revenge his foul and most unnatural murder.
HAMLET: Murder!
GHOST: Murder most foul, as in the best it is;
  But this most foul, strange, and unnatural.
HAMLET: Haste me to know 't, that I, with wings as swift
  As meditation or the thoughts of love,
  May sweep to my revenge.
GHOST: I find thee apt;
  And duller shouldst thou be than the fat weed
  That rots itself in ease on Lethe wharf,

Wouldst thou not stir in this. Now, Hamlet, hear:
'Tis given out that, sleeping in mine orchard,
A serpent stung me; so the whole ear of Denmark
Is by a forged process of my death
Rankly abus'd; but know, thou noble youth,
The serpent that did sting thy father's life
Now wears his crown.

HAMLET: O my prophetic soul!
My uncle!

GHOST: Ay, that incestuous, that adulterate beast,
With witchcraft of his wit, with traitorous gifts,—
O wicked wit and gifts, that have the power
So to seduce!—won to his shameful lust
The will of my most seeming-virtuous queen.
O Hamlet! what a falling-off was there;
From me, whose love was of that dignity
That it went hand in hand even with the vow
I made to her in marriage; and to decline
Upon a wretch whose natural gifts were poor
To those of mine!
But virtue, as it never will be mov'd,
Though lewdness court it in a shape of heaven,
So lust, though to a radiant angel link'd,
Will sate itself in a celestial bed,
And prey on garbage.
But, soft! methinks I scent the morning air;
Brief let me be. Sleeping within mine orchard,
My custom always in the afternoon,
Upon my secure hour thy uncle stole,
With juice of cursed hebona in a vial,
And in the porches of mine ears did pour
The leperous distilment; whose effect
Holds such an enmity with blood of man
That swift as quicksilver it courses through
The natural gates and alleys of the body,
And with a sudden vigour it doth posset

And curd, like eager droppings into milk,
The thin and wholesome blood: so did it mine;
And a most instant tetter bark'd about,
Most lazar-like, with vile and loathsome crust,
All my smooth body.
Thus was I, sleeping, by a brother's hand,
Of life, of crown, of queen, at once dispatch'd;
Cut off even in the blossoms of my sin,
Unhousel'd, disappointed, unanel'd,[8]
No reckoning made, but sent to my account
With all my imperfections on my head:
O, horrible! O, horrible! most horrible!
If thou hast nature in thee, bear it not;
Let not the royal bed of Denmark be
A couch for luxury and damned incest.
But, howsoever thou pursu'st this act,
Taint not thy mind, nor let thy soul contrive
Against thy mother aught; leave her to heaven,
And to those thorns that in her bosom lodge,
To prick and sting her. Fare thee well at once!
The glow-worm shows the matin to be near,
And 'gins to pale his uneffectual fire;
Adieu, adieu! Hamlet, remember me.   *Exit.*
HAMLET: O all you host of heaven! O earth! What else?
And shall I couple hell? O fie! Hold, hold, my heart!
And you, my sinews, grow not instant old,
But bear me stiffly up! Remember thee!
Ay, thou poor ghost, while memory holds a seat
In this distracted globe. Remember thee!
Yea, from the table of my memory
I'll wipe away all trivial fond records,
All saws of books, all forms, all pressures past,
That youth and observation copied there;

---

[8] [*Unhousel'd:* without having received the Holy Communion; *disappointed:*
unprepared; *unanel'd:* without having received extreme unction.]

And thy commandment all alone shall live
Within the book and volume of my brain,
Unmix'd with baser matter: yes, by heaven!
O most pernicious woman!
O villain, villain, smiling, damned villain!
My tables, my tables,—meet it is I set it down,
That one may smile, and smile, and be a villain;
At least I'm sure it may be so in Denmark: [*Writing.*]
So, uncle, there you are. Now to my word;
It is, "Adieu, adieu! remember me."
I have sworn 't.

HORATIO *and* MARCELLUS (*within*): My lord! my lord!

Enter HORATIO *and* MARCELLUS.

MARCELLUS: Lord Hamlet!
HORATIO: Heaven secure him!
MARCELLUS: So be it!
HORATIO: Hillo, ho, ho, my lord!
HAMLET: Hillo, ho, ho, boy! come, bird, come.
MARCELLUS: How is 't, my noble lord?
HORATIO: What news, my lord?
HAMLET: O! wonderful.
HORATIO: Good my lord, tell it.
HAMLET: No; you will reveal it.
HORATIO: Not I, my lord, by heaven!
MARCELLUS: Nor I, my lord.
HAMLET: How say you, then; would heart of man once think
    it?
    But you'll be secret?
HORATIO, MARCELLUS: Ay, by heaven, my lord.
HAMLET: There's ne'er a villain dwelling in all Denmark,
    But he 's an arrant knave.
HORATIO: There needs no ghost, my lord, come from the grave,
    To tell us this.
HAMLET: Why, right; you are i' the right;
    And so, without more circumstance at all,

I hold it fit that we shake hands and part;
You, as your business and desire shall point you, —
For every man hath business and desire,
Such as it is, — and, for mine own poor part,
Look you, I'll go pray.

HORATIO: These are but wild and hurling words, my lord.

HAMLET: I am sorry they offend you, heartily;
Yes, faith, heartily.

HORATIO: There's no offence, my lord.

HAMLET: Yes, by Saint Patrick, but there is, Horatio,
And much offence, too. Touchng this vision here,
It is an honest ghost, that let me tell you;
For your desire to know what is between us,
O'ermaster 't as you may. And now, good friends,
As you are friends, scholars, and soldiers,
Give me one poor request.

HORATIO: What is 't, my lord? we will.

HAMLET: Never make known what you have seen to-night.

HORATIO, MARCELLUS: My lord, we will not.

HAMLET: Nay, but swear 't.

HORATIO: In faith,
My lord, not I.

MARCELLUS: Nor I, my lord, in faith.

HAMLET: Upon my sword.

MARCELLUS: We have sworn, my lord, already.

HAMLET: Indeed, upon my sword, indeed.

                    GHOST *cries under the stage.*

GHOST: Swear.

HAMLET: Ah, ha, boy! sayst thou so? art thou there, true-penny?
Come on, — you hear this fellow in the cellarage, —
Consent to swear.

HORATIO: Propose the oath, my lord.

HAMLET: Never to speak of this that you have seen,
Swear by my sword.

GHOST [*beneath*]: Swear.
HAMLET: *Hic et ubique?* then we'll shift our ground.
Come hither, gentlemen,
And lay your hands again upon my sword:
Never to speak of this that you have heard,
Swear by my sword.
GHOST [*beneath*]: Swear.
HAMLET: Well said, old mole! canst work i' the earth so fast?
A worthy pioneer! once more remove, good friends.
HORATIO: O day and night, but this is wondrous strange!
HAMLET: And therefore as a stranger give it welcome.
There are more things in heaven and earth, Horatio,
Than are dreamt of in your philosophy.
But come;
Here, as before, never, so help you mercy,
How strange or odd soe'er I bear myself,
As I perchance hereafter shall think meet
To put an antic disposition on,
That you, at such times seeing me, never shall,
With arms encumber'd thus, or thus, head shake,
Or by pronouncing of some doubtful phrase,
As, "Well, well, we know," or, "We could, an if we would";
Or, "If we list to speak," or, "There be, an if they might";
Or such ambiguous giving out, to note
That you know aught of me: this not to do,
So grace and mercy at your most need help you,
Swear.
GHOST [*beneath*]: Swear.   [*They swear.*]
HAMLET: Rest, rest, perturbed spirit! So, gentlemen,
With all my love I do commend me to you:
And what so poor a man as Hamlet is
May do, to express his love and friending to you,
God willing, shall not lack. Let us go in together;
And still your fingers on your lips, I pray.
The time is out of joint; O cursed spite,
That ever I was born to set it right!
Nay, come, let's go together.   *Exeunt.*

ACT II

SCENE ONE—POLONIUS' *Apartment in the Castle.*

Enter POLONIUS *and* REYNALDO.

POLONIUS: Give him this money and these notes, Reynaldo.
REYNALDO: I will, my lord.
POLONIUS: You shall do marvellous wisely, good Reynaldo,
Before you visit him, to make inquiry
Of his behaviour.
REYNALDO: My lord, I did intend it.
POLONIUS: Marry, well said, very well said. Look you, sir,
Inquire me first what Danskers are in Paris;
And how, and who, what means, and where they keep,
What company, at what expense; and finding
By this encompassment and drift of question
That they do know my son, come you more nearer
Than your particular demands will touch it:
Take you, as 'twere, some distant knowledge of him;
As thus, "I know his father, and his friends,
And, in part, him"; do you mark this, Reynaldo?
REYNALDO: Ay, very well, my lord.
POLONIUS: "And, in part, him; but," you may say, "not well:
But if 't be he I mean, he's very wild,
Addicted so and so"; and there put on him
What forgeries you please; marry, none so rank
As may dishonour him; take heed of that;
But, sir, such wanton, wild, and usual slips
As are companions noted and most known
To youth and liberty.
REYNALDO: As gaming, my lord?
POLONIUS: Ay, or drinking, fencing, swearing, quarrelling,
Drabbing; you may go so far.
REYNALDO: My lord, that would dishonour him.
POLONIUS: Faith, no; as you may season it in the charge.
You must not put another scandal on him,

That he is open to incontinency;
That's not my meaning; but breathe his faults so quaintly
That they may seem the taints of liberty,
The flash and outbreak of a fiery mind,
A savageness in unreclaimed blood,
Of general assault.

REYNALDO: But, my good lord,—
POLONIUS: Wherefore should you do this?
REYNALDO: Ay, my lord,
    I would know that.
POLONIUS: Marry, sir, here's my drift;
    And, I believe, it is a fetch of warrant:
    You laying these slight sullies on my son,
    As 'twere a thing a little soil'd i' the working,
    Mark you,
    Your party in converse, him you would sound,
    Having ever seen in the prenominate crimes
    The youth you breathe of guilty, be assur'd,
    He closes with you in this consequence;
    "Good sir," or so; or "friend," or "gentleman,"
    According to the phrase or the addition
    Of man and country.
REYNALDO: Very good, my lord.
POLONIUS: And then, sir, does he this,—he does,—what was
    I about to say? By the mass I was about to say something:
    where did I leave?
REYNALDO: At "closes in the consequence."
    At "friend or so," and "gentleman."
POLONIUS: At "closes in the consequence," ay, marry;
    He closes with you thus: "I know the gentleman;
    I saw him yesterday, or t' other day,
    Or then, or then; with such, or such; and, as you say,
    There was a' gaming; there o'ertook in 's rouse;
    There falling out at tennis"; or perchance,
    "I saw him enter such a house of sale,"
    Videlicet, a brothel, or so forth.

See you now;
Your bait of falsehood takes this carp of truth;
And thus do we of wisdom and of reach,
With windlasses, and with assays of bias,
By indirections find directions out:
So by my former lecture and advice
Shall you my son. You have me, have you not?
REYNALDO: My lord, I have.
POLONIUS: God be wi' you; fare you well.
REYNALDO: Good my lord!
POLONIUS: Observe his inclination in yourself.
REYNALDO: I shall, my lord.
POLONIUS: And let him ply his music.
REYNALDO: Well, my lord.
POLONIUS: Farewell!   *Exit* REYNALDO.
Enter OPHELIA.
                    How now, Ophelia! what's the matter?
OPHELIA: Alas! my lord, I have been so affrighted.
POLONIUS: With what, in the name of God?
OPHELIA: My lord, as I was sewing in my closet,
Lord Hamlet, with his doublet all unbrac'd;
No hat upon his head; his stockings foul'd,
Ungarter'd, and down-gyved to his ankle;
Pale as his shirt; his knees knocking each other;
And with a look so piteous in purport
As if he had been loosed out of hell
To speak of horrors, he comes before me.
POLONIUS: Mad for thy love?
OPHELIA: My lord, I do not know;
But truly I do fear it.
POLONIUS: What said he?
OPHELIA: He took me by the wrist and held me hard,
Then goes he to the length of all his arm,

And, with his other hand thus o'er his brow,
He falls to such perusal of my face
As he would draw it. Long stay'd he so;
At last, a little shaking of mine arm,
And thrice his head thus waving up and down,
He rais'd a sigh so piteous and profound
That it did seem to shatter all his bulk
And end his being. That done, he lets me go,
And, with his head over his shoulder turn'd,
He seem'd to find his way without his eyes;
For out o' doors he went without their help,
And to the last bended their light on me.

POLONIUS: Come, go with me; I will go seek the king.
This is the very ecstasy of love,
Whose violent property fordoes itself
And leads the will to desperate undertakings
As oft as any passion under heaven
That does afflict our natures. I am sorry.
What! have you given him any hard words of late?

OPHELIA: No, my good lord; but, as you did command,
I did repel his letters and denied
His access to me.

POLONIUS: That hath made him mad.
I am sorry that with better heed and judgment
I had not quoted him; I fear'd he did but trifle,
And meant to wrack thee; but, beshrew my jealousy!
By heaven, it is as proper to our age
To cast beyond ourselves in our opinions
As it is common for the younger sort
To lack discretion. Come, go we to the king:
This must be known; which, being kept close, might move
More grief to hide than hate to utter love.
Come.   *Exeunt.*

SCENE TWO—*A Room in the Castle.*

Enter KING, QUEEN, ROSENCRANTZ, GUILDENSTERN, *with others.*

KING: Welcome, dear Rosencrantz and Guildenstern!
Moreover that we much did long to see you,
The need we have to use you did provoke
Our hasty sending. Something have you heard
Of Hamlet's transformation; so I call it,
Since nor the exterior nor the inward man
Resembles that it was. What it should be
More than his father's death, that thus hath put him
So much from the understanding of himself,
I cannot dream of: I entreat you both,
That, being of so young days brought up with him,
And since so neighbour'd to his youth and humour,
That you vouchsafe your rest here in our court
Some little time; so by your companies
To draw him on to pleasures, and to gather,
So much as from occasion you may glean,
Whether aught to us unknown afflicts him thus,
That, open'd, lies within our remedy.
QUEEN: Good gentlemen, he hath much talk'd of you;
And sure I am two men there are not living
To whom he more adheres. If it will please you
To show us so much gentry and good will
As to expend your time with us awhile,
For the supply and profit of our hope,
Your visitation shall receive such thanks
As fits a king's remembrance.
ROSENCRANTZ: Both your majesties
Might, by the sovereign power you have of us,
Put your dread pleasures more into command
Than to entreaty.
GUILDENSTERN: But we both obey,
And here give up ourselves, in the full bent,

To lay our service freely at your feet,
To be commanded.

KING: Thanks, Rosencrantz and gentle Guildenstern.

QUEEN: Thanks, Guildenstern and gentle Rosencrantz;
And I beseech you instantly to visit
My too much changed son. Go, some of you,
And bring these gentlemen where Hamlet is.

GUILDENSTERN: Heavens make our presence, and our practices
Pleasant and helpful to him!

QUEEN: Ay, amen!

Exeunt ROSENCRANTZ,
GUILDENSTERN, [*and some* Attendants].

Enter POLONIUS.

POLONIUS: The ambassadors from Norway, my good lord,
Are joyfully return'd.

KING: Thou still hast been the father of good news.

POLONIUS: Have I, my lord? Assure you, my good liege,
I hold my duty, as I hold my soul,
Both to my God, one to my gracious king;
And I do think—or else this brain of mine
Hunts not the trail of policy so sure
As it hath us'd to do—that I have found
The very cause of Hamlet's lunacy.

KING: O! speak of that; that do I long to hear.

POLONIUS: Give first admittance to the ambassadors;
My news shall be the fruit to that great feast.

KING: Thyself do grace to them, and bring them in.
[*Exit* POLONIUS.]
He tells me, my sweet queen, that he hath found
The head and source of all your son's distemper.

QUEEN: I doubt it is no other but the main;
His father's death, and our o'erhasty marriage.

KING: Well, we shall sift him.

Enter POLONIUS, VOLTIMAND, *and* CORNELIUS.

                                    Welcome, my good friends!
     Say, Voltimand, what from our brother Norway?
VOLTIMAND: Most fair return of greetings, and desires.
     Upon our first, he sent out to suppress
     His nephew's levies, which to him appear'd
     To be a preparation 'gainst the Polack;
     But, better look'd into, he truly found
     It was against your highness: whereat griev'd,
     That so his sickness, age, and impotence
     Was falsely borne in hand, sends out arrests
     On Fortinbras; which he, in brief, obeys,
     Receives rebuke from Norway, and, in fine,
     Makes vow before his uncle never more
     To give the assay of arms against your majesty.
     Whereon old Norway, overcome with joy,
     Gives him three thousand crowns in annual fee,
     And his commission to employ those soldiers,
     So levied as before, against the Polack;
     With an entreaty, herein further shown,   [*Giving a paper.*]
     That it might please you to give quiet pass
     Through your dominions for this enterprise,
     On such regards of safety and allowance
     As therein are set down.
KING: It likes us well;
     And at our more consider'd time we'll read,
     Answer, and think upon this business:
     Meantime we thank you for your well-took labour.
     Go to your rest; at night we'll feast together:
     Most welcome home.
                              Exeunt Ambassadors
                         [VOLTIMAND *and* CORNELIUS].

POLONIUS: This business is well ended.
     My liege, and madam, to expostulate
     What majesty should be, what duty is,
     Why day is day, night night, and time is time,

Were nothing but to waste night, day, and time.
Therefore, since brevity is the soul of wit,
And tediousness the limbs and outward flourishes,
I will be brief. Your noble son is mad:
Mad call I it; for, to define true madness,
What is 't but to be nothing else but mad?
But let that go.

QUEEN: More matter, with less art.

POLONIUS: Madam, I swear I use no art at all.
That he is mad, 'tis true; 'tis true 'tis pity;
And pity 'tis 'tis true: a foolish figure;
But farewell it, for I will use no art.
Mad let us grant him, then; and now remains
That we find out the cause of this effect,
Or rather say, the cause of this defect,
For this effect defective comes by cause;
Thus it remains, and the remainder thus.
Perpend.
I have a daughter, have while she is mine;
Who, in her duty and obedience, mark,
Hath given me this: now, gather, and surmise.   [*Reads.*]
"To the celestial, and my soul's idol, the most beautified
    Ophelia. —"
That's an ill phrase, a vile phrase; "beautified" is a vile phrase;
    but you shall hear. Thus:
"In her excellent white bosom, these, &c. —"

QUEEN: Came this from Hamlet to her?

POLONIUS: Good madam, stay awhile; I will be faithful.

> "Doubt thou the stars are fire;
>   Doubt that the sun doth move;
> Doubt truth to be a liar;
>   But never doubt I love.

O dear Ophelia! I am ill at these numbers: I have not art to
reckon my groans; but that I love thee best, O most best!
believe it. Adieu.

> Thine evermore, most dear lady, whilst
> this machine is to him,
>
>   HAMLET."

This in obedience hath my daughter shown me;
And more above, hath his solicitings,
As they fell out by time, by means, and place,
All given to mine ear.

KING: But how hath she
Receiv'd his love?

POLONIUS: What do you think of me?

KING: As of a man faithful and honourable.

POLONIUS: I would fain prove so. But what might you think,
When I had seen this hot love on the wing, —
As I perceiv'd it, I must tell you that,
Before my daughter told me, — what might you,
Or my dear majesty, your queen here, think,
If I had play'd the desk or table-book,
Or given my heart a winking, mute and dumb,
Or look'd upon this love with idle sight;
What might you think? No, I went round to work,
And my young mistress thus I did bespeak:
"Lord Hamlet is a prince, out of thy star;
This must not be": and then I precepts gave her,
That she should lock herself from his resort,
Admit no messengers, receive no tokens.
Which done, she took the fruits of my advice;
And he, repulsed, — a short tale to make, —
Fell into a sadness, then into a fast,
Thence to a watch, thence into a weakness,
Thence to a lightness; and by this declension
Into the madness wherein now he raves,
And all we wail for.

KING: Do you think 'tis this?

QUEEN: It may be, very likely.

POLONIUS: Hath there been such a time, — I'd fain know
that, —

That I have positively said, " 'Tis so,"
When it prov'd otherwise?
KING: Not that I know.
POLONIUS [*pointing to his head and shoulder*]: Take this from
    this, if this be otherwise:
If circumstances lead me, I will find
Where truth is hid, though it were hid indeed
Within the centre.
KING: How may we try it further?
POLONIUS: You know sometimes he walks four hours together
    Here in the lobby.
QUEEN: So he does indeed.
POLONIUS: At such a time I'll loose my daughter to him;
    Be you and I behind an arras then;
Mark the encounter; if he love her not,
And be not from his reason fallen thereon,
Let me be no assistant for a state,
But keep a farm, and carters.
KING: We will try it.

Enter HAMLET *reading on a book.*

QUEEN: But look, where sadly the poor wretch comes reading.
POLONIUS: Away! I do beseech you, both away.
    I'll board him presently.
                     Exeunt KING, QUEEN, [*and* Attendants].
                  O! give me leave.
    How does my good Lord Hamlet?
HAMLET: Well, God a-mercy.
POLONIUS: Do you know me, my lord?
HAMLET: Excellent well; you are a fishmonger.
POLONIUS: Not I, my lord.
HAMLET: Then I would you were so honest a man.
POLONIUS: Honest, my lord!
HAMLET: Ay, sir; to be honest, as this world goes, is to be one
    man picked out of ten thousand.

POLONIUS: That's very true, my lord.

HAMLET: For if the sun breed maggots in a dead dog, being a good kissing carrion,—Have you a daughter?

POLONIUS: I have, my lord.

HAMLET: Let her not walk i' the sun: conception is a blessing; but not as your daughter may conceive. Friend, look to 't.

POLONIUS [aside]: How say you by that? Still harping on my daughter: yet he knew me not at first; he said I was a fishmonger: he is far gone, far gone: and truly in my youth I suffered much extremity for love; very near this. I'll speak to him again. What do you read, my lord?

HAMLET: Words, words, words.

POLONIUS: What is the matter, my lord?

HAMLET: Between who?

POLONIUS: I mean the matter that you read, my lord.

HAMLET: Slanders, sir: for the satirical rogue says here that old men have grey beards, that their faces are wrinkled, their eyes purging thick amber and plum-tree gum, and that they have a plentiful lack of wit, together with most weak hams: all which, sir, though I most powerfully and potently believe, yet I hold it not honesty to have it thus set down; for you yourself, sir, should be old as I am, if, like a crab, you could go backward.

POLONIUS [aside]: Though this be madness, yet there is method in 't. Will you walk out of the air, my lord?

HAMLET: Into my grave?

POLONIUS: Indeed, that is out of the air. [Aside.] How pregnant sometimes his replies are! a happiness that often madness hits on, which reason and sanity could not so prosperously be delivered of. I will leave him, and suddenly contrive the means of meeting between him and my daughter. My honourable lord, I will most humbly take my leave of you.

HAMLET: You cannot, sir, take from me any thing that I will more willingly part withal; except my life, except my life, except my life.

POLONIUS: Fare you well, my lord.   [*Going.*]
HAMLET: These tedious old fools!

Enter ROSENCRANTZ *and* GUILDENSTERN.

POLONIUS: You go to seek the Lord Hamlet; there he is.
ROSENCRANTZ [*to* POLONIUS]: God save you, sir!
                                        [*Exit* POLONIUS.]
GUILDENSTERN: Mine honoured lord!
ROSENCRANTZ: My most dear lord!
HAMLET: My excellent good friends! How dost thou, Guilden-
stern? Ah, Rosencrantz! Good lads, how do ye both?
ROSENCRANTZ: As the indifferent children of the earth.
GUILDENSTERN: Happy in that we are not over happy; on For-
tune's cap we are not the very button.
HAMLET: Nor the soles of her shoe?
ROSENCRANTZ: Neither, my lord.
HAMLET: Then you live about her waist, or in the middle of
her favours?
GUILDENSTERN: Faith, her privates we.
HAMLET: In the secret parts of Fortune? O! most true; she is a
strumpet. What news?
ROSENCRANTZ: None, my lord, but that the world's grown
honest.
HAMLET: Then is doomsday near; but your news is not true.
Let me question more in particular: what have you, my
good friends, deserved at the hands of Fortune, that she
sends you to prison hither?
GUILDENSTERN: Prison, my lord!
HAMLET: Denmark's a prison.
ROSENCRANTZ: Then is the world one.
HAMLET: A goodly one; in which there are many confines, wards,
and dungeons, Denmark being one o' the worst.
ROSENCRANTZ: We think not so, my lord.
HAMLET: Why, then, 'tis none to you; for there is nothing either
good or bad, but thinking makes it so: to me it is a prison.

ROSENCRANTZ: Why, then your ambition makes it one; 'tis too narrow for your mind.

HAMLET: O God! I could be bounded in a nutshell, and count myself a king of infinite space, were it not that I have bad dreams.

GUILDENSTERN: Which dreams, indeed, are ambition, for the very substance of the ambitious is merely the shadow of a dream.

HAMLET: A dream itself is but a shadow.

ROSENCRANTZ: Truly, and I hold ambition of so airy and light a quality that it is but a shadow's shadow.

HAMLET: Then are our beggars bodies, and our monarchs and outstretched heroes the beggars' shadows. Shall we to the court? for, by my fay, I cannot reason.

ROSENCRANTZ, GUILDENSTERN: We'll wait upon you.

HAMLET: No such matter; I will not sort you with the rest of my servants, for, to speak to you like an honest man, I am most dreadfully attended. But, in the beaten way of friendship, what make you at Elsinore?

ROSENCRANTZ: To visit you, my lord; no other occasion.

HAMLET: Beggar that I am, I am even poor in thanks; but I thank you: and sure, dear friends, my thanks are too dear a halfpenny. Were you not sent for? Is it your own inclining? Is it a free visitation? Come, come, deal justly with me: come, come; nay, speak.

GUILDENSTERN: What should we say, my lord?

HAMLET: Why anything, but to the purpose. You were sent for; and there is a kind of confession in your looks which your modesties have not craft enough to colour: I know the good king and queen have sent for you.

ROSENCRANTZ: To what end, my lord?

HAMLET: That you must teach me. But let me conjure you, by the rights of our fellowship, by the consonancy of our youth, by the obligation of our ever-preserved love, and by what more dear a better proposer could charge you withal, be even and direct with me, whether you were sent for or no!

ROSENCRANTZ [*aside to* GUILDENSTERN]: What say you?

HAMLET: Nay, then, I have an eye of you. If you love me, hold not off.

GUILDENSTERN: My lord, we were sent for.

HAMLET: I will tell you why; so shall my anticipation prevent your discovery, and your secrecy to the king and queen moult no feather. I have of late,—but wherefore I know not,—lost all my mirth, forgone all custom of exercises; and indeed it goes so heavily with my disposition that this goodly frame, the earth, seems to me a sterile promontory; this most excellent canopy, the air, look you, this brave o'erhanging firmament, this majestical roof fretted with golden fire, why, it appears no other thing to me but a foul and pestilent congregation of vapours. What a piece of work is a man! How noble in reason! how infinite in faculty! in form and moving, how express and admirable! in action how like an angel! in apprehension how like a god! the beauty of the world! the paragon of animals! And yet, to me, what is this quintessence of dust? man delights not me; no, nor woman neither, though, by your smiling, you seem to say so.

ROSENCRANTZ: My lord, there was no such stuff in my thoughts.

HAMLET: Why did you laugh then, when I said "man delights not me?"

ROSENCRANTZ: To think, my lord, if you delight not in man, what lenten entertainment the players shall receive from you: we coted them on the way; and hither are they coming, to offer you service.

HAMLET: He that plays the king shall be welcome; his majesty shall have tribute of me; the adventurous knight shall use his foil and target; the lover shall not sigh gratis; the humorous man shall end his part in peace; the clown shall make those laugh whose lungs are tickle o' the sere;[9] and

---

[9] [*tickle o' the sere:* yield easily to any impulse.]

the lady shall say her mind freely, or the blank verse shall halt for 't. What players are they?

ROSENCRANTZ: Even those you were wont to take delight in, the tragedians of the city.

HAMLET: How chances it they travel? their residence, both in reputation and profit, was better both ways.

ROSENCRANTZ: I think their inhibition comes by the means of the late innovation.

HAMLET: Do they hold the same estimation they did when I was in the city? Are they so followed?

ROSENCRANTZ: No, indeed they are not.

HAMLET: How comes it? Do they grow rusty?

ROSENCRANTZ: Nay, their endeavour keeps in the wonted pace: but there is, sir, an aery of children, little eyases, that cry out on the top of question,[10] and are most tyrannically clapped for 't: these are now the fashion, and so berattle the common stages,—so they call them,—that many wearing rapiers are afraid of goose-quills,[11] and dare scarce come thither.

HAMLET: What! are they children? who maintains 'em? how are they escoted? Will they pursue the quality no longer than they can sing? will they not say afterwards, if they should grow themselves to common players,—as it is most like, if their means are no better,— their writers do them wrong, to make them exclaim against their own succession?

ROSENCRANTZ: Faith, there has been much to-do on both sides: and the nation holds it no sin to tarre them to controversy: there was, for a while, no money bid for argument,[12] unless the poet and the player went to cuffs in the question.

---

[10] [*eyases:* young hawks; *cry . . . question:* recite at the highest pitch of the voice.]

[11] [*afraid of goose-quills:* afraid of being satirized.]

[12] [*argument:* subject matter, plot.]

HAMLET: Is it possible?

GUILDENSTERN: O! there has been much throwing about of brains.

HAMLET: Do the boys carry it away?

ROSENCRANTZ: Ay, that they do, my lord; Hercules and his load too.

HAMLET: It is not strange; for my uncle is King of Denmark, and those that would make mows at him while my father lived, give twenty, forty, fifty, a hundred ducats a-piece for his picture in little. 'Sblood, there is something in this more than natural, if philosophy could find it out.

Flourish for the Players.

GUILDENSTERN: There are the players.

HAMLET: Gentlemen, you are welcome to Elsinore. Your hands, come then; the appurtenance of welcome is fashion and ceremony: let me comply with you in this garb, lest my extent to the players—which, I tell you, must show fairly outward—should more appear like entertainment than yours. You are welcome; but my uncle-father and aunt-mother are deceived.

GUILDENSTERN: In what, my dear lord?

HAMLET: I am but mad north-north-west: when the wind is southerly I know a hawk from a handsaw.

Enter POLONIUS.

POLONIUS: Well be with you, gentlemen!

HAMLET: Hark you, Guildenstern; and you too; at each ear a hearer: that great baby you see there is not yet out of his swaddling-clouts.

ROSENCRANTZ: Happily he's the second time come to them; for they say an old man is twice a child.

HAMLET: I will prophesy he comes to tell me of the players; mark it. You say right, sir; o' Monday morning; 'twas so indeed.

POLONIUS: My lord, I have news to tell you.
HAMLET: My lord, I have news to tell you. When Roscius was an actor in Rome, —
POLONIUS: The actors are come hither, my lord.
HAMLET: Buzz, buzz!
POLONIUS: Upon my honour, —
HAMLET: Then came each actor on his ass, —
POLONIUS: The best actors in the world, either for tragedy, comedy, history, pastoral, pastoral-comical, historical-pastoral, tragical-historical, tragical-comical-historical-pastoral, scene individable, or poem unlimited: Seneca cannot be too heavy, nor Plautus too light. For the law of writ and the liberty, these are the only men.
HAMLET: O Jephthah, judge of Israel, what a treasure hadst thou!
POLONIUS: What a treasure had he, my lord?
HAMLET: Why

> "One fair daughter and no more,
> The which he loved passing well."

POLONIUS [aside]: Still on my daughter.
HAMLET: Am I not i' the right, old Jephthah?
POLONIUS: If you call me Jephthah, my lord, I have a daughter that I love passing well.
HAMLET: Nay, that follows not.
POLONIUS: What follows, then, my lord?
HAMLET: Why,

> "As by lot, God wot."

And then, you know,

> "It came to pass, as most like it was. —"

The first row of the pious chanson will show you more; for look where my abridgments come.

Enter four or five Players.

You are welcome, masters; welcome, all. I am glad to see thee well: welcome, good friends. O, my old friend! Thy face is valanced since I saw thee last: comest thou to beard me in Denmark? What! my young lady and mistress! By 'r lady, your ladyship is nearer heaven than when I saw you last, by the altitude of a chopine.[13] Pray God, your voice, like a piece of uncurrent gold, be not cracked within the ring. Masters, you are welcome. We'll e'en to 't like French falconers, fly at anything we see: we'll have a speech straight. Come, give us a taste of your quality; come, a passionate speech.

FIRST PLAYER: What speech, my lord?

HAMLET: I heard thee speak me a speech once, but it was never acted; or, if it was, not above once; for the play, I remember, pleased not the million; 'twas caviare to the general: but it was—as I received it, and others, whose judgments in such matters cried in the top of mine—an excellent play, well digested in the scenes, set down with as much modesty as cunning. I remember one said there were no sallets in the lines to make the matter savoury, nor no matter in the phrase that might indict the author of affectation; but called it an honest method, as wholesome as sweet, and by very much more handsome than fine. One speech in it I chiefly loved; 'twas Aeneas' tale to Dido; and thereabout of it especially, where he speaks of Priam's slaughter. If it live in your memory, begin at this line: let me see, let me see:—

"The rugged Pyrrhus, like the Hyrcanian beast,—"
'Tis not so, it begins with Pyrrhus:—
"The rugged Pyrrhus, he, whose sable arms,
Black as his purpose, did the night resemble
When he lay couched in the ominous horse,
Hath now this dread and black complexion smear'd
With heraldry more dismal; head to foot
Now is he total gules; horridly trick'd[14]

---

[13] [*chopine:* a Venetian raised shoe often worn by actors.]
[14] [*gules:* red, in heraldry; *trick'd:* painted.]

With blood of fathers, mothers, daughters, sons,
Bak'd and impasted with the parching streets,
That lend a tyrannous and damned light
To their vile murders: roasted in wrath and fire,
And thus o'er-sized with coagulate gore,
With eyes like carbuncles, the hellish Pyrrhus
Old grandsire Priam seeks."
So proceed you.

POLONIUS: 'Fore God, my lord, well spoken; with good accent and good discretion.

FIRST PLAYER: "Anon, he finds him
Striking too short at Greeks; his antique sword,
Rebellious to his arm, lies where it falls,
Repugnant to command. Unequal match'd,
Pyrrhus at Priam drives; in rage strikes wide;
But with the whiff and wind of his fell sword
The unnerved father falls. Then senseless Ilium,
Seeming to feel this blow, with flaming top
Stoops to his base, and with a hideous crash
Takes prisoner Pyrrhus' ear: for lo! his sword,
Which was declining on the milky head
Of reverend Priam, seem'd i' the air to stick:
So, as a painted tyrant, Pyrrhus stood,
And like a neutral to his will and matter,
Did nothing.
But, as we often see, against some storm,
A silence in the heavens, the rack stand still,
The bold winds speechless and the orb below
As hush as death, anon the dreadful thunder
Doth rend the region; so, after Pyrrhus' pause,
Aroused vengeance sets him new a-work;
And never did the Cyclops' hammers fall
On Mars's armour, forg'd for proof eterne,
With less remorse than Pyrrhus' bleeding sword
Now falls on Priam.
Out, out, thou strumpet, Fortune! All you gods,

In general synod, take away her power;
Break all the spokes and fellies from her wheel,
And bowl the round nave down the hill of heaven,
As low as to the fiends!"

POLONIUS: This is too long.

HAMLET: It shall to the barber's, with your beard. Prithee, say
on: he's for a jig or a tale of bawdry, or he sleeps. Say on;
come to Hecuba.

FIRST PLAYER: "But who, O! who had seen the mobled[15]
queen—"

HAMLET: "The mobled queen?"—

POLONIUS: That's good; "mobled queen" is good.

FIRST PLAYER: "Run barefoot up and down, threat'ning the
flames
With bisson rheum; a clout upon that head
Where late the diadem stood; and, for a robe,
About her lank and all o'er-teemed loins,
A blanket, in the alarm of fear caught up;
Who this had seen, with tongue in venom steep'd,
'Gainst Fortune's state would treason have pronounc'd:
But if the gods themselves did see her then,
When she saw Pyrrhus make malicious sport
In mincing with his sword her husband's limbs,
The instant burst of clamour that she made—
Unless things mortal move them not at all—
Would have made milch the burning eyes of heaven,
And passion in the gods."

POLONIUS: Look! wh'er he has not turned his colour and has
tears in 's eyes. Prithee, no more.

GUILDENSTERN: 'Tis well; I'll have thee speak out the rest soon.
Good my lord, will you see the players well bestowed? Do
you hear, let them be well used; for they are the abstracts
and brief chronicles of the time: after your death you were

---

[15] [*mobled*: muffled.]

better have a bad epitaph than their ill report while you
live.

POLONIUS: My lord, I will use them according to their desert.

HAMLET: God's bodikins, man, much better; use every man
after his desert, and who should 'scape whipping? Use them
after your own honour and dignity: the less they deserve,
the more merit is in your bounty. Take them in.

POLONIUS: Come, sirs.

HAMLET: Follow him, friends: we'll hear a play to-morrow. *Exit*
POLONIUS [*with all the* Players *but the* FIRST]. Dost thou
hear me, old friend; can you play the Murder of Gonzago?

FIRST PLAYER: Ay, my lord.

HAMLET: We'll ha 't to-morrow night. You could, for a need,
study a speech of some dozen or sixteen lines, which I
would set down and insert in 't, could you not?

FIRST PLAYER: Ay, my lord.

HAMLET: Very well. Follow that lord; and look you mock him
not. [*Exit* FIRST PLAYER. *To* ROSENCRANTZ *and* GUILDEN-
STERN.] My good friends, I'll leave you till night; you are
welcome to Elsinore.

ROSENCRANTZ: Good my lord!

Exeunt [ROSENCRANTZ *and* GUILDENSTERN].

HAMLET: Ay, so, God be wi' ye! Now I am alone.
O! what a rogue and peasant slave am I:
Is it not monstrous that this player here,
But in a fiction, in a dream of passion,
Could force his soul so to his own conceit
That from her working all his visage wann'd,
Tears in his eyes, distraction in 's aspect,
A broken voice, and his whole function suiting
With forms to his conceit? and all for nothing!
For Hecuba!
What's Hecuba to him or he to Hecuba
That he should weep for her? What would he do
Had he the motive and the cue for passion

That I have? He would drown the stage with tears,
And cleave the general ear with horrid speech,
Make mad the guilty and appal the free,
Confound the ignorant, and amaze indeed
The very faculties of eyes and ears.
Yet I,
A dull and muddy-mettled rascal, peak,
Like John-a-dreams, unpregnant of my cause,
And can say nothing; no, not for a king,
Upon whose property and most dear life
A damn'd defeat was made. Am I a coward?
Who calls me villain? breaks my pate across?
Plucks off my beard and blows it in my face?
Tweaks me by the nose? gives me the lie i' the throat,
As deep as to the lungs? Who does me this?
Ha!
'Swounds, I should take it, for it cannot be
But I am pigeon-liver'd, and lack gall
To make oppression bitter, or ere this
I should have fatted all the region kites
With this slave's offal. Bloody, bawdy villain!
Remorseless, treacherous, lecherous, kindless villain!
O! vengeance!
Why, what an ass am I! This is most brave
That I, the son of a dear father murder'd,
Prompted to my revenge by heaven and hell,
Must, like a whore, unpack my heart with words,
And fall a-cursing, like a very drab,
A scullion!
Fie upon 't! foh! About, my brain! I have heard,
That guilty creatures sitting at a play
Have by the very cunning of the scene
Been struck so to the soul that presently
They have proclaim'd their malefactions;
For murder, though it have no tongue, will speak
With most miraculous organ. I'll have these players

Play something like the murder of my father
Before mine uncle; I'll observe his looks;
I'll tent him to the quick: if he but blench
I know my course. The spirit that I have seen
May be the devil: and the devil hath power
To assume a pleasing shape; yea, and perhaps
Out of my weakness and my melancholy—
As he is very potent with such spirits—
Abuses me to damn me. I'll have grounds
More relative than this: the play's the thing
Wherein I'll catch the conscience of the king.   *Exit.*

ACT III

SCENE ONE—*A Room in the Castle.*

Enter KING, QUEEN, POLONIUS, OPHELIA, ROSENCRANTZ, GUILDENSTERN, *and* Lords.

KING: And can you, by no drift of circumstance,
Get from him why he puts on this confusion,
Grating so harshly all his days of quiet
With turbulent and dangerous lunacy?
ROSENCRANTZ: He does confess he feels himself distracted;
But from what cause he will by no means speak.
GUILDENSTERN: Nor do we find him forward to be sounded,
But, with a crafty madness, keeps aloof,
When we would bring him on to some confession
Of his true state.
QUEEN: Did he receive you well?
ROSENCRANTZ: Most like a gentleman.
GUILDENSTERN: But with much forcing of his disposition.
ROSENCRANTZ: Niggard of question, but of our demands
Most free in his reply.
QUEEN: Did you assay him
To any pastime?
ROSENCRANTZ: Madam, it so fell out that certain players
We o'er-raught on the way; of these we told him,
And there did seem in him a kind of joy
To hear of it: they are about the court,
And, as I think, they have already order
This night to play before him.
POLONIUS: 'Tis most true;
And he beseech'd me to entreat your majesties
To hear and see the matter.
KING: With all my heart; and it doth much content me
To hear him so inclin'd.
Good gentlemen, give him a further edge,
And drive his purpose on to these delights.

ROSENCRANTZ: We shall, my lord.

Exeunt [ROSENCRANTZ *and* GUILDENSTERN].

KING: Sweet Gertrude, leave us too;
For we have closely sent for Hamlet hither,
That he, as 'twere by accident, may here
Affront Ophelia.
Her father and myself, lawful espials,
Will so bestow ourselves, that, seeing, unseen,
We may of their encounter frankly judge,
And gather by him, as he is behav'd,
If 't be the affliction of his love or no
That thus he suffers for.

QUEEN: I shall obey you.
And for your part, Ophelia, I do wish
That your good beauties be the happy cause
Of Hamlet's wildness; so shall I hope your virtues
Will bring him to his wonted way again,
To both your honours.

OPHELIA: Madam, I wish it may.

[*Exit* QUEEN.]

POLONIUS: Ophelia, walk you here. Gracious, so please you,
We will bestow ourselves. [*To* OPHELIA.] Read on this book;
That show of such an exercise may colour
Your loneliness. We are oft to blame in this,
'Tis too much prov'd, that with devotion's visage
And pious action we do sugar o'er
The devil himself.

KING [*aside*]: O! 'tis too true;
How smart a lash that speech doth give my conscience!
The harlot's cheek, beautied with plastering art,
Is not more ugly to the thing that helps it
Than is my deed to my most painted word:
O heavy burden!

POLONIUS: I hear him coming; let's withdraw, my lord.

Exeunt [KING *and* POLONIUS].

Enter HAMLET.

HAMLET: To be, or not to be: that is the question:
Whether 'tis nobler in the mind to suffer
The slings and arrows of outrageous fortune,
Or to take arms against a sea of troubles,
And by opposing end them? To die, to sleep;
No more; and, by a sleep to say we end
The heart-ache and the thousand natural shocks
That flesh is heir to, 'tis a consummation
Devoutly to be wish'd. To die, to sleep;
To sleep, perchance to dream: ay, there's the rub;
For in that sleep of death what dreams may come
When we have shuffled off this mortal coil,
Must give us pause. There's the respect
That makes calamity of so long life;
For who would bear the whips and scorns of time,
The oppressor's wrong, the proud man's contumely,
The pangs of dispriz'd love, the law's delay,
The insolence of office, and the spurns
That patient merit of the unworthy takes,
When he himself might his quietus make
With a bare bodkin? who would fardels bear,[16]
To grunt and sweat under a weary life,
But that the dread of something after death,
The undiscover'd country from whose bourn
No traveller returns, puzzles the will,
And makes us rather bear those ills we have
Than fly to others that we know not of?
Thus conscience does make cowards of us all;
And thus the native hue of resolution

---

[16] [*bodkin:* dagger; *fardels:* burdens.]

Is sicklied o'er with pale cast of thought,
And enterprises of great pith and moment
With this regard their currents turn awry,
And lose the name of action. Soft you now!
The fair Ophelia! Nymph, in thy orisons
Be all my sins remember'd.

OPHELIA: Good my lord,
How does your honour for this many a day?

HAMLET: I humbly thank you; well, well, well.

OPHELIA: My lord, I have remembrances of yours,
That I have longed long to re-deliver;
I pray you, now receive them.

HAMLET: No, not I;
I never gave you aught.

OPHELIA: My honour'd lord, you know right well you did;
And, with them, words of so sweet breath compos'd
As made the things more rich: their perfume lost,
Take these again; for to the noble mind
Rich gifts wax poor when givers prove unkind.
There, my lord.

HAMLET: Ha, ha! are you honest?[17]

OPHELIA: My lord!

HAMLET: Are you fair?

OPHELIA: What means your lordship?

HAMLET: That if you be honest and fair, your honesty should
admit no discourse to your beauty.

OPHELIA: Could beauty, my lord, have better commerce than
with honesty?

HAMLET: Ay, truly; for the power of beauty will sooner trans-
form honesty from what it is to a bawd than the force of
honesty can translate beauty into his likeness: this was
sometime a paradox, but now the time gives it proof. I
did love you once.

---

[17] [*honest:* chaste.]

OPHELIA: Indeed, my lord, you made me believe so.

HAMLET: You should not have believed me; for virtue cannot so inoculate our old stock but we shall relish of it: I loved you not.

OPHELIA: I was the more deceived.

HAMLET: Get thee to a nunnery: why wouldst thou be a breeder of sinners? I am myself indifferent honest; but yet I could accuse me of such things that it were better my mother had not borne me. I am very proud, revengeful, ambitious; with more offences at my beck than I have thoughts to put them in, imagination to give them shape, or time to act them in. What should such fellows as I do crawling between heaven and earth? We are arrant knaves, all; believe none of us. Go thy ways to a nunnery. Where's your father?

OPHELIA: At home, my lord.

HAMLET: Let the doors be shut upon him, that he may play the fool nowhere but in 's own house. Farewell.

OPHELIA: O! help him, you sweet heavens!

HAMLET: If thou dost marry, I'll give thee this plague for thy dowry: be thou as chaste as ice, as pure as snow, thou shalt not escape calumny. Get thee to a nunnery, go; farewell. Or, if thou wilt needs marry, marry a fool; for wise men know well enough what monsters you make of them. To a nunnery, go; and quickly too. Farewell.

OPHELIA: O heavenly powers, restore him!

HAMLET: I have heard of your paintings too, well enough; God hath given you one face, and you make yourselves another: you jig, you amble, and you lisp, and nickname God's creatures, and make your wantonness your ignorance. Go to, I'll no more on 't; it hath made me mad. I say, we will have no more marriages; those that are married already, all but one, shall live; the rest shall keep as they are. To a nunnery, go. *Exit* HAMLET.

OPHELIA: O! what a noble mind is here o'erthrown:
The courtier's, soldier's, scholar's, eye, tongue, sword;
The expectancy and rose of the fair state,
The glass of fashion and the mould of form,
The observ'd of all observers, quite, quite down!
And I, of ladies most deject and wretched,
That suck'd the honey of his music vows,
Now see that noble and most sovereign reason,
Like sweet bells jangled, out of tune and harsh;
That unmatch'd form and feature of blown youth
Blasted with ecstasy: O! woe is me,
To have seen what I have seen, see what I see!

Enter KING *and* POLONIUS.

KING: Love! his affections do not that way tend;
Nor what he spake, though it lack'd form a little,
Was not like madness. There's something in his soul
O'er which his melancholy sits on brood;
And, I do doubt, the hatch and the disclose
Will be some danger; which for to prevent,
I have in quick determination
Thus set it down: he shall with speed to England,
For the demand of our neglected tribute:
Haply the seas and countries different
With variable objects shall expel
This something-settled matter in his heart,
Whereon his brains still beating puts him thus
From fashion of himself. What think you on 't?
POLONIUS: It shall do well: but yet do I believe
The origin and commencement of his grief
Sprung from neglected love. How now, Ophelia!
You need not tell us what Lord Hamlet said;
We heard it all. My lord, do as you please;
But, if you hold it fit, after the play,
Let his queen mother all alone entreat him
To show his griefs: let her be round with him;

And I'll be plac'd, so please you, in the ear
Of all their conference. If she find him not,
To England send him, or confine him where
Your wisdom best shall think.
KING: It shall be so:
Madness in great ones must not unwatch'd go.   *Exeunt.*

SCENE TWO—*A Hall in the Castle.*

Enter HAMLET *and two or three of the* Players.

HAMLET: Speak the speech, I pray you, as I pronounced it to
you, trippingly on the tongue; but if you mouth it, as
many of your players do, I had as lief the town-crier spoke
my lines. Nor do not saw the air too much with your hand,
thus; but use all gently: for in the very torrent, tempest,
and—as I may say—whirlwind of passion, you must acquire and beget a temperance, that may give it smoothness.
O! it offends me to the soul to hear a robustious periwig-
pated fellow tear a passion to tatters, to very rags, to split
the ears of the groundlings, who for the most part are
capable of nothing but inexplicable dumb-shows and noise:
I would have such a fellow whipped for o'er-doing Ter-
magant; it out-herods Herod: pray you, avoid it.

FIRST PLAYER: I warrant your honour.

HAMLET: Be not too tame neither, but let your own discretion
be your tutor: suit the action to the word, the word to the
action; with this special observance, that you o'erstep not
the modesty of nature; for anything so overdone is from
the purpose of playing, whose end, both at the first and
now, was and is, to hold, as 'twere, the mirror up to nature;
to show virtue her own feature, scorn her own image, and
the very age and body of the time his form and pressure.
Now, this overdone, or come tardy off, though it make
the unskilful laugh, cannot but make the judicious grieve;
the censure of which one must in your allowance o'erweigh

a whole theatre of others. O! there be players that I have seen play, and heard others praise, and that highly, not to speak it profanely, that, neither having the accent of Christians nor the gait of Christian, pagan, nor man, have so strutted and bellowed that I have thought some of nature's journeymen had made men and not made them well, they imitated humanity so abominably.

FIRST PLAYER: I hope we have reformed that indifferently with us, sir.

HAMLET: O! reform it altogether. And let those that play your clowns speak no more than is set down for them; for there be of them that will themselves laugh, to set on some quantity of barren spectators to laugh too, though in the mean time some necessary question of the play be then to be considered; that's villainous, and shows a most pitiful ambition in the fool that uses it. Go, make you ready.

Exeunt Players.

Enter POLONIUS, ROSENCRANTZ, *and* GUILDENSTERN.

How now, my lord! will the king hear this piece of work?

POLONIUS: And the queen too, and that presently.

HAMLET: Bid the players make haste.   *Exit* POLONIUS.
Will you two help to hasten them?

ROSENCRANTZ *and* GUILDENSTERN: We will, my lord.

Exeunt [ROSENCRANTZ *and* GUILDENSTERN].

HAMLET: What, ho! Horatio!

Enter HORATIO.

HORATIO: Here, sweet lord, at your service.

HAMLET: Horatio, thou art e'en as just a man
As e'er my conversation cop'd withal.

HORATIO: O! my dear lord,—

HAMLET: Nay, do not think I flatter;
For what advancement may I hope from thee,
That no revenue hast but thy good spirits

To feed and clothe thee? Why should the poor be flatter'd?
No; let the candied tongue lick absurd pomp,
And crook the pregnant hinges of the knee
Where thrift may follow fawning. Dost thou hear?
Since my dear soul was mistress of her choice
And could of men distinguish, her election
Hath seal'd thee for herself; for thou hast been
As one, in suffering all, that suffers nothing,
A man that fortune's buffets and rewards
Hast ta'en with equal thanks; and bless'd are those
Whose blood and judgment are so well co-mingled
That they are not a pipe for fortune's finger
To sound what stop she please. Give me that man
That is not passion's slave, and I will wear him
In my heart's core, ay, in my heart of heart,
As I do thee. Something too much of this.
There is a play to-night before the king;
One scene of it comes near the circumstance
Which I have told thee of my father's death:
I prithee, when thou seest that act afoot,
Even with the very comment of thy soul
Observe mine uncle; if his occulted guilt
Do not itself unkennel in one speech,
It is a damned ghost that we have seen,
And my imaginations are as foul
As Vulcan's stithy. Give him heedful note;
For I mine eyes will rivet to his face,
And after we will both our judgments join
In censure of his seeming.
HORATIO: Well, my lord:
  If he steal aught the whilst this play is playing,
  And 'scape detecting, I will pay the theft.
HAMLET: They are coming to the play; I must be idle:
  Get you a place.

Enter KING, QUEEN, POLONIUS, OPHELIA, ROSENCRANTZ,

GUILDENSTERN, *and other* Lords *attendant, with his* Guard *carrying torches. Danish March. Sound a Flourish.*

KING: How fares our cousin Hamlet?

HAMLET: Excellent, i' faith; of the chameleon's dish: I eat the air, promise-crammed; you cannot feed capons so.

KING: I have nothing with this answer, Hamlet; these words are not mine.

HAMLET: No, nor mine now. [*To* POLONIUS.] My lord, you played once i' the university, you say?

POLONIUS: That did I, my lord, and was accounted a good actor.

HAMLET: And what did you enact?

POLONIUS: I did enact Julius Caesar: I was killed i' the Capitol; Brutus killed me.

HAMLET: It was a brute part of him to kill so capital a calf there. Be the players ready?

ROSENCRANTZ: Ay, my lord; they stay upon your patience.

QUEEN: Come hither, my good Hamlet, sit by me.

HAMLET: No, good mother, here's metal more attractive.

POLONIUS [*to the* KING]: O ho! do you mark that?

HAMLET: Lady, shall I lie in your lap?

[*Lying down at* OPHELIA's *feet.*]

OPHELIA: No, my lord.

HAMLET: I mean, my head upon your lap?

OPHELIA: Ay, my lord.

HAMLET: Do you think I meant country matters?

OPHELIA: I think nothing, my lord.

HAMLET: That's a fair thought to lie between maids' legs.

OPHELIA: What is, my lord?

HAMLET: Nothing.

OPHELIA: You are merry, my lord.

HAMLET: Who, I?

OPHELIA: Ay, my lord.

HAMLET: O God, your only jig-maker. What should a man do but be merry? for, look you, how cheerfully my mother looks, and my father died within's two hours.

OPHELIA: Nay, 'tis twice two months, my lord.

HAMLET: So long? Nay, then, let the devil wear black, for I'll have a suit of sables. O heavens! die two months ago, and not forgotten yet? Then there's hope a great man's memory may outlive his life half a year; but, by 'r lady, he must build churches then, or else shall he suffer not thinking on, with the hobby-horse, whose epitaph is, "For, O! for, O! the hobby-horse is forgot."

Hautboys play. The dumb-show enters.

Enter a King and a Queen, very lovingly; the Queen embracing him, and he her. She kneels, and makes show of protestation unto him. He takes her up, and declines his head upon her neck; lays him down upon a bank of flowers: she, seeing him asleep, leaves him. Anon comes in a fellow, takes off his crown, kisses it, and pours poison in the King's ears, and exit. The Queen returns, finds the King dead, and makes passionate action. The Poisoner, with some two or three Mutes, comes in again, seeming to lament with her. The dead body is carried away. The Poisoner wooes the Queen with gifts; she seems loath and unwilling awhile, but in the end accepts his love. Exeunt.

OPHELIA: What means this, my lord?

HAMLET: Marry, this is miching mallecho; it means mischief.

OPHELIA: Belike this show imports the argument of the play.

Enter PROLOGUE.

HAMLET: We shall know by this fellow: the players cannot keep counsel; they'll tell all.

OPHELIA: Will he tell us what this show meant?

HAMLET: Ay, or any show that you'll show him; be not you ashamed to show, he'll not shame to tell you what it means.

OPHELIA: You are naught, you are naught. I'll mark the play.
PROLOGUE: *For us and for our tragedy,*
Here stooping to your clemency,
We beg your hearing patiently.
HAMLET: Is this a prologue, or the posy of a ring?
OPHELIA: 'Tis brief, my lord.
HAMLET: As woman's love.

Enter [two Players *as]* King *and his* Queen.

King: *Full thirty times hath Phoebus' cart gone round*
Neptune's salt wash and Tellus' orbed ground,
And thirty dozen moons with borrow'd sheen
About the world have times twelve thirties been,
Since love our hearts and Hymen did our hands
Unite commutual in most sacred bands.
Queen: *So many journeys may the sun and moon*
Make us again count o'er ere love be done!
But, woe is me! you are so sick of late,
So far from cheer and from your former state,
That I distrust you. Yet, though I distrust,
Discomfort you, my lord, it nothing must;
For women's fear and love holds quantity,
In neither aught, or in extremity.
Now, what my love is, proof hath made you know;
And as my love is siz'd, my fear is so.
Where love is great, the littlest doubts are fear;
Where little fears grow great, great love grows there.
King: *Faith, I must leave thee, love, and shortly too;*
My operant powers their functions leave to do:
And thou shalt live in this fair world behind,
Honour'd, belov'd; and haply one as kind
For husband shalt thou—
Queen: *O! confound the rest;*
Such love must needs be treason in my breast:
In second husband let me be accurst;
None wed the second but who kill'd the first.

HAMLET [*aside*]: Wormwood, wormwood.

Queen: *The instances that second marriage move,*
Are base respects of thrift, but none of love;
A second time I kill my husband dead,
When second husband kisses me in bed.

King: *I do believe you think what now you speak;*
But what we do determine oft we break.
Purpose is but the slave to memory,
Of violent birth, but poor validity;
Which now, like fruit unripe, sticks on the tree,
But fall unshaken when they mellow be.
Most necessary 'tis that we forget
To pay ourselves what to ourselves is debt;
What to ourselves in passion we propose,
The passion ending, doth the purpose lose.
The violence of either grief or joy
Their own enactures with themselves destroy;
Where joy most revels grief doth most lament,
Grief joys, joy grieves, on slender accident.
This world is not for aye, nor 'tis not strange,
That even our loves should with our fortunes change;
For 'tis a question left us yet to prove
Whether love lead fortune or else fortune love.
The great man down, you mark his favourite flies;
The poor advanc'd makes friends of enemies.
And hitherto doth love on fortune tend,
For who not needs shall never lack a friend;
And who in want a hollow friend doth try
Directly seasons him his enemy.
But, orderly to end where I begun,
Our wills and fates do so contrary run
That our devices still are overthrown,
Our thoughts are ours, their ends none of our own:
So think thou wilt no second husband wed;
But die thy thoughts when thy first lord is dead.

Queen: Nor earth to me give food, nor heaven light!
  Sport and repose lock from me day and night!
  To desperation turn my trust and hope!
  An anchor's cheer in prison be my scope!
  Each opposite that blanks the face of joy
  Meet what I would have well, and it destroy!
  Both here and hence pursue me lasting strife,
  If, once a widow, ever I be wife!
HAMLET: If she should break it now!
King: 'Tis deeply sworn. Sweet, leave me here awhile;
  My spirits grow dull, and fain I would beguile
  The tedious day with sleep.   *(Sleeps.)*
Queen: *Sleep rock thy brain;*
  And never come mischance between us twain!   *Exit.*
HAMLET: Madam, how like you this play?
QUEEN: The lady doth protest too much, methinks.
HAMLET: O! but she'll keep her word.
KING: Have you heard the argument? Is there no offence in 't?
HAMLET: No, no, they do but jest, poison in jest; no offence i'
  the world.
KING: What do you call the play?
HAMLET: The Mouse-trap. Marry, how? Tropically.[18] This play
  is the image of a murder done in Vienna: Gonzago is the
  duke's name; his wife, Baptista. You shall see anon; 'tis
  a knavish piece of work: but what of that? your majesty
  and we that have free souls, it touches us not: let the galled
  jade wince, our withers are unwrung.

Enter [Player as] Lucianus.

  This is one Lucianus, nephew to the king.
OPHELIA: You are a good chorus, my lord.
HAMLET: I could interpret between you and your love, if I could
  see the puppets dallying.

---

[18] [*Tropically:* figuratively.]

OPHELIA: You are keen, my lord, you are keen.

HAMLET: It would cost you a groaning to take off my edge.

OPHELIA: Still better, and worse.

HAMLET: So you must take your husbands. Begin, murderer; pox, leave thy damnable faces, and begin. Come; the croaking raven doth bellow for revenge.

Lucianus: Thoughts black, hands apt, drugs fit, and time agreeing;
Confederate season, else no creature seeing;
Thou mixture rank, of midnight weeds collected,
With Hecate's ban thrice blasted, thrice infected,
Thy natural magic and dire property,
On wholesome life usurp immediately.

(*Pours the poison in his ears.*)

HAMLET: He poisons him i' the garden for 's estate. His name's Gonzago; the story is extant, and writ in very choice Italian. You shall see anon how the murderer gets the love of Gonzago's wife.

OPHELIA: The king rises.

HAMLET: What! frighted with false fire?

QUEEN: How fares my lord?

POLONIUS: Give o'er the play.

KING: Give me some light: away!

ALL: Lights, lights, lights!

Exeunt all but HAMLET *and* HORATIO.

HAMLET:

"Why, let the stricken deer go weep,
    The hart ungalled play;
For some must watch, while some must sleep:
    So runs the world away."

Would not this, sir, and a forest of feathers, if the rest of my fortunes turn Turk with me, with two Provincial roses on my razed shoes, get me a fellowship in a cry of players, sir?

HORATIO: Half a share.
HAMLET: A whole one, I.

> "For thou dost know, O Damon dear,
> This realm dismantled was
> Of Jove himself; and now reigns here
> A very, very—pajock."[19]

HORATIO: You might have rimed.
HAMLET: O good Horatio! I'll take the ghost's word for a thousand pound. Didst perceive?
HORATIO: Very well, my lord.
HAMLET: Upon the talk of the poisoning?
HORATIO: I did very well note him.
HAMLET: Ah, ha! Come, some music! come, the recorders!

> "For if the king like not the comedy,
> Why then, belike he likes it not, perdy."[20]

Come, some music!

Enter ROSENCRANTZ *and* GUILDENSTERN.

GUILDENSTERN: Good my lord, vouchsafe me a word with you.
HAMLET: Sir, a whole history.
GUILDENSTERN: The king, sir,—
HAMLET: Ay, sir, what of him?
GUILDENSTERN: Is in his retirement marvellous distempered.
HAMLET: With drink, sir?
GUILDENSTERN: No, my lord, rather with choler.
HAMLET: Your wisdom should show itself more richer to signify this to his doctor; for, for me to put him to his purgation would perhaps plunge him into far more choler.
GUILDENSTERN: Good my lord, put your discourse into some frame, and start not so wildly from my affair.

---

[19] [*pajock:* peacock (?).]
[20] [*perdy:* a corruption of *par Dieu* ("by God").]

HAMLET: I am tame, sir; pronounce.

GUILDENSTERN: The queen, your mother, in most great affliction of spirit, hath sent me to you.

HAMLET: You are welcome.

GUILDENSTERN: Nay, good my lord, this courtesy is not of the right breed. If it shall please you to make me a wholesome answer, I will do your mother's commandment; if not, your pardon and my return shall be the end of my business.

HAMLET: Sir, I cannot.

GUILDENSTERN: What, my lord?

HAMLET: Make you a wholesome answer; my wit's diseased; but, sir, such answer as I can make, you shall command; or, rather, as you say, my mother: therefore no more, but to the matter: my mother, you say,—

ROSENCRANTZ: Then, thus she says: your behaviour hath struck her into amazement and admiration.

HAMLET: O wonderful son, that can so astonish a mother! But is there no sequel at the heels of this mother's admiration? Impart.

ROSENCRANTZ: She desires to speak with you in her closet ere you go to bed.

HAMLET: We shall obey, were she ten times our mother. Have you any further trade with us?

ROSENCRANTZ: My lord, you once did love me.

HAMLET: So I do still, by these pickers and stealers.[21]

ROSENCRANTZ: Good my lord, what is your cause of distemper? you do surely bar the door upon your own liberty, if you deny your griefs to your friend.

HAMLET: Sir, I lack advancement.

ROSENCRANTZ: How can that be when you have the voice of the king himself for your succession in Denmark?

HAMLET: Ay, sir, but "While the grass grows,"—the proverb is something musty.

Enter the Players, *with recorders.*

---

[21] [*pickers and stealers:* hands.]

O! the recorders: let me see one. To withdraw with you: why do you go about to recover the wind of me, as if you would drive me into a toil?

GUILDENSTERN: O! my lord, if my duty be too bold, my love is too unmannerly.

HAMLET: I do not well understand that. Will you play upon this pipe?

GUILDENSTERN: My lord, I cannot.

HAMLET: I pray you.

GUILDENSTERN: Believe me, I cannot.

HAMLET: I beseech you.

GUILDENSTERN: I know no touch of it, my lord.

HAMLET: 'Tis as easy as lying; govern these ventages with your finger and thumb, give it breath with your mouth, and it will discourse most excellent music. Look you, these are the stops.

GUILDENSTERN: But these cannot I command to any utterance of harmony; I have not the skill.

HAMLET: Why, look you now, how unworthy a thing you make of me. You would play upon me; you would seem to know my stops; you would pluck out the heart of my mystery; you would sound me from my lowest note to the top of my compass; and there is much music, excellent voice, in this little organ, yet cannot you make it speak. 'Sblood, do you think I am easier to be played on than a pipe? Call me what instrument you will, though you can fret me, you cannot play upon me.

Enter POLONIUS.

God bless you, sir!

POLONIUS: My lord, the queen would speak with you, and presently.

HAMLET: Do you see yonder cloud that's almost in shape of a camel?

POLONIUS: By the mass, and 'tis like a camel, indeed.

HAMLET: Methinks it is like a weasel.

POLONIUS: It is backed like a weasel.

HAMLET: Or like a whale?

POLONIUS: Very like a whale.

HAMLET: Then I will come to my mother by and by. [*Aside.*] They fool me to the top of my bent. [*Aloud.*] I will come by and by.

POLONIUS: I will say so.   *Exit.*

HAMLET: By and by is easily said. Leave me, friends.

                              [*Exeunt all but* HAMLET.]
  'Tis now the very witching time of night,
When churchyards yawn and hell itself breathes out
Contagion to this world: now could I drink hot blood,
And so such bitter business as the day
Would quake to look on. Soft! now to my mother.
O heart! lose not thy nature; let not ever
The soul of Nero enter this firm bosom;
Let me be cruel, not unnatural;
I will speak daggers to her, but use none;
My tongue and soul in this be hypocrites;
How in my words soever she be shent,
To give them seals never, my soul, consent!   *Exit.*

SCENE THREE—*A Room in the Castle.*

Enter KING, ROSENCRANTZ, *and* GUILDENSTERN.

KING: I like him not, nor stands it safe with us
  To let his madness range. Therefore prepare you;
  I your commission will forthwith dispatch,
  And he to England shall along with you.
  The terms of our estate may not endure
  Hazard so dangerous as doth hourly grow
  Out of his lunacies.

GUILDENSTERN: We will ourselves provide.
  Most holy and religious fear it is
  To keep those many many bodies safe
  That live and feed upon your majesty.
ROSENCRANTZ: The single and peculiar life is bound
  With all the strength and armour of the mind
  To keep itself from noyance; but much more
  That spirit upon whose weal depend and rest
  The lives of many. The cease of majesty
  Dies not alone, but, like a gulf doth draw
  What's near it with it; it is a massy wheel,
  Fix'd on the summit of the highest mount,
  To whose huge spokes ten thousand lesser things
  Are mortis'd and adjoin'd; which, when it falls,
  Each small annexment, petty consequence,
  Attends the boisterous ruin. Never alone
  Did the king sigh, but with a general groan.
KING: Arm you, I pray you, to this speedy voyage;
  For we will fetters put upon this fear,
  Which now goes too free-footed.
ROSENCRANTZ: We will haste us.
          Exeunt [ROSENCRANTZ *and* GUILDENSTERN].

Enter POLONIUS.

POLONIUS: My lord, he's going to his mother's closet:
  Behind the arras I'll convey myself
  To hear the process; I'll warrant she'll tax him home;
  And, as you said, and wisely was it said,
  'Tis meet that some more audience than a mother,
  Since nature makes them partial, should o'erhear
  The speech, of vantage. Fare you well, my liege:
  I'll call upon you ere you go to bed
  And tell you what I know.
KING: Thanks, dear my lord.
                              Exit [POLONIUS].
  O! my offence is rank, it smells to heaven;

It hath the primal eldest curse upon 't;
A brother's murder! Pray can I not,
Though inclination be as sharp as will:
My stronger guilt defeats my strong intent;
And, like a man to double business bound,
I stand in pause where I shall first begin,
And both neglect. What if this cursed hand
Were thicker than itself with brother's blood,
Is there not rain enough in the sweet heavens
To wash it white as snow? Whereto serves mercy
But to confront the visage of offence?
And what's in prayer but this two-fold force,
To be forestalled, ere we come to fall,
Or pardon'd, being down? Then, I'll look up;
My fault is past. But, O! what form of prayer
Can serve my turn? "Forgive me my foul murder?"
That cannot be; since I am still possess'd
Of those effects for which I did the murder,
My crown, mine own ambition, and my queen.
May one be pardon'd and retain the offence?
In the corrupted currents of this world
Offence's gilded hand may shove by justice,
And oft 'tis seen the wicked prize itself
Buys out the law; but 'tis not so above;
There is no shuffling, there the action lies
In his true nature, and we ourselves compell'd
Even to the teeth and forehead of our faults
To give in evidence. What then? what rests?
Try what repentance can: what can it not?
Yet what can it, when one cannot repent?
O wretched state! O bosom black as death!
O limed soul, that struggling to be free
Art more engaged! Help, angels! make assay;
Bow, stubborn knees; and heart with strings of steel
Be soft as sinews of the new-born babe.
All may be well.   [*Retires and kneels.*]

Enter HAMLET.

HAMLET: Now might I do it pat, now he is praying;
  And now I'll do 't: and so he goes to heaven;
  And so am I reveng'd. That would be scann'd:
  A villain kills my father; and for that,
  I, his sole son, do this same villain send
  To heaven.
  Why, this is hire and salary, not revenge.
  He took my father grossly, full of bread,
  With all his crimes broad blown, as flush as May;
  And how his audit stands who knows save heaven?
  But in our circumstance and course of thought
  'Tis heavy with him. And am I then reveng'd,
  To take him in the purging of his soul,
  When he is fit and season'd for his passage?
  No!
  Up, sword, and know thou a more horrid hent;
  When he is drunk asleep, or in his rage,
  Or in the incestuous pleasure of his bed,
  At gaming, swearing, or about some act
  That has no relish of salvation in 't;
  Then trip him, that his heels may kick at heaven,
  And that his soul may be as damn'd and black
  As hell, whereto it goes. My mother stays:
  This physic but prolongs thy sickly days.   *Exit.*
                    [*The* KING *rises and advances.*]

KING: My words fly up, my thoughts remain below:
  Words without thoughts never to heaven go.   *Exit.*

SCENE FOUR — *The* QUEEN's *Closet.*

Enter QUEEN *and* POLONIUS.

POLONIUS: He will come straight. Look you lay home to him;
  Tell him his pranks have been too broad to bear with,
  And that your Grace hath screen'd and stood between

Much heat and him. I'll silence me e'en here.
Pray you, be round with him.
HAMLET (*within*): Mother, mother, mother!
QUEEN: I'll warrant you;
Fear me not. Withdraw, I hear him coming.
[POLONIUS *hides behind the arras.*]

Enter HAMLET.

HAMLET: Now, mother, what's the matter?
QUEEN: Hamlet, thou hast thy father much offended.
HAMLET: Mother, you have my father much offended.
QUEEN: Come, come, you answer with an idle tongue.
HAMLET: Go, go, you question with a wicked tongue.
QUEEN: Why, how now, Hamlet!
HAMLET: What's the matter now?
QUEEN: Have you forgot me?
HAMLET: No, by the rood, not so:
You are the queen, your husband's brother's wife;
And,—would it were not so!—you are my mother.
QUEEN: Nay then, I'll set those to you that can speak.
HAMLET: Come, come, and sit you down; you shall not budge;
You go not, till I set you up a glass
Where you may see the inmost part of you.
QUEEN: What wilt thou do? thou wilt not murder me?
Help, help, ho!
POLONIUS [*behind*]: What, ho! help! help! help!
HAMLET [*draws*]: How now! a rat? Dead, for a ducat, dead!
[*Makes a thrust through the arras.*]   *Kills* POLONIUS.
POLONIUS [*behind*]: O! I am slain.
QUEEN: O me, what hast thou done?
HAMLET: Nay, I know not: is it the king?
QUEEN: O! what a rash and bloody deed is this!
HAMLET: A bloody deed! almost as bad, good mother,
As kill a king, and marry with his brother.

QUEEN: As kill a king!

HAMLET: Ay, lady, 'twas my word.

[*Lifts up the arras and discovers* POLONIUS.]

[*To* POLONIUS.] Thou wretched, rash, intruding fool, farewell!
I took thee for thy better; take thy fortune;
Thou find'st to be too busy is some danger.
[*To the* QUEEN.] Leave wringing of your hands: peace! sit you
    down,
And let me wring your heart; for so I shall
If it be made of penetrable stuff,
If damned custom have not brass'd it so
That it is proof and bulwark against sense.

QUEEN: What have I done that thou dar'st wag thy tongue
In noise so rude against me?

HAMLET: Such an act
That blurs the grace and blush of modesty,
Calls virtue hypocrite, takes off the rose
From the fair forehead of an innocent love
And sets a blister there, makes marriage vows
As false as dicers' oaths; O! such a deed
As from the body of contraction plucks
The very soul, and sweet religion makes
A rhapsody of words; heaven's face doth glow,
Yea, this solidity and compound mass,
With tristful visage, as against the doom,
Is thought-sick at the act.

QUEEN: Ay me! what act,
That roars so loud and thunders in the index?

HAMLET: Look here, upon this picture, and on this;
The counterfeit presentment of two brothers.
See, what a grace was seated on this brow;
Hyperion's curls, the front of Jove himself,
An eye like Mars, to threaten and command,
A station like the herald Mercury
New-lighted on a heaven-kissing hill,
A combination and a form indeed,

Where every god did seem to set his seal,
To give the world assurance of a man.
This was your husband: look you now, what follows.
Here is your husband; like a mildew'd ear,
Blasting his wholesome brother. Have you eyes?
Could you on this fair mountain leave to feed,
And batten on this moor? Ha! have you eyes?
You cannot call it love, for at your age
The hey-day in the blood is tame, it's humble,
And waits upon the judgment; and what judgment
Would step from this to this? Sense, sure, you have,
Else could you not have motion; but sure, that sense
Is apoplex'd; for madness would not err,
Nor sense to ecstasy was ne'er so thrall'd
But it reserv'd some quantity of choice,
To serve in such a difference. What devil was 't
That thus hath cozen'd you at hoodman-blind?
Eyes without feeling, feeling without sight,
Ears without hands or eyes, smelling sans all,
Or but a sickly part of one true sense
Could not so mope.
O shame! where is thy blush? Rebellious hell,
If thou canst mutine in a matron's bones,
To flaming youth let virtue be as wax,
And melt in her own fire: proclaim no shame
When the compulsive ardour gives the charge,
Since frost itself as actively doth burn,
And reason panders will.

QUEEN: O Hamlet! speak no more;
Thou turn'st mine eyes into my very soul;
And there I see such black and grained spots
As will not leave their tinct.

HAMLET: Nay, but to live
In the rank sweat of an enseamed bed,
Stew'd in corruption, honeying and making love
Over the nasty sty—

QUEEN: O! speak to me no more;
These words like daggers enter in mine ears;
No more, sweet Hamlet!
HAMLET: A murderer, and a villain;
A slave that is not twentieth part the tithe
Of your precedent lord; a vice of kings;
A cut-purse of the empire and the rule,
That from a shelf the precious diadem stole,
And put it in his pocket!
QUEEN: No more!
HAMLET: A king of shreds and patches,—

Enter GHOST.

Save me, and hover o'er me with your wings,
You heavenly guards! What would your gracious figure?
QUEEN: Alas! he's mad!
HAMLET: Do you not come your tardy son to chide,
That, laps'd in time and passion, lets go by
The important acting of your dread command?
O! say.
GHOST: Do not forget: this visitation
Is but to whet thy almost blunted purpose.
But, look! amazement on thy mother sits;
O! step between her and her fighting soul;
Conceit in weakest bodies strongest works:
Speak to her, Hamlet.
HAMLET: How is it with you, lady?
QUEEN: Alas! how is 't with you,
That you do bend your eye on vacancy
And with the incorporal air do hold discourse?
Forth at your eyes your spirits wildly peep;
And, as the sleeping soldiers in the alarm,
Your bedded hair, like life in excrements,
Starts up and stands an end. O gentle son!
Upon the heat and flame of thy distemper
Sprinkle cool patience. Whereon do you look?

HAMLET: On him, on him! Look you, how pale he glares!
His form and cause conjoin'd, preaching to stones,
Would make them capable. Do not look upon me;
Lest with this piteous action you convert
My stern effects: then what I have to do
Will want true colour; tears perchance for blood.
QUEEN: To whom do you speak this?
HAMLET: Do you see nothing there?
QUEEN: Nothing at all; yet all that is I see.
HAMLET: Nor did you nothing hear?
QUEEN: No, nothing but ourselves.
HAMLET: Why, look you there! look, how it steals away;
My father, in his habit as he liv'd;
Look! where he goes, even now, out at the portal.

                                                Exit GHOST.

QUEEN: This is the very coinage of your brain:
This bodiless creation ecstasy
Is very cunning in.
HAMLET: Ecstasy!
My pulse, as yours, doth temperately keep time,
And makes as healthful music. It is not madness
That I have utter'd: bring me to the test,
And I the matter will re-word, which madness
Would gambol from. Mother, for love of grace,
Lay not that flattering unction to your soul,
That not your trespass but my madness speaks;
It will but skin and film the ulcerous place,
Whiles rank corruption, mining all within,
Infects unseen. Confess yourself to heaven;
Repent what's past; avoid what is to come;
And do not spread the compost on the weeds
To make them ranker. Forgive me this my virtue;
For in the fatness of these pursy times
Virtue itself of vice must pardon beg,
Yea, curb and woo for leave to do him good.

QUEEN: O Hamlet! thou hast cleft my heart in twain.
HAMLET: O! throw away the worser part of it,
And live the purer with the other half.
Good-night; but go not to mine uncle's bed;
Assume a virtue, if you have it not.
That monster, custom, who all sense doth eat,
Of habits devil, is angel yet in this,
That to the use of actions fair and good
He likewise gives a frock or livery,
That aptly is put on. Refrain to-night;
And that shall lend a kind of easiness
To the next abstinence: the next more easy;
For use almost can change the stamp of nature,
And master ev'n the devil or throw him out
With wondrous potency. Once more, good-night:
And when you are desirous to be bless'd,
I'll blessing beg of you. For this same lord,
                           [*Pointing to* POLONIUS.]
I do repent: but heaven hath pleas'd it so,
To punish me with this, and this with me,
That I must be their scourge and minister.
I will bestow him, and will answer well
The death I gave him. So, again, good-night.
I must be cruel only to be kind:
Thus bad begins and worse remains behind.
One word more, good lady.
QUEEN: What shall I do?
HAMLET: Not this, by no means, that I bid you do:
Let the bloat king tempt you again to bed;
Pinch wanton on your cheek; call you his mouse;
And let him, for a pair of reechy kisses,
Or paddling in your neck with his damn'd fingers,
Make you to ravel all this matter out,
That I essentially am not in madness,
But mad in craft. 'Twere good you let him know;
For who that's but a queen, fair, sober, wise,

Would from a paddock, from a bat, a gib,
Such dear concernings hide? who would do so?
No, in despite of sense and secrecy,
Unpeg the basket on the house's top,
Let the birds fly, and, like the famous ape,
To try conclusions, in the basket creep,
And break your own neck down.

QUEEN: Be thou assur'd, if words be made of breath,
And breath of life, I have no life to breathe
What thou hast said to me.

HAMLET: I must to England; you know that?

QUEEN: Alack!
I had forgot: 'tis so concluded on.

HAMLET: There's letters seal'd; and my two schoolfellows,
Whom I will trust as I will adders fang'd,
They bear the mandate; they must sweep my way,
And marshal me to knavery. Let it work;
For 'tis the sport to have the enginer
Hoist with his own petar:²² and it shall go hard
But I will delve one yard below their mines,
And blow them at the moon. O! 'tis most sweet,
When in one line two crafts directly meet.
This man shall set me packing;
I'll lug the guts into the neighbour room.
Mother, good-night. Indeed this counselor
Is now most still, most secret, and most grave,
Who was in life a foolish prating knave.
Come, sir, to draw toward an end with you.
Good-night, mother.   *Exit* HAMLET *tugging in* POLONIUS.

---

²² [*Hoist:* blown up; *petar:* small bomb.]

ACT IV

SCENE ONE—*A Room in the Castle.*

Enter KING, [*and* QUEEN, *with* ROSENCRANTZ *and* GUILDENSTERN].

KING: There's matter in these sighs, these profound heaves:
You must translate; 'tis fit we understand them.
Where is your son?
QUEEN: Bestow this place on us a little while.
               [*Exeunt* ROSENCRANTZ *and* GUILDENSTERN.]
Ah! my good lord, what have I seen to-night!
KING: What, Gertrude? How does Hamlet?
QUEEN: Mad as the sea and wind, when both contend
Which is the mightier. In his lawless fit,
Behind the arras hearing something stir,
Whips out his rapier, cries, "A rat! a rat!"
And, in his brainish apprehension, kills
The unseen good old man.
KING: O heavy deed!
It had been so with us had we been there.
His liberty is full of threats to all;
To you yourself, to us, to every one.
Alas! how shall this bloody deed be answer'd?
It will be laid to us, whose providence
Should have kept short, restrain'd, and out of haunt,
This mad young man: but so much was our love,
We would not understand what was most fit,
But, like the owner of a foul disease,
To keep it from divulging, let it feed
Even on the pith of life. Where is he gone?
QUEEN: To draw apart the body he hath kill'd,
O'er whom his very madness, like some ore
Among a mineral of metals base,
Shows itself pure: he weeps for what is done.

KING: O Gertrude! come away.
The sun no sooner shall the mountains touch
But we will ship him hence; and this vile deed
We must, with all our majesty and skill,
Both countenance and excuse. Ho! Guildenstern!

Enter ROSENCRANTZ *and* GUILDENSTERN.

Friends both, go join you with some further aid:
Hamlet in madness hath Polonius slain,
And from his mother's closet hath he dragg'd him:
Go seek him out; speak fair, and bring the body
Into the chapel. I pray you, haste in this.
                    Exeunt [ROSENCRANTZ *and* GUILDENSTERN].
Come, Gertrude, we'll call up our wisest friends;
And let them know both what we mean to do,
And what's untimely done: so, haply, slander,
Whose whisper o'er the world's diameter,
As level as the cannon to his blank
Transports his poison'd shot, may miss our name,
And hit the woundless air. O! come away;
My soul is full of discord and dismay.   *Exeunt.*

SCENE TWO—*Another Room in the Castle.*

Enter HAMLET.

HAMLET: Safely stowed.
ROSENCRANTZ *and* GUILDENSTERN (*within*): Hamlet! Lord
    Hamlet!
HAMLET: What noise? who calls on Hamlet?
    O! here they come.

Enter ROSENCRANTZ *and* GUILDENSTERN.

ROSENCRANTZ: What have you done, my lord, with the dead
    body?

HAMLET: Compounded it with dust, whereto 'tis kin.

ROSENCRANTZ: Tell us where 'tis, that we may take it thence
And bear it to the chapel.

HAMLET: Do not believe it.

ROSENCRANTZ: Believe what?

HAMLET: That I can keep your counsel and not mine own.
Besides, to be demanded of a sponge! what replication
should be made by the son of a king?

ROSENCRANTZ: Take you me for a sponge, my lord?

HAMLET: Ay, sir, that soaks up the king's countenance, his
rewards, his authorities. But such officers do the king best
service in the end: he keeps them, like an ape, in the corner
of his jaw; first mouthed, to be last swallowed: when he
needs what you have gleaned, it is but squeezing you, and,
sponge, you shall be dry again.

ROSENCRANTZ: I understand you not, my lord.

HAMLET: I am glad of it: a knavish speech sleeps in a foolish
ear.

ROSENCRANTZ: My lord, you must tell us where the body is,
and go with us to the king.

HAMLET: The body is with the king, but the king is not with
the body. The king is a thing—

GUILDENSTERN: A thing, my lord!

HAMLET: Of nothing: bring me to him. Hide fox, and all
after.   *Exeunt.*

SCENE THREE—*Another Room in the Castle.*

Enter KING, [*attended*].

KING: I have sent to seek him, and to find the body.
How dangerous is it that this man goes loose!
Yet must not we put the strong law on him:
He's lov'd of the distracted multitude,
Who like not in their judgment, but their eyes;
And where 'tis so, the offender's scourge is weigh'd,

But never the offence. To bear all smooth and even,
This sudden sending him away must seem
Deliberate pause: diseases desperate grown
By desperate appliance are reliev'd,
Or not at all.

Enter ROSENCRANTZ.

              How now! what hath befall'n?
ROSENCRANTZ: Where the dead body is bestow'd, my lord,
We cannot get from him.
KING: But where is he?
ROSENCRANTZ: Without, my lord; guarded, to know your
   pleasure.
KING: Bring him before us.
ROSENCRANTZ: Ho, Guildenstern! bring in my lord.

Enter HAMLET *and* GUILDENSTERN.

KING: Now, Hamlet, where's Polonius?
HAMLET: At supper.
KING: At supper! Where?
HAMLET: Not where he eats, but where he is eaten: a certain
   convocation of politic worms are e'en at him. Your worm
   is your only emperor for diet: we fat all creatures else to
   fat us, and we fat ourselves for maggots: your fat king and
   your lean beggar is but variable service; two dishes, but
   to one table: that's the end.
KING: Alas, alas!
HAMLET: A man may fish with the worm that hath eat of a
   king, and eat of the fish that hath fed of that worm.
KING: What dost thou mean by this?
HAMLET: Nothing, but to show you how a king may go a
   progress through the guts of a beggar.
KING: Where is Polonius?
HAMLET: In heaven; send thither to see: if your messenger find
   him not there, seek him i' the other place yourself. But,

indeed, if you find him not within this month, you shall
nose him as you go up the stairs into the lobby.

KING [*to some* Attendants]: Go seek him there.

HAMLET: He will stay till you come.   [*Exeunt* Attendants.]

KING: Hamlet, this deed, for thine especial safety,
    Which we do tender, as we dearly grieve
    For that which thou hast done, must send thee hence
    With fiery quickness: therefore prepare thyself;
    The bark is ready, and the wind at help,
    The associates tend, and every thing is bent
    For England.

HAMLET: For England!

KING: Ay, Hamlet.

HAMLET: Good.

KING: So is it, if thou knew'st our purposes.

HAMLET: I see a cherub that sees them. But, come; for England!
    Farewell, dear mother.

KING: Thy loving father, Hamlet.

HAMLET: My mother: father and mother is man and wife, man
    and wife is one flesh, and so, my mother. Come, for
    England!   *Exit.*

KING: Follow him at foot; tempt him with speed aboard:
    Delay it not, I'll have him hence to-night.
    Away! for every thing is seal'd and done
    That else leans on the affair: pray you, make haste.
              [*Exeunt* ROSENCRANTZ *and* GUILDENSTERN.]
    And, England, if my love thou hold'st at aught,—
    As my great power thereof may give thee sense,
    Since yet thy cicatrice looks raw and red
    After the Danish sword, and thy free awe
    Pays homage to us,—thou mayst not coldly set
    Our sovereign process, which imports at full,
    By letters conjuring to that effect,
    The present death of Hamlet. Do it, England;
    For like the hectic in my blood he rages,

And thou must cure me. Till I know 'tis done,
Howe'er my haps, my joys were ne'er begun.   *Exit.*

SCENE FOUR — *Near Elsinore.*

Enter FORTINBRAS *with an army.*

FORTINBRAS: Go, captain, from me greet the Danish king;
Tell him that, by his licence, Fortinbras
Claims the conveyance of a promis'd march
Over his kingdom. You know the rendezvous.
If that his majesty would aught with us,
We shall express our duty in his eye,
And let him know so.
CAPTAIN: I will do 't, my lord.
FORTINBRAS: Go softly on.
                    [*Exeunt* FORTINBRAS *and* Soldiers.]

[*Enter* HAMLET, ROSENCRANTZ, *&c.*]

HAMLET: Good sir, whose powers are these?
CAPTAIN: They are of Norway, sir.
HAMLET: How purpos'd, sir, I pray you?
CAPTAIN: Against some part of Poland.
HAMLET: Who commands them, sir?
CAPTAIN: The nephew of old Norway, Fortinbras.
HAMLET: Goes it against the main of Poland, sir,
Or for some frontier?
CAPTAIN: Truly to speak, and with no addition,
We go to gain a little patch of ground
That hath in it no profit but the name.
To pay five ducats, five, I would not farm it;
Nor will it yield to Norway or the Pole
A ranker rate, should it be sold in fee.
HAMLET: Why, then the Polack never will defend it.

CAPTAIN: Yes, 'tis already garrison'd.

HAMLET: Two thousand souls and twenty thousand ducats
Will not debate the question of this straw:
This is the imposthume of much wealth and peace,
That inward breaks, and shows no cause without
Why the man dies. I humbly thank you, sir.

CAPTAIN: God be wi' you, sir.   [*Exit.*]

ROSENCRANTZ: Will 't please you go, my lord?

HAMLET: I'll be with you straight. Go a little before.
                    [*Exeunt all except* HAMLET.]
How all occasions do inform against me,
And spur my dull revenge! What is a man,
If his chief good and market of his time
Be but to sleep and feed? a beast, no more.
Sure he that made us with such large discourse,
Looking before and after, gave us not
That capability and god-like reason
To fust in us unus'd. Now, whether it be
Bestial oblivion, or some craven scruple
Of thinking too precisely on the event,
A thought, which, quarter'd, hath but one part wisdom,
And ever three parts coward, I do not know
Why yet I live to say "This thing's to do";
Sith I have cause and will and strength and means
To do 't. Examples gross as earth exhort me:
Witness this army of such mass and charge
Led by a delicate and tender prince,
Whose spirit with divine ambition puff'd
Makes mouths at the invisible event,
Exposing what is mortal and unsure
To all that fortune, death and danger dare,
Even for an egg-shell. Rightly to be great
Is not to stir without great argument,
But greatly to find quarrel in a straw
When honour's at the stake. How stand I then,
That have a father kill'd, a mother stain'd,

Excitements of my reason and my blood,
And let all sleep, while, to my shame, I see
The imminent death of twenty thousand men,
That, for a fantasy and trick of fame,
Go to their graves like beds, fight for a plot
Whereon the numbers cannot try the cause,
Which is not tomb enough and continent
To hide the slain? O! from this time forth,
My thoughts be bloody, or be nothing worth!   *Exit.*

SCENE FIVE—*Elsinore. A Room in the Castle.*

Enter QUEEN *and* HORATIO, [*with a* GENTLEMAN].

QUEEN: I will not speak with her.
GENTLEMAN: She is importunate, indeed distract:
   Her mood will needs be pitied.
QUEEN: What would she have?
GENTLEMAN: She speaks much of her father; says she hears
   There's tricks i' the world; and hems, and beats her heart;
   Spurns enviously at straws; speaks things in doubt,
   That carry but half sense: her speech is nothing,
   Yet the unshaped use of it doth move
   The hearers to collection; they aim at it,
   And botch the words up fit to their own thoughts;
   Which, as her winks, and nods, and gestures yield them,
   Indeed would make one think there might be thought,
   Though nothing sure, yet much unhappily.
HORATIO: 'Twere good she were spoken with, for she may strew
   Dangerous conjectures in ill-breeding minds.
QUEEN: Let her come in.   [*Exit* GENTLEMAN.]
   To my sick soul, as sin's true nature is,
   Each toy seems prologue to some great amiss:
   So full of artless jealousy is guilt,
   It spills itself in fearing to be spilt.

Enter OPHELIA *distracted.*

OPHELIA: Where is the beauteous majesty of Denmark?

QUEEN: How now, Ophelia!

OPHELIA [*singing*]:

> "How should I your true love know
> From another one?
> By his cockle hat and staff,
> And his sandal shoon."

QUEEN: Alas! sweet lady, what imports this song?

OPHELIA: Say you? nay, pray you, mark.

> "He is dead and gone, lady,
> He is dead and gone;
> At his head a grass-green turf;
> At his heels a stone."

O, ho!

QUEEN: Nay, but Ophelia,—

OPHELIA: Pray you, mark. [*Sings:*]

> "White his shroud as the mountain snow,—"

Enter KING.

QUEEN: Alas! look here, my lord.

OPHELIA:

> "Larded with sweet flowers;
> Which bewept to the grave did go
> With true-love showers."

KING: How do you, pretty lady?

OPHELIA: Well, God 'ild you! They say the owl was a baker's daughter. Lord! we know what we are, but not what we may be. God be at your table!

KING: Conceit upon her father.

OPHELIA: Pray you, let's have no words of this; but when they ask you what it means, say you this:

"To-morrow is Saint Valentine's day,
All in the morning betime,
And I a maid at your window,
To be your Valentine:
Then up he rose, and donn'd his clothes,
And dupp'd the chamber door;
Let in the maid, that out a maid
Never departed more."

KING: Pretty Ophelia!

OPHELIA: Indeed, la! without an oath, I'll make an end on 't:

"By Gis and by Saint Charity,
Alack, and fie for shame!
Young men will do 't, if they come to 't;
By Cock they are to blame.
Quoth she, before you tumbled me,
You promis'd me to wed.
So would I ha' done, by yonder sun,
An thou hadst not come to my bed."

KING: How long hath she been thus?

OPHELIA: I hope all will be well. We must be patient: but I
cannot choose but weep, to think they should lay him i'
the cold ground. My brother shall know of it: and so I
thank you for your good counsel. Come, my coach! Good-
night, ladies; good-night, sweet ladies; good-night, good-
night.   *Exit.*

KING: Follow her close; give her good watch, I pray you.

[*Exit* HORATIO.]

O! this is the poison of deep grief; it springs
All from her father's death. O Gertrude, Gertrude!
When sorrows come, they come not single spies,
But in battalions. First, her father slain;
Next, your son gone; but he most violent author
Of his own just remove: the people muddied,
Thick and unwholesome in their thoughts and whispers,

For good Polonius' death; and we have done but greenly,
In hugger-mugger to inter him: poor Ophelia
Divided from herself and her fair judgment,
Without the which we are pictures, or mere beasts:
Last, and as much containing as all these,
Her brother is in secret come from France,
Feeds on his wonder, keeps himself in clouds,
And wants not buzzers to infect his ear
With pestilent speeches of his father's death;
Wherein necessity, of matter beggar'd,
Will nothing stick our person to arraign
In ear and ear. O my dear Gertrude! this,
Like to a murdering-piece, in many places
Gives me superfluous death.   *A noise within.*
QUEEN: Alack! what noise is this?

Enter a MESSENGER.

KING: Where are my Switzers? Let them guard the door.
    What is the matter?
MESSENGER: Save yourself, my lord;
    The ocean, overpeering of his list,
    Eats not the flats with more impetuous haste
    Than young Laertes, in a riotous head,
    O'erbears your officers. The rabble call him lord;
    And, as the world were now but to begin,
    Antiquity forgot, custom not known,
    The ratifiers and props of every word,
    They cry, "Choose we; Laertes shall be king!"
    Caps, hands, and tongues, applaud it to the clouds,
    "Laertes shall be king, Laertes king!"
QUEEN: How cheerfully on the false trail they cry!
    O! this is counter, you false Danish dogs!
KING: The doors are broke.   *Noise within.*

Enter LAERTES *with others.*

LAERTES: Where is the king? Sirs, stand you all without.

ALL: No, let's come in.

LAERTES: I pray you, give me leave.

ALL: We will, we will.   [*They retire without the door.*]

LAERTES: I thank you: keep the door. O thou vile king!
  Give me my father.

QUEEN: Calmly, good Laertes.

LAERTES: That drop of blood that's calm proclaims me bastard,
  Cries cuckold to my father, brands the harlot
  Even here, between the chaste unsmirched brow
  Of my true mother.

KING: What is the cause, Laertes,
  That thy rebellion looks so giant-like?
  Let him go, Gertrude; do not fear our person:
  There's such divinity doth hedge a king,
  That treason can but peep to what it would,
  Acts little of his will. Tell me, Laertes,
  Why thou art thus incens'd. Let him go, Gertrude.
  Speak, man.

LAERTES: Where is my father?

KING: Dead.

QUEEN: But not by him.

KING: Let him demand his fill.

LAERTES: How came he dead? I'll not be juggled with.
  To hell, allegiance! vows, to the blackest devil!
  Conscience and grace, to the profoundest pit!
  I dare damnation. To this point I stand,
  That both the worlds I give to negligence,
  Let come what comes; only I'll be reveng'd
  Most throughly for my father.

KING: Who shall stay you?

LAERTES: My will, not all the world:
  And, for my means, I'll husband them so well,
  They shall go far with little.

KING: Good Laertes,
  If you desire to know the certainty

Of your dear father's death, is 't writ in your revenge,
That, swoopstake, you will draw both friend and foe,
Winner and loser?
LAERTES: None but his enemies.
KING: Will you know them then?
LAERTES: To his good friends thus wide I'll ope my arms;
And like the kind life-rendering pelican,
Repast them with my blood.
KING: Why, now you speak
Like a good child and a true gentleman.
That I am guiltless of your father's death,
And am most sensibly in grief for it,
It shall as level to your judgment pierce
As day does to your eye.
A noise within. [*Voices.*] Let her come in.
LAERTES: How now! what noise is that?

Enter OPHELIA.

O heat, dry up my brains! tears seven times salt,
Burn out the sense and virtue of mine eye!
By heaven, thy madness shall be paid by weight,
Till our scale turn the beam. O rose of May!
Dear maid, kind sister, sweet Ophelia!
O heavens! is 't possible a young maid's wits
Should be as mortal as an old man's life?
Nature is fine in love, and where 'tis fine
It sends some precious instance of itself
After the thing it loves.
OPHELIA:

"They bore him barefac'd on the bier;
Hey non nonny, nonny, hey nonny;
And in his grave rain'd many a tear; —"

Fare you well, my dove!

LAERTES: Hadst thou thy wits, and didst persuade revenge,
It could not move thus.

OPHELIA:

"You must sing, a-down a-down,
And you call him a-down-a."

O how the wheel becomes it! It is the false steward that stole
his master's daughter.

LAERTES: This nothing's more than matter.

OPHELIA: There's rosemary, that's for remembrance; pray, love,
remember: and there is pansies, that's for thoughts.

LAERTES: A document in madness, thoughts and remembrance
fitted.

OPHELIA: There's fennel for you, and columbines; there's rue
for you; and here's some for me; we may call it herb of
grace o' Sundays. O! you must wear your rue with a difference. There's a daisy; I would give you some violets,
but they withered all when my father died. They say he
made a good end, —   [*Sings:*]

"For bonny sweet Robin is all my joy."

LAERTES: Thought and affliction, passion, hell itself,
She turns to favour and to prettiness.

OPHELIA:

"And will he not come again?
And will he not come again?
No, no, he is dead;
Go to thy death-bed,
He never will come again.

His beard was as white as snow
All flaxen was his poll,
He is gone, he is gone,
And we cast away moan:
God ha' mercy on his soul!"

And of all Christian souls! I pray God. God be wi' ye!

Exit OPHELIA.

LAERTES: Do you see this, O God?

KING: Laertes, I must common with your grief,
Or you deny me right. Go but apart,
Make choice of whom your wisest friends you will,
And they shall hear and judge 'twixt you and me.
If by direct or by collateral hand
They find us touch'd, we will our kingdom give,
Our crown, our life, and all that we call ours,
To you in satisfaction; but if not,
Be you content to lend your patience to us,
And we shall jointly labour with your soul
To give it due content.

LAERTES: Let this be so:
His means of death, his obscure burial,
No trophy, sword, nor hatchment o'er his bones,
No noble rite nor formal ostentation,
Cry to be heard, as 'twere from heaven to earth,
That I must call 't in question.

KING: So you shall;
And where the offence is let the great axe fall.
I pray you go with me.   *Exeunt.*

SCENE SIX—*Another Room in the Castle.*

Enter HORATIO *with an* ATTENDANT.

HORATIO: What are they that would speak with me?
ATTENDANT: Sailors, sir: they say, they have letters for you.
HORATIO: Let them come in.   [*Exit* ATTENDANT.]
I do not know from what part of the world
I should be greeted, if not from Lord Hamlet.

Enter SAILOR.

SAILOR: God bless you, sir.

HORATIO: Let him bless thee too.

SAILOR: He shall, sir, an 't please him. There's a letter for you, sir;—it comes from the ambassador that was bound for England;—if your name be Horatio, as I am let to know it is.

HORATIO (*reads the letter*): "Horatio, when thou shalt have overlooked this, give these fellows some means to the king: they have letters for him. Ere we were two days old at sea, a pirate of very war-like appointment gave us chase. Finding ourselves too slow of sail, we put on a compelled valour; in the grapple I boarded them. On the instant they got clear of our ship, so I alone became their prisoner. They have dealt with me like thieves of mercy, but they knew what they did; I am to do a good turn for them. Let the king have the letters I have sent; and repair thou to me with as much haste as thou wouldst fly death. I have words to speak in thine ear will make thee dumb; yet are they much too light for the bore of the matter. These good fellows will bring thee where I am. Rosencrantz and Guildenstern hold their course for England: of them I have much to tell thee. Farewell.

　　　　He that thou knowest thine,

　　　　　　HAMLET."

Come, I will give you way for these your letters;
And do 't the speedier, that you may direct me
To him from whom you brought them.　　　*Exeunt.*

SCENE SEVEN—*A Room in the Castle.*

Enter KING *and* LAERTES.

KING: Now must your conscience my acquittance seal,
And you must put me in your heart for friend,
Sith you have heard, and with a knowing ear,

That he which hath your noble father slain
Pursu'd my life.

LAERTES: It well appears: but tell me
Why you proceeded not against these feats,
So crimeful and so capital in nature,
As by your safety, wisdom, all things else,
You mainly were stirr'd up.

KING: O! for two special reasons;
Which may to you, perhaps, seem much unsinew'd,
But yet to me they are strong. The queen his mother
Lives almost by his looks, and for myself,—
My virtue or my plague, be it either which,—
She's so conjunctive to my life and soul,
That, as the star moves not but in his sphere,
I could not but by her. The other motive,
Why to a public count I might not go,
Is the great love the general gender bear him;
Who, dipping all his faults in their affection,
Would, like the spring that turneth wood to stone,
Convert his gyves to graces; so that my arrows,
Too slightly timber'd for so loud a wind,
Would have reverted to my bow again,
And not where I had aim'd them.

LAERTES: And so have I a noble father lost;
A sister driven into desperate terms,
Whose worth, if praises may go back again,
Stood challenger on mount of all the age
For her perfections. But my revenge will come.

KING: Break not your sleeps for that; you must not think
That we are made of stuff so flat and dull
That we can let our beard be shook with danger
And think it pastime. You shortly shall hear more;
I lov'd your father, and we love ourself,
And that, I hope, will teach you to imagine,—

Enter a MESSENGER.

How now! what news?

MESSENGER: Letters, my lord, from Hamlet:
This to your majesty; this to the queen.

KING: From Hamlet! who brought them?

MESSENGER: Sailors, my lord, they say; I saw them not:
They were given me by Claudio, he receiv'd them
Of him that brought them.

KING: Laertes, you shall hear them.
Leave us. *Exit* MESSENGER.

"High and mighty, you shall know I am set naked on
your kingdom. To-morrow shall I beg leave to see your
kingly eyes; when I shall, first asking your pardon ther-
eunto, recount the occasions of my sudden and more
strange return. HAMLET."

What should this mean? Are all the rest come back?
Or is it some abuse and no such thing?

LAERTES: Know you the hand?

KING: 'Tis Hamlet's character. "Naked,"
And in a postscript here, he says, "alone."
Can you advise me?

LAERTES: I'm lost in it, my lord. But let him come:
It warms the very sickness in my heart,
That I shall live and tell him to his teeth,
"Thus didst thou."

KING: If it be so, Laertes,
As how should it be so? how otherwise?
Will you be rul'd by me?

LAERTES: Ay, my lord;
So you will not o'er-rule me to a peace.

KING: To thine own peace. If he be now return'd,
As checking at his voyage, and that he means
No more to undertake it, I will work him
To an exploit, now ripe in my device,

Under the which he shall not choose but fall;
And for his death no wind of blame shall breathe,
But even his mother shall uncharge the practice
And call it accident.

LAERTES: My lord, I will be rul'd;
The rather, if you could devise it so
That I might be the organ.

KING: It falls right.
You have been talk'd of since your travel much,
And that in Hamlet's hearing, for a quality
Wherein, they say, you shine; your sum of parts
Did not together pluck such envy from him
As did that one, and that, in my regard,
Of the unworthiest siege.

LAERTES: What part is that, my lord?

KING: A very riband in the cap of youth,
Yet needful too; for youth no less becomes
The light and careless livery that it wears
Than settled age his sables and his weeds,
Importing health and graveness. Two months since
Here was a gentleman of Normandy.
I've seen myself, and serv'd against the French,
And they can well on horseback; but this gallant
Had witchcraft in 't, he grew unto his seat,
And to such wondrous doing brought his horse,
As he had been incorps'd and demi-natur'd
With the brave beast; so far he topp'd my thought,
That I, in forgery of shapes and tricks,
Come short of what he did.

LAERTES: A Norman was 't?

KING: A Norman.

LAERTES: Upon my life, Lamond.

KING: The very same.

LAERTES: I know him well; he is the brooch indeed
And gem of all the nation.

KING: He made confession of you,
  And gave you such a masterly report
  For art and exercise in your defence,
  And for your rapier most especially,
  That he cried out, 'twould be a sight indeed
  If one could match you; the scrimers of their nation,
  He swore, had neither motion, guard, nor eye,
  If you oppos'd them. Sir, this report of his
  Did Hamlet so envenom with his envy
  That he could nothing do but wish and beg
  Your sudden coming o'er, to play with him.
  Now, out of this, —
LAERTES: What out of this, my lord?
KING: Laertes, was your father dear to you?
  Or are you like the painting of a sorrow,
  A face without a heart?
LAERTES: Why ask you this?
KING: Not that I think you did not love your father,
  But that I know love is begun by time,
  And that I see, in passages of proof,
  Time qualifies the spark and fire of it.
  There lives within the very flame of love
  A kind of wick or snuff that will abate it,
  And nothing is at a like goodness still,
  For goodness, growing to a plurisy,
  Dies in his own too-much. That we would do,
  We should do when we would, for this "would" changes,
  And hath abatements and delays as many
  As there are tongues, are hands, are accidents;
  And then this "should" is like a spendthrift sigh,
  That hurts by easing. But, to the quick o' the ulcer;
  Hamlet comes back; what would you undertake
  To show yourself your father's son in deed
  More than in words?
LAERTES: To cut his throat i' the church.

KING: No place, indeed, should murder sanctuarize;
Revenge should have no bounds. But, good Laertes,
Will you do this, keep close within your chamber.
Hamlet return'd shall know you are come home;
We'll put on those shall praise your excellence,
And set a double varnish on the fame
The Frenchman gave you, bring you, in fine, together,
And wager on your heads: he, being remiss,
Most generous and free from all contriving,
Will not peruse the foils; so that, with ease
Or with a little shuffling, you may choose
A sword unbated, and, in a pass of practice
Requite him for your father.

LAERTES: I will do 't;
And, for that purpose, I'll anoint my sword.
I bought an unction of a mountebank,
So mortal that, but dip a knife in it,
Where it draws blood no cataplasm so rare,
Collected from all simples that have virtue
Under the moon, can save the thing from death
That is but scratch'd withal; I'll touch my point
With this contagion, that, if I gall him slightly,
It may be death.

KING: Let's further think of this;
Weigh what convenience both of time and means
May fit us to our shape. If this should fail,
And that our drift look through our bad performance
'Twere better not assay'd; therefore this project
Should have a back or second, that might hold,
If this should blast in proof. Soft! let me see;
We'll make a solemn wager on your cunnings:
I ha 't:
When in your motion you are hot and dry,—
As make your bouts more violent to that end,—
And that he calls for drink, I'll have prepar'd him
A chalice for the nonce, whereon but sipping,

If he by chance escape your venom'd stuck,
Our purpose may hold there. But stay! what noise?

Enter QUEEN.

How now, sweet queen!
QUEEN: One woe doth tread upon another's heel,
So fast they follow: your sister's drown'd, Laertes.
LAERTES: Drown'd! O, where?
QUEEN: There is a willow grows aslant a brook,
That shows his hoar leaves in the glassy steam;
There with fantastic garlands did she come,
Of crow-flowers, nettles, daisies, and long purples,
That liberal shepherds give a grosser name,
But our cold maids do dead men's fingers call them:
There, on the pendent boughs her coronet weeds
Clambering to hang, an envious sliver broke,
When down her weedy trophies and herself
Fell in the weeping brook. Her clothes spread wide,
And, mermaid-like, awhile they bore her up;
Which time she chanted snatches of old tunes,
As one incapable of her own distress,
Or like a creature native and indu'd
Unto that element; but long it could not be
Till that her garments, heavy with their drink,
Pull'd the poor wretch from her melodious lay
To muddy death.
LAERTES: Alas! then, she is drown'd?
QUEEN: Drown'd, drown'd.
LAERTES: Too much of water hast thou, poor Ophelia,
And therefore I forbid my tears; but yet
It is our trick, nature her custom holds,
Let shame say what it will; when these are gone
The woman will be out. Adieu, my lord!
I have a speech of fire, that fain would blaze,
But that this folly douts it.   *Exit.*

KING: Let's follow, Gertrude.
How much I had to do to calm his rage!
Now fear I this will give it start again;
Therefore let's follow.   *Exeunt.*

ACT V

Scene One—*A Churchyard.*

Enter two CLOWNS.[23]

FIRST CLOWN: Is she to be buried in Christian burial that wilfully seeks her own salvation?

SECOND CLOWN: I tell thee she is; and therefore make her grave straight: the crowner hath sat on her,[24] and finds it Christian burial.

FIRST CLOWN: How can that be, unless she drowned herself in her own defence?

SECOND CLOWN: Why, 'tis found so.

FIRST CLOWN: It must be *se offendendo;* it cannot be else. For here lies the point: if I drown myself wittingly it argues an act; and an act hath three branches; it is, to act, to do, and to perform: argal, she drowned herself wittingly.

SECOND CLOWN: Nay, but hear you, goodman delver,—

FIRST CLOWN: Give me leave. Here lies the water; good: here stands the man; good: if the man go to this water, and drown himself, it is, will he, nill he, he goes; mark you that? but if the water come to him, and drown him, he

---

[23] [*Clowns:* peasants.]
[24] [*Crowner:* coroner; *sat on:* passed on.]

drowns not himself: argal, he that is not guilty of his own death shortens not his own life.

SECOND CLOWN: But is this law?

FIRST CLOWN: Ay, marry, is 't; crowner's quest law.

SECOND CLOWN: Will you ha' the truth on 't? If this had not been a gentlewoman she should have been buried out o' Christian burial.

FIRST CLOWN: Why, there thou sayest; and the more pity that great folk should have countenance in this world to drown or hang themselves more than their even Christian. Come, my spade. There is no ancient gentlemen but gardeners, ditchers, and grave-makers; they hold up Adam's profession.

SECOND CLOWN: Was he a gentleman?

FIRST CLOWN: A' was the first that ever bore arms.

SECOND CLOWN: Why, he had none.

FIRST CLOWN: What! art a heathen? How dost thou understand the Scripture? The Scripture says, Adam digged; could he dig without arms? I'll put another question to thee; if thou answerest me not to the purpose, confess thyself—

SECOND CLOWN: Go to.

FIRST CLOWN: What is he that builds stronger than either the mason, the shipwright, or the carpenter?

SECOND CLOWN: The gallows-maker; for that frame outlives a thousand tenants.

FIRST CLOWN: I like thy wit well, in good faith; the gallows does well, but how does it well? it does well to those that do ill; now thou dost ill to say the gallows is built stronger than the church: argal, the gallows may do well to thee. To 't again; come.

SECOND CLOWN: Who builds stronger than a mason, a shipwright, or a carpenter?

FIRST CLOWN: Ay, tell me that, and unyoke.

SECOND CLOWN: Marry, now I can tell.

FIRST CLOWN: To 't.

SECOND CLOWN: Mass, I cannot tell.

Enter HAMLET *and* HORATIO *afar off.*

FIRST CLOWN: Cudgel thy brains no more about it, for your dull ass will not mend his pace with beating; and, when you are asked this question next, say, "a grave-maker": the houses that he makes last till doomsday. Go, get thee to Yaughan; fetch me a stoup of liquor.

[*Exit* SECOND CLOWN.

FIRST CLOWN *digs, and*] *sings:*

> "In youth, when I did love, did love,
>   Methought it was very sweet,
>   To contract, O! the time, for-a my behove,
>   O! methought there was nothing meet."

HAMLET: Has this fellow no feeling of his business, that he sings at grave-making?

HORATIO: Custom hath made it in him a property of easiness.

HAMLET: 'Tis e'en so; the hand of little employment hath the daintier sense.

CLOWN *sings:*

> "But age, with his stealing steps,
>   Hath claw'd me in his clutch,
>   And hath shipped me intil the land,
>   As if I had never been such."

[*Throws up a skull.*]

HAMLET: That skull had a tongue in it, and could sing once; how the knave jowls it to the ground, as if it were Cain's jaw-bone, that did the first murder! This might be the pate of a politician, which this ass now o'er-offices, one that would circumvent God, might it not?

HORATIO: It might, my lord.

HAMLET: Or of a courtier, which could say, "Good morrow, sweet lord! How dost thou, good lord?" This might be my Lord Such-a-one, that praised my Lord Such-a-one's horse, when he meant to beg it, might it not?

HORATIO: Ay, my lord.

HAMLET: Why, e'en so, and now my Lady Worm's; chapless, and knocked about the mazzard with a sexton's spade. Here's fine revolution, an we had the trick to see 't. Did these bones cost no more the breeding but to play at loggats with 'em? mine ache to think on 't.

CLOWN *sings:*

> "A pick-axe, and a spade, a spade,
> For and a shrouding sheet;
> O! a pit of clay for to be made
> For such a guest is meet."

> [*Throws up another skull.*]

HAMLET: There's another; why may not that be the skull of a lawyer? Where be his quiddities now, his quillets, his cases, his tenures, and his tricks? why does he suffer this rude knave now to knock him about the sconce with a dirty shovel, and will not tell him of his action of battery? Hum! This fellow might be in 's time a great buyer of land, with his statutes, his recognizances, his fines, his double vouchers, his recoveries; is this the fine of his fines, and the recovery of his recoveries, to have his fine pate full of fine dirt? will his vouchers vouch him no more of his purchases, and double ones too, than the length and breadth of a pair of indentures? The very conveyance of his lands will hardly lie in this box, and must the inheritor himself have no more, ha?

HORATIO: Not a jot more, my lord.

HAMLET: Is not parchment made of sheep-skins?

HORATIO: Ay, my lord, and of calf-skins, too.

HAMLET: They are sheep and calves which seek out assurance in that. I will speak to this fellow. Whose grave 's this, sir?

FIRST CLOWN: Mine, sir,

> "O! a pit of clay for to be made
> For such a guest is meet."

HAMLET: I think it be thine, indeed; for thou liest in 't.

FIRST CLOWN: You lie out on 't, sir, and therefore it is not yours; for my part, I do not lie in 't, and yet it is mine.

HAMLET: Thou doest lie in 't, to be in 't and say it is thine: 'tis for the dead, not for the quick; therefore thou liest.

FIRST CLOWN: 'Tis a quick lie, sir; 'twill away again, from me to you.

HAMLET: What man dost thou dig it for?

FIRST CLOWN: For no man, sir.

HAMLET: What woman, then?

FIRST CLOWN: For none, neither.

HAMLET: Who is to be buried in 't?

FIRST CLOWN: One that was a woman, sir; but rest her soul, she's dead.

HAMLET: How absolute the knave is! we must speak by the card, or equivocation will undo us. By the Lord, Horatio, these three years I have taken note of it; the age is grown so picked that the toe of the peasant comes so near the heel of the courtier, he galls his kibe. How long hast thou been a grave-maker?

FIRST CLOWN: Of all the days i' the year, I came to 't that day that our last King Hamlet overcame Fortinbras.

HAMLET: How long is that since?

FIRST CLOWN: Cannot you tell that? every fool can tell that; it was the very day that young Hamlet was born; he that is mad, and sent into England.

HAMLET: Ay, marry; why was he sent into England?

FIRST CLOWN: Why, because he was mad: he shall recover his wits there; or, if he do not, 'tis no great matter there.

HAMLET: Why?

FIRST CLOWN: 'Twill not be seen in him there; there the men are as mad as he.

HAMLET: How came he mad?

FIRST CLOWN: Very strangely, they say.

HAMLET: How strangely?

FIRST CLOWN: Faith, e'en with losing his wits.

HAMLET: Upon what ground?

FIRST CLOWN: Why, here in Denmark; I have been sexton here, man and boy, thirty years.

HAMLET: How long will a man lie i' the earth ere he rot?

FIRST CLOWN: Faith, if he be not rotten before he die,—as we have many pocky corses now-a-days, that will scarce hold the laying in,—he will last you some eight year or nine year; a tanner will last you nine year.

HAMLET: Why he more than another?

FIRST CLOWN: Why, sir, his hide is so tanned with his trade that he will keep out water a great while, and your water is a sore decayer of your whoreson dead body. Here's a skull now; this skull hath lain you i' the earth three-and-twenty years.

HAMLET: Whose was it?

FIRST CLOWN: A whoreson mad fellow's it was: whose do you think it was?

HAMLET: Nay, I know not.

FIRST CLOWN: A pestilence on him for a mad rogue! a' poured a flagon of Rhenish on my head once. This same skull, sir, was Yorick's skull, the king's jester.

HAMLET: This!

FIRST CLOWN: E'en that.

HAMLET: Let me see.—[*Takes the skull.*]—Alas! poor Yorick. I knew him, Horatio; a fellow of infinite jest, of most excellent fancy; he hath borne me on his back a thousand

times; and now, how abhorred in my imagination it is!
my gorge rises at it. Here hung those lips that I have kissed
I know not how oft. Where be your gibes now? your
gambols? your songs? your flashes of merriment, that were
wont to set the table on a roar? Not one now, to mock
your own grinning? quite chapfallen? Now get you to my
lady's chamber, and tell her, let her paint an inch thick,
to this favour she must come; make her laugh at that.
Prithee, Horatio, tell me one thing.

HORATIO: What's that, my lord?

HAMLET: Dost thou think Alexander looked o' this fashion i'
the earth?

HORATIO: E'en so.

HAMLET: And smelt so? pah!   [Puts down the skull.]

HORATIO: E'en so, my lord.

HAMLET: To what base uses we may return, Horatio! Why may
not imagination trace the noble dust of Alexander, till he
find it stopping a bung-hole?

HORATIO: 'Twere to consider too curiously, to consider so.

HAMLET: No, faith, not a jot; but to follow him thither with
modesty enough, and likelihood to lead it; as thus: Alexander died, Alexander was buried, Alexander returneth into
dust; the dust is earth; of earth we make loam, and why
of that loam, whereto he was converted, might they not
stop a beer-barrel?

Imperious Caesar, dead and turn'd to clay,
Might stop a hole to keep the wind away:
O! that that earth, which kept the world in awe,
Should patch a wall to expel the winter's flaw.
But soft! but soft! aside: here comes the king.

Enter KING, QUEEN, LAERTES, [*a* PRIEST,] *and a Coffin, with*
Lords *attendant*.

The queen, the courtiers: who is that they follow?
And with such maimed rites? This doth betoken
The corse they follow did with desperate hand

Fordo it own life; 'twas of some estate.
Couch we awhile, and mark.   [*Retiring with* HORATIO.]
LAERTES: What ceremony else?
HAMLET: That is Laertes,
  A very noble youth: mark.
LAERTES: What ceremony else?
PRIEST: Her obsequies have been as far enlarg'd
  As we have warrantise: her death was doubtful,
  And, but that great command o'ersways the order,
  She should in ground unsanctified have lodg'd
  Till the last trumpet; for charitable prayers,
  Shards, flints, and pebbles should be thrown on her;
  Yet here she is allow'd her virgin crants,
  Her maiden strewments, and the bringing home
  Of bell and burial.
LAERTES: Must there no more be done?
PRIEST: No more be done:
  We should profane the service of the dead,
  To sing a requiem, and such rest to her
  As to peace-parted souls.
LAERTES: Lay her i' the earth;
  And from her fair and unpolluted flesh
  May violets spring! I tell thee, churlish priest,
  A ministering angel shall my sister be,
  When thou liest howling.
HAMLET: What! the fair Ophelia?
QUEEN: Sweets to the sweet: farewell!   [*Scattering flowers.*]
  I hop'd thou shouldst have been my Hamlet's wife;
  I thought thy bride-bed to have deck'd, sweet maid,
  And not have strew'd thy grave.
LAERTES: O! treble woe
  Fall ten times treble on that cursed head
  Whose wicked deed thy most ingenious sense
  Depriv'd thee of. Hold off the earth awhile,
  Till I have caught her once more in mine arms.
                Leaps into the grave.

Now pile your dust upon the quick and dead,
Till of this flat a mountain you have made,
To o'er-top old Pelion or the skyish head
Of blue Olympus.
HAMLET [*advancing*]: What is he whose grief
Bears such an emphasis? whose phrase of sorrow
Conjures the wandering stars, and makes them stand
Like wonder-wounded hearers? this is I,
Hamlet the Dane.   [*Leaps into the grave.*]
LAERTES: The devil take thy soul!
                                    [*Grapples with him.*]
HAMLET: Thou pray'st not well.
I prithee, take thy fingers from my throat;
For though I am not splenetive and rash
Yet have I in me something dangerous,
Which let thy wisdom fear. Away thy hand!
KING: Pluck them asunder.
QUEEN: Hamlet! Hamlet!
ALL: Gentlemen,—
HORATIO: Good my lord, be quiet.
                    [*The* Attendants *part them, and
                    they come out of the grave.*]
HAMLET: Why, I will fight with him upon this theme
Until my eyelids will no longer wag.
QUEEN: O my son! what theme?
HAMLET: I lov'd Ophelia: forty thousand brothers
Could not, with all their quantity of love,
Make up my sum. What wilt thou do for her?
KING: O! he is mad, Laertes.
QUEEN: For love of God, forbear him.
HAMLET: 'Swounds, show me what thou'lt do:
Woo't weep? woo't fight? woo't fast? woo't tear thyself?
Woo't drink up eisel? eat a crocodile?
I'll do 't. Dost thou come here to whine?
To outface me with leaping in her grave?

Be buried quick with her, and so will I:
And, if thou prate of mountains, let them throw
Millions of acres on us, till our ground,
Singeing his pate against the burning zone,
Make Ossa like a wart! Nay, an thou'lt mouth,
I'll rant as well as thou.
QUEEN: This is mere madness:
And thus a while the fit will work on him;
Anon, as patient as the female dove,
When that her golden couplets are disclos'd,
His silence will sit drooping.
HAMLET: Hear you, sir;
What is the reason that you use me thus?
I lov'd you ever: but it is no matter;
Let Hercules himself do what he may,
The cat will mew and dog will have his day.   *Exit.*
KING: I pray you, good Horatio, wait upon him.
                                        [*Exit* HORATIO.]
[*To* LAERTES.] Strengthen your patience in our last night's
   speech;
We'll put the matter to the present push.
Good Gertrude, set some watch over your son.
This grave shall have a living monument:
An hour of quiet shortly shall we see;
Till then, in patience our proceeding be.   *Exeunt.*

SCENE TWO—*A Hall in the Castle.*

Enter HAMLET *and* HORATIO.

HAMLET: So much for this, sir: now shall you see the other;
   You do remember all the circumstance?
HORATIO: Remember it, my lord?
HAMLET: Sir, in my heart there was a kind of fighting
   That would not let me sleep; methought I lay

Worse than the mutines in the bilboes.[25] Rashly,—
And prais'd be rashness for it, let us know,
Our indiscretion sometimes serves us well
When our deep plots do pall; and that should teach us
There's a divinity that shapes our ends,
Rough-hew them how we will.

HORATIO: That is most certain.

HAMLET: Up from my cabin,
My sea-gown scarf'd about me, in the dark
Grop'd I to find out them, had my desire,
Finger'd their packet, and in fine withdrew
To mine own room again; making so bold—
My fears forgetting manners—to unseal
Their grand commission; where I found, Horatio,
O royal knavery! an exact command,
Larded with many several sorts of reasons
Importing Denmark's health, and England's too,
With, ho! such bugs and goblins in my life,
That, on the supervise, no leisure bated,
No, not to stay the grinding of the axe,
My head should be struck off.

HORATIO: Is 't possible?

HAMLET: Here's the commission: read it at more leisure.
But wilt thou hear me how I did proceed?

HORATIO: I beseech you.

HAMLET: Being thus be-netted round with villainies,—
Ere I could make a prologue to my brains
They had begun the play,—I sat me down,
Devis'd a new commission, wrote it fair;
I once did hold it, as our statists do,
A baseness to write fair, and labour'd much
How to forget that learning; but, sir, now
It did me yeoman's service. Wilt thou know
The effect of what I wrote?

---

[25] [*bilboes*: shackles.]

HORATIO: Ay, good my lord.
HAMLET: An earnest conjuration from the king,
  As England was his faithful tributary,
  As love between them like the palm should flourish,
  As peace should still her wheaten garland wear,
  And stand a comma 'tween their amities,
  And many such-like "As"es of great charge,
  That, on the view and knowing of these contents,
  Without debatement further, more or less,
  He should the bearers put to sudden death,
  Not shriving-time allow'd.
HORATIO: How was this seal'd?
HAMLET: Why, even in that was heaven ordinant.
  I had my father's signet in my purse,
  Which was the model of that Danish seal;
  Folded the writ up in form of the other,
  Subscrib'd it, gave 't th' impression, plac'd it safely,
  The changeling never known. Now, the next day
  Was our sea-fight, and what to this was sequent
  Thou know'st already.
HORATIO: So Guildenstern and Rosencrantz go to 't.
HAMLET: Why, man, they did make love to this employment;
  They are not near my conscience; their defeat
  Does by their own insinuation grow.
  'Tis dangerous when the baser nature comes
  Between the pass and fell-incensed points
  Of mighty opposites.
HORATIO: Why, what a king is this!
HAMLET: Does it not, think'st thee, stand me now upon—
  He that hath kill'd my king and whor'd my mother,
  Popp'd in between the election and my hopes,
  Thrown out his angle for my proper life,
  And with such cozenage—is 't not perfect conscience
  To quit him with this arm? and is 't not to be damn'd
  To let this canker of our nature come
  In further evil?

HORATIO: It must be shortly known to him from England
What is the issue of the business there.
HAMLET: It will be short: the interim is mine;
And a man's life's no more than to say "One."
But I am very sorry, good Horatio,
That to Laertes I forgot myself;
For, by the image of my cause, I see
The portraiture of his: I'll count his favours:
But, sure, the bravery of his grief did put me
Into a towering passion.
HORATIO: Peace! who comes here?

Enter young OSRIC.

OSRIC: Your lordship is right welcome back to Denmark.
HAMLET: I humbly thank you, sir. [*Aside to* HORATIO.] Dost
know this water-fly?
HORATIO [*aside to* HAMLET]: No, my good lord.
HAMLET [*aside to* HORATIO]: Thy state is the more gracious;
for 'tis a vice to know him. He hath much land, and
fertile: let a beast be lord of beasts, and his crib shall stand
at the king's mess: 'tis a chough;[26] but, as I say, spacious
in the possession of dirt.
OSRIC: Sweet lord, if your lordship were at leisure, I should
impart a thing to you from his majesty.
HAMLET: I will receive it, sir, with all diligence of spirit. Your
bonnet to his right use; 'tis for the head.
OSRIC: I thank your lordship, 'tis very hot.
HAMLET: No, believe me, 'tis very cold; the wind is northerly.
OSRIC: It is indifferent cold, my lord, indeed.
HAMLET: But yet methinks it is very sultry and hot for my
complexion.
OSRIC: Exceedingly, my lord; it is very sultry, as 'twere, I cannot
tell how. But, my lord, his majesty bade me signify to you

---

[26] [*chough:* small chattering bird.]

that he has laid a great wager on your head. Sir, this is
the matter, —

HAMLET: I beseech you, remember —

> [HAMLET *moves him to put on his hat.*]

OSRIC: Nay, good my lord; for mine ease, in good faith. Sir,
here is newly come to court Laertes; believe me, an absolute
gentleman, full of most excellent differences, of very soft
society and great showing; indeed, to speak feelingly of
him, he is the card or calendar of gentry, for you shall find
in him the continent of what part a gentleman would see.

HAMLET: Sir, his definement suffers no perdition in you; though,
I know, to divide him inventorially would dizzy the arith-
metic of memory, and yet but yaw[27] neither, in respect of
his quick sail. But, in the verity of extolment, I take him
to be a soul of great article; and his infusion of such dearth
and rareness, as, to make true diction of him, his semblable
is his mirror; and who else would trace him, his umbrage,
nothing more.

OSRIC: Your lordship speaks most infallibly of him.

HAMLET: The concernancy, sir? why do we wrap the gentleman
in our more rawer breath?

OSRIC: Sir?

HORATIO: Is 't not possible to understand in another tongue?
You will do 't, sir, really.

HAMLET: What imports the nomination of this gentleman?

OSRIC: Of Laertes?

HORATIO [*aside to* HAMLET]: His purse is empty already; all 's
golden words are spent.

HAMLET: Of him, sir.

OSRIC: I know you are not ignorant —

HAMLET: I would you did, sir; in faith, if you did, it would
not much approve me. Well, sir.

---

[27] [*yaw:* stagger.]

OSRIC: You are not ignorant of what excellence Laertes is—

HAMLET: I dare not confess that, lest I should compare with him in excellence; but, to know a man well, were to know himself.

OSRIC: I mean, sir, for his weapon; but in the imputation laid on him by them, in his meed he's unfellowed.

HAMLET: What's his weapon?

OSRIC: Rapier and dagger.

HAMLET: That's two of his weapons; but, well.

OSRIC: The king, sir, hath wagered with him six Barbary horses; against the which he has imponed, as I take it, six French rapiers and poniards, with their assigns, as girdle, hangers, and so: three of the carriages, in faith, are very dear to fancy, very responsive to the hilts, most delicate carriages, and of very liberal conceit.

HAMLET: What call you the carriages?

HORATIO [*aside to* HAMLET]: I knew you must be edified by the margent, ere you had done.

OSRIC: The carriages, sir, are the hangers.

HAMLET: The phrase would be more german to the matter, if we could carry cannon by our sides; I would it might be hangers till then. But, on; six Barbary horses against six French swords, their assigns, and three liberal-conceited carriages; that's the French bet against the Danish. Why is this "imponed," as you call it?

OSRIC: The king sir, hath laid, that in a dozen passes between yourself and him, he shall not exceed you three hits; he hath laid on twelve for nine, and it would come to immediate trial, if your lordship would vouchsafe the answer.

HAMLET: How if I answer no?

OSRIC: I mean, my lord, the opposition of your person in trial.

HAMLET: Sir, I will walk here in the hall; if it please his majesty, 'tis the breathing time of day with me; let the foils be brought; the gentleman willing, and the king hold his purpose, I will win for him an I can; if not, I will gain nothing but my shame and the odd hits.

OSRIC: Shall I re-deliver you so?

HAMLET: To this effect, sir; after what flourish your nature will.

OSRIC: I commend my duty to your lordship.

HAMLET: Yours, yours. [*Exit* OSRIC.] He does well to commend
it himself; there are no tongues else for 's turn.

HORATIO: This lapwing runs away with the shell on his head.

HAMLET: He did comply with his dug before he sucked it.
Thus has he—and many more of the same bevy, that I
know the drossy age dotes on—only got the tune of the
time and outward habit of encounter, a kind of yesty collection which carries them through and through the most
fond and winnowed opinions; and do but blow them to
their trial, the bubbles are out.

Enter a LORD.

LORD: My lord, his majesty commended him to you by young
Osric, who brings back to him, that you attend him in
the hall; he sends to know if your pleasure hold to play
with Laertes, or that you will take longer time.

HAMLET: I am constant to my purposes; they follow the king's
pleasure: if his fitness speaks, mine is ready; now, or whensoever, provided I be so able as now.

LORD: The king, and queen, and all are coming down.

HAMLET: In happy time.

LORD: The queen desires you to use some gentle entertainment
to Laertes before you fall to play.

HAMLET: She well instructs me.   [*Exit* LORD.]

HORATIO: You will lose this wager, my lord.

HAMLET: I do not think so; since he went into France, I have
been in continual practice; I shall win at the odds. But
thou wouldst not think how ill all 's here about my heart;
but it is no matter.

HORATIO: Nay, good my lord,—

HAMLET: It is but foolery; but it is such a kind of gain-giving
as would perhaps trouble a woman.

HORATIO: If your mind dislike any thing, obey it; I will forestall their repair hither, and say you are not fit.

HAMLET: Not a whit, we defy augury; there's a special providence in the fall of a sparrow. If it be now, 'tis not to come; if it be not to come, it will be now; if it be not now, yet it will come: the readiness is all. Since no man has aught of what he leaves, what is 't to leave betimes? Let be.

Enter KING, QUEEN, LAERTES *and* Lords, *with other* Attendants *with foils and gauntlets, a table and flagons of wine on it.*

KING: Come, Hamlet, come, and take this hand from me.
> [*The* KING *puts the hand of* LAERTES
> *into that of* HAMLET.]

HAMLET: Give me your pardon, sir; I've done you wrong;
But pardon 't, as you are a gentleman.
This presence knows,
And you must needs have heard, how I am punish'd
With sore distraction. What J have done,
That might your nature, honour and exception
Roughly awake, I here proclaim was madness.
Was 't Hamlet wrong'd Laertes? Never Hamlet:
If Hamlet from himself be ta'en away,
And when he's not himself does wrong Laertes,
Then Hamlet does it not; Hamlet denies it.
Who does it then? His madness. If 't be so,
Hamlet is of the faction that is wrong'd;
His madness is poor Hamlet's enemy.
Sir, in this audience,
Let my disclaiming from a purpos'd evil
Free me so far in your most generous thoughts,
That I have shot mine arrow o'er the house,
And hurt my brother.

LAERTES: I am satisfied in nature,
Whose motive, in this case, should stir me most

To my revenge; but in my terms of honour
I stand aloof, and will no reconcilement,
Till by some elder masters, of known honour,
I have a voice and precedent of peace,
To keep my name ungor'd. But till that time,
I do receive your offer'd love like love,
And will not wrong it.

HAMLET: I embrace it freely;
And will this brother's wager frankly play.
Give us the foils. Come on.

LAERTES: Come, one for me.

HAMLET: I'll be your foil, Laertes; in mine ignorance
Your skill shall, like a star i' the darkest night,
Stick fiery off indeed.

LAERTES: You mock me, sir.

HAMLET: No, by this hand.

KING: Give them the foils, young Osric. Cousin Hamlet,
You know the wager?

HAMLET: Very well, my lord;
Your Grace hath laid the odds o' the weaker side.

KING: I do not fear it; I have seen you both;
But since he is better'd, we have therefore odds.

LAERTES: This is too heavy; let me see another.

HAMLET: This likes me well. These foils have all a length?

OSRIC: Ay, my good lord.   *Prepare to play.*

KING: Set me the stoups of wine upon that table.
If Hamlet give the first or second hit,
Or quit in answer of the third exchange,
Let all the battlements their ordnance fire;
The king shall drink to Hamlet's better breath;
And in the cup an union shall he throw,
Richer than that which four successive kings
In Denmark's crown have worn. Give me the cups;
And let the kettle to the trumpet speak,
The trumpet to the cannoneer without,
The cannons to the heavens, the heavens to earth,

"Now the king drinks to Hamlet!" Come, begin;
And you, the judges, bear a wary eye.

HAMLET: Come on, sir.

LAERTES: Come, my lord.   *They play.*

HAMLET: One.

LAERTES: No.

HAMLET: Judgment.

OSRIC: A hit, a very palpable hit.

LAERTES: Well; again.

KING: Stay; give me drink. Hamlet, this pearl is thine;
Here's to thy health. Give him the cup.
                              Trumpets sound; and shot goes off.

HAMLET: I'll play this bout first; set it by awhile.
Come. [*They play.*] Another hit; what say you?

LAERTES: A touch, a touch, I do confess.

KING: Our son shall win.

QUEEN: He's fat, and scant of breath.
Here, Hamlet, take my napkin, rub thy brows;
The queen carouses to thy fortune, Hamlet.

HAMLET: Good madam!

KING: Gertrude, do not drink.

QUEEN: I will, my lord; I pray you, pardon me.

KING [*aside*]: It is the poison'd cup! it is too late.

HAMLET: I dare not drink yet, madam; by and by.

QUEEN: Come, let me wipe thy face.

LAERTES: My lord, I'll hit him now.

KING: I do not think 't.

LAERTES [*aside*]: And yet 'tis almost 'gainst my conscience.

HAMLET: Come, for the third, Laertes. You but dally;
I pray you, pass with your best violence.
I am afeard you make a wanton of me.

LAERTES: Say you so? come on.   [*They*] *play.*

OSRIC: Nothing, neither way.

LAERTES: Have at you now.   *In scuffling they change rapiers.*

KING: Part them! they are incens'd.

HAMLET: Nay, come, again.   [*The* QUEEN *falls.*]

OSRIC: Look to the queen there, ho!

HORATIO: They bleed on both sides. How is it, my lord?

OSRIC: How is it, Laertes?

LAERTES: Why, as a woodcock to mine own springe, Osric;
I am justly kill'd with mine own treachery.

HAMLET: How does the queen?

KING: She swounds to see them bleed.

QUEEN: No, no, the drink, the drink,—O my dear Hamlet!
The drink, the drink; I am poison'd.   [*Dies.*]

HAMLET: O villainy! Ho! let the door be lock'd:
Treachery! seek it out.   [LAERTES *falls.*]

LAERTES: It is here, Hamlet. Hamlet, thou art slain;
No medicine in the world can do thee good;
In thee there is not half an hour of life;
The treacherous instrument is in thy hand,
Unbated and envenom'd. The foul practice
Hath turn'd itself on me; lo! here I lie,
Never to rise again. Thy mother's poison'd.
I can no more. The king, the king's to blame.

HAMLET: The point envenom'd too!—
Then, venom, to thy work.   *Hurts the* KING.

ALL: Treason! treason!

KING: O! yet defend me, friends; I am but hurt.

HAMLET: Here, thou incestuous, murderous, damned Dane,
Drink off this potion;—is thy union here?
Follow my mother.   KING *dies.*

LAERTES: He is justly serv'd;
It is a poison temper'd by himself.
Exchange forgiveness with me, noble Hamlet:
Mine and my father's death come not upon thee,
Nor thine on me!   *Dies.*

HAMLET: Heaven make thee free of it! I follow thee.
I am dead, Horatio. Wretched queen, adieu!
You that look pale and tremble at this chance,

That are but mutes or audience to this act,
Had I but time,—as this fell sergeant, death,
Is strict in his arrest,—O! I could tell you—
But let it be. Horatio, I am dead;
Thou liv'st; report me and my cause aright
To the unsatisfied.

HORATIO: Never believe it;
I am more an antique Roman than a Dane:
Here's yet some liquor left.

HAMLET: As thou'rt a man,
Give me the cup: let go; by heaven, I'll have 't.
O good Horatio, what a wounded name,
Things standing thus unknown, shall live behind me.
If thou didst ever hold me in thy heart,
Absent thee from felicity awhile,
And in this harsh world draw thy breath in pain,
To tell my story.   *March afar off, and shout within.*
            What war-like noise is this?

Enter OSRIC.

OSRIC: Young Fortinbras, with conquest come from Poland,
To the ambassadors of England gives
This war-like volley.

HAMLET: O! I die, Horatio;
The potent poison quite o'er-crows my spirit:
I cannot live to hear the news from England,
But I do prophesy the election lights
On Fortinbras: he has my dying voice;
So tell him, with the occurrents, more and less,
Which have solicited.—The rest is silence.   *Dies.*

HORATIO: Now cracks a noble heart. Good-night, sweet prince,
And flights of angels sing thee to thy rest!
Why does the drum come hither?

Enter FORTINBRAS, *and* ENGLISH AMBASSADOR, *with drum, col-
ours, and* Attendants.

FORTINBRAS: Where is this sight?

HORATIO: What is it ye would see?
If aught of woe or wonder, cease your search.

FORTINBRAS: This quarry cries on havoc. O proud death!
What feast is toward in thine eternal cell,
That thou so many princes at a shot
So bloodily hast struck?

AMBASSADOR: The sight is dismal;
And our affairs from England come too late:
The ears are senseless that should give us hearing,
To tell him his commandment is fulfill'd,
That Rosencrantz and Guildenstern are dead.
Where should we have our thanks?

HORATIO: Not from his mouth,
Had it the ability of life to thank you:
He never gave commandment for their death.
But since, so jump upon this bloody question,
You from the Polack wars, and you from England,
Are here arriv'd, give order that these bodies
High on a stage be placed to the view;
And let me speak to the yet unknowing world
How these things came about: so shall you hear
Of carnal, bloody, and unnatural acts,
Of accidental judgments, casual slaughters;
Of deaths put on by cunning and forc'd cause,
And, in this upshot, purposes mistook
Fall'n on the inventors' heads; all this can I
Truly deliver.

FORTINBRAS: Let us haste to hear it,
And call the noblest to the audience.
For me, with sorrow I embrace my fortune;
I have some rights of memory in this kingdom,
Which now to claim my vantage doth invite me.

HORATIO: Of that I shall have also cause to speak,
And from his mouth whose voice will draw on more:
But let this same be presently perform'd,

Even while men's minds are wild, lest more mischance
On plots and errors happen.

FORTINBRAS: Let four captains
Bear Hamlet, like a soldier, to the stage;
For he was likely, had he been put on,
To have prov'd most royally: and, for his passage,
The soldiers' music and the rites of war
Speak loudly for him.
Take up the bodies: such a sight as this
Becomes the field, but here shows much amiss.
Go, bid the soldiers shoot.

Exeunt marching, after the which,
a peal of ordnance are shot off.

A selection from "The Gospel According to Mark" in *The Holy Bible,* King James Version. Publisher: Meridian Books, The World Publishing Co., 1964. Chapters: 1:1–39; 2:1–17; 3:1–19; 4; 5:1–20; 6:30–43; 8:27–38; 9:1–10; 10:17–34; 11:1–27; 12:13–34; 14; 15; 16:1–8.

The Gospel of Mark

The beginning of the gospel of Jesus Christ, the Son of God; As it is written in the prophets, Behold, I send my messenger before thy face, which shall prepare thy way before thee. The voice of one crying in the wilderness, Prepare ye the way of the Lord, make his paths straight.

John did baptize in the wilderness, and preach the baptism of repentance for the remission of sins. And there went out unto him all the land of Judaea, and they of Jerusalem, and were all baptized of him in the river of Jordan, confessing their sins. And John was clothed with camel's hair, and with a girdle of a skin about his loins; and he did eat locusts and wild honey; and preached, saying, There cometh one mightier than I after me, the latchet of whose shoes I am not worthy to stoop down and unloose. I indeed have baptized you with water: but he shall baptize you with the Holy Ghost.

And it came to pass in those days, that Jesus came from Nazareth of Galilee, and was baptized of John in Jordan. And straightway coming up out of the water, he saw the heavens opened, and the Spirit like a dove descending upon him: and there came a voice from heaven, saying, Thou art my beloved Son, in whom I am well pleased.

And immediately the spirit driveth him into the wilderness. And he was there in the wilderness forty days, tempted of Satan; and was with the wild beasts; and the angels ministered unto him.

Now after that John was put in prison, Jesus came into Galilee, preaching the gospel of the kingdom of God, and saying, The time is fulfilled, and the kingdom of God is at hand: repent ye, and believe the gospel.

Now as he walked by the sea of Galilee, he saw Simon and Andrew his brother casting a net into the sea: for they were fishers. And Jesus said unto them, Come ye after me, and I will make you to become fishers of men. And straightway they forsook their nets, and followed him. And when he had gone a little farther thence, he saw James the son of Zebedee, and John his brother, who also were in the ship mending their nets. And straightway he called them: and they left their father Zebedee in the ship with the hired servants, and went after him.

And they went into Capernaum; and straightway on the sabbath day he entered into the synagogue, and taught. And they were astonished at his doctrine: for he taught them as one that had authority, and not as the scribes. And there was in their synagogue a man with an unclean spirit; and he cried out, saying, Let us alone; what have we to do with thee, thou Jesus of Nazareth? art thou come to destroy us? I know thee who thou art, the Holy One of God. And Jesus rebuked him, saying, Hold thy peace, and come out of him. And when the unclean spirit had torn him, and cried with a loud voice, he came out of him. And they were all amazed, insomuch that they questioned among themselves, saying, What thing is this? what new doctrine is this? for with authority commandeth he even the unclean spirits, and they do obey him. And immediately his fame spread abroad throughout all the region round about Galilee.

And forthwith, when they were come out of the synagogue, they entered into the house of Simon and Andrew, with James and John. But Simon's wife's mother lay sick of a fever, and anon they tell him of her. And he came and took her by the hand, and lifted her up; and immediately the fever left her, and she ministered unto them.

And at even, when the sun did set, they brought unto him all that were diseased, and them that were possessed with devils. And all the city was gathered together at the door. And he healed many that were sick of divers diseases, and cast out many devils; and suffered not the devils to speak, because they knew him.

And in the morning, rising up a great while before day, he went out, and departed into a solitary place, and there prayed. And Simon and they that were with him followed after him. And when they had found him, they said unto him, All men seek for thee. And he said unto them, Let us go into the next towns, that I may preach there also: for therefore came I forth. And he preached in their synagogues throughout all Galilee, and cast out devils. . . .

And again he entered into Capernaum after some days; and it was noised that he was in the house. And straightway many were gathered together, insomuch that there was no room to receive them, no, not so much as about the door: and he preached the word unto them. And they come unto him, bringing one sick of the palsy, which was borne of four. And when they could not come nigh unto him for the press, they uncovered the roof where he was: and when they had broken it up, they let down the bed wherein the sick of the palsy lay. When Jesus saw their faith, he said unto the sick of the palsy, Son, thy sins be forgiven thee. But there were certain of the scribes sitting there, and reasoning in their hearts, Why doth this man thus speak blasphemies? who can forgive sins but God only? And immediately when Jesus perceived in his spirit that they so reasoned within themselves, he said unto them, Why reason ye these things in your hearts? Whether is it easier to say to the sick of the palsy, Thy sins be forgiven thee; or to say, Arise, and take up thy bed, and walk? But that ye may know that the Son of man hath power on earth to forgive sins (he saith to the sick of the palsy),

I say unto thee, Arise, and take up thy bed, and go thy way into thine house. And immediately he arose, took up the bed, and went forth before them all; insomuch that they were all amazed, and glorified God, saying, We never saw it on this fashion.

And he went forth again by the sea side; and all the multitude resorted unto him, and he taught them. And as he passed by, he saw Levi the son of Alphaeus sitting at the receipt of custom, and said unto him, Follow me. And he arose and followed him.

And it came to pass, that, as Jesus sat at meat in his house, many publicans and sinners sat also together with Jesus and his disciples: for there were many, and they followed him. And when the scribes and Pharisees saw him eat with publicans and sinners, they said unto his disciples, How is it that he eateth and drinketh with publicans and sinners? When Jesus heard it, he saith unto them, They that are whole have no need of the physician, but they that are sick: I came not to call the righteous, but sinners to repentance. . . .

And he entered again into the synagogue; and there was a man there which had a withered hand. And they watched him, whether he would heal him on the sabbath day; that they might accuse him. And he saith unto the man which had the withered hand, Stand forth. And he saith unto them, Is it lawful to do good on the sabbath days, or to do evil? to save life, or to kill? But they held their peace. And when he had looked round about on them with anger, being grieved for the hardness of their hearts, he saith unto the man, Stretch forth thine hand. And he stretched it out: and his hand was restored whole as the other. And the Pharisees went forth, and straightway took counsel with the Herodians against him, how they might destroy him.

But Jesus withdrew himself with his disciples to the sea: and a great multitude from Galilee followed him, and from Judaea, and from Jerusalem, and from Idumaea, and from beyond Jordan;

and they about Tyre and Sidon, a great multitude, when they had heard what great things he did, came unto him. And he spake to his disciples, that a small ship should wait on him because of the multitude, lest they should throng him. For he had healed many; insomuch that they pressed upon him for to touch him, as many as had plagues. And unclean spirits, when they saw him, fell down before him, and cried, saying, Thou art the Son of God. And he straitly charged them that they should not make him known.

And he goeth up into a mountain, and calleth unto him whom he would: and they came unto him. And he ordained twelve, that they should be with him, and that he might send them forth to preach, and to have power to heal sicknesses, and to cast out devils: and Simon he surnamed Peter; and James the son of Zebedee, and John the brother of James; and he surnamed them Boanerges, which is, The sons of thunder: and Andrew, and Philip, and Bartholomew, and Matthew, and Thomas, and James the son of Alphaeus, and Thaddaeus, and Simon the Canaanite, and Judas Iscariot, which also betrayed him: and they went into an house. . . .

And he began again to teach by the sea side: and there was gathered unto him a great multitude, so that he entered into a ship, and sat in the sea; and the whole multitude was by the sea on the land. And he taught them many things by parables, and said unto them in his doctrine, Hearken; Behold, there went out a sower to sow: and it came to pass, as he sowed, some fell by the way side, and the fowls of the air came and devoured it up. And some fell on stony ground, where it had not much earth; and immediately it sprang up, because it had no depth of earth. But when the sun was up, it was scorched; and because it had no root, it withered away. And some fell among thorns, and the thorns grew up, and choked it, and it yielded no fruit. And other fell on good ground, and did yield fruit that sprang up and increased; and brought forth, some thirty, and some sixty, and some an hundred. And he said unto them, He that hath ears to hear, let him hear.

And when he was alone, they that were about him with the twelve asked of him the parable. And he said unto them, Unto you it is given to know the mystery of the kingdom of God: but unto them that are without, all these things are done in parables: that seeing they may see, and not perceive; and hearing they may hear, and not understand; lest at any time they should be converted, and their sins should be forgiven them. And he said unto them, Know ye not this parable? and how then will ye know all parables?

The sower soweth the word. And these are they by the way side, where the word is sown; but when they have heard, Satan cometh immediately, and taketh away the word that was sown in their hearts. And these are they likewise which are sown on stony ground; who, when they have heard the word, immediately receive it with gladness; and have no root in themselves, and so endure but for a time: afterward, when affliction or persecution ariseth for the word's sake, immediately they are offended. And these are they which are sown among thorns; such as hear the word, and the cares of this world, and the deceitfulness of riches, and the lusts of other things entering in, choke the word, and it becometh unfruitful. And these are they which are sown on good ground; such as hear the word, and receive it, and bring forth fruit, some thirtyfold, some sixty, and some an hundred.

And he said unto them, Is a candle brought to be put under a bushel, or under a bed? and not to be set on a candlestick? For there is nothing hid, which shall not be manifested; neither was any thing kept secret, but that it should come abroad. If any man have ears to hear, let him hear. And he said unto them, Take heed what ye hear: with what measure ye mete, it shall be measured to you: and unto you that hear shall more be given. For he that hath, to him shall be given: and he that hath not, from him shall be taken even that which he hath.

And he said, So is the kingdom of God, as if a man should cast seed into the ground; and should sleep, and rise night and day, and the seed should spring and grow up, he knoweth not how. For the earth bringeth forth fruit of herself; first the blade, then the ear, after that the full corn in the ear. But when the fruit is brought forth, immediately he putteth in the sickle, because the harvest is come.

And he said, Whereunto shall we liken the kingdom of God? or with what comparison shall we compare it? It is like a grain of mustard seed, which, when it is sown in the earth, is less than all the seeds that be in the earth. But when it is sown, it growth up, and becometh greater than all herbs, and shooteth out great branches; so that the fowls of the air may lodge under the shadow of it.

And with many such parables spake he the word unto them, as they were able to hear it. But without a parable spake he not unto them: and when they were alone, he expounded all things to his disciples.

And the same day, when the even was come, he saith unto them, Let us pass over unto the other side. And when they had sent away the multitude, they took him even as he was in the ship. And there were also with him other little ships. And there arose a great storm of wind, and the waves beat into the ship, so that it was now full. And he was in the hinder part of the ship, asleep on a pillow: and they awake him, and say unto him, Master, carest thou not that we perish? And he arose, and rebuked the wind, and said unto the sea, Peace, be still. And the wind ceased, and there was a great calm. And he said unto them, Why are ye so fearful? how is it that ye have no faith? And they feared exceedingly, and said one to another, What manner of man is this, that even the wind and the sea obey him?

And they came over unto the other side of the sea, into the country of the Gadarenes. And when he was come out of the

ship, immediately there met him out of the tombs a man with
an unclean spirit, who had his dwelling among the tombs; and
no man could bind him, no, not with chains: because that he
had been often bound with fetters and chains, and the chains
had been plucked asunder by him, and the fetters broken in
pieces: neither could any man tame him. And always, night and
day, he was in the mountains, and in the tombs, crying, and
cutting himself with stones. But when he saw Jesus afar off, he
ran and worshipped him, and cried with a loud voice, and said,
What have I to do with thee, Jesus, thou Son of the most high
God? I adjure thee by God, that thou torment me not. For he
said unto him, Come out of the man, thou unclean spirit. And
he asked him, What is thy name? And he answered, saying,
My name is Legion: for we are many. And he besought him
much that he would not send them away out of the country.
Now there was there nigh unto the mountains a great herd of
swine feeding. And all the devils besought him, saying, Send
us into the swine, that we may enter into them. And forthwith
Jesus gave them leave. And the unclean spirits went out, and
entered into the swine: and the herd ran violently down a steep
place into the sea (they were about two thousand); and were
choked in the sea.

And they that fed the swine fled, and told it in the city, and
in the country. And they went out to see what it was that was
done. And they come to Jesus, and see him that was possessed
with the devil, and had the legion, sitting, and clothed, and in
his right mind: and they were afraid. And they that saw it told
them how it befell to him that was possessed with the devil,
and also concerning the swine. And they began to pray him to
depart out of their coasts. And when he was come into the ship,
he that had been possessed with the devil prayed him that he
might be with him. Howbeit Jesus suffered him not, but saith
unto him, Go home to thy friends, and tell them how great
things the Lord hath done for thee, and hath had compassion

on thee. And he departed, and began to publish in Decapolis how great things Jesus had done for him: and all men did marvel. . . .

The apostles gathered themselves together unto Jesus, and told him all things, both what they had done, and what they had taught. And he said unto them, Come ye yourselves apart into a desert place, and rest a while: for there were many coming and going, and they had no leisure so much as to eat. And they departed into a desert place by ship privately. And the people saw them departing, and many knew him, and ran afoot thither out of all cities, and outwent them, and came together unto him. And Jesus, when he came out, saw much people, and was moved with compassion toward them, because they were as sheep not having a shepherd: and he began to teach them many things. And when the day was now far spent, his disciples came unto him, and said, This is a desert place, and now the time is far passed: send them away, that they may go into the country round about, and into the villages, and buy themselves bread: for they have nothing to eat.

He answered and said unto them, Give ye them to eat. And they say unto him, Shall we go and buy two hundred penny-worth of bread, and give them to eat? He saith unto them, How many loaves have ye? go and see. And when they knew, they say, Five, and two fishes. And he commanded them to make all sit down by companies upon the green grass. And they sat down in ranks, by hundreds, and by fifties. And when he had taken the five loaves and the two fishes, he looked up to heaven, and blessed, and brake the loaves, and gave them to his disciples to set before them; and the two fishes divided he among them all. And they did all eat, and were filled. And they took up twelve baskets full of the fragments, and of the fishes. And they that did eat of the loaves were about five thousand men. . . .

And Jesus went out, and his disciples, into the towns of Caesarea Philippi: and by the way he asked his disciples, saying unto them, Whom do men say that I am? And they answered, John the Baptist: but some say, Elias; and others, One of the prophets. And he saith unto them, But whom say ye that I am? And Peter answereth and saith unto him, Thou art the Christ. And he charged them that they should tell no man of him.

And he began to teach them, that the Son of man must suffer many things, and be rejected of the elders, and of the chief priests, and scribes, and be killed, and after three days rise again. And he spake that saying openly. And Peter took him, and began to rebuke him. But when he had turned about and looked on his disciples, he rebuked Peter, saying, Get thee behind me, Satan: for thou savourest not the things that be of God, but the things that be of men.

And when he had called the people unto him with his disciples also, he said unto them, Whosoever will come after me, let him deny himself, and take up his cross, and follow me. For whosoever will save his life shall lose it; but whosoever shall lose his life for my sake and the gospel's, the same shall save it. For what shall it profit a man, if he shall gain the whole world, and lose his own soul? Or what shall a man give in exchange for his soul?

Whosoever therefore shall be ashamed of me and of my words in this adulterous and sinful generation; of him also shall the Son of man be ashamed, when he cometh in the glory of his Father with the holy angels.

And he said unto them, Verily I say unto you, That there be some of them that stand here, which shall not taste of death, till they have seen the kingdom of God come with power.

And after six days Jesus taketh with him Peter, and James, and John, and leadeth them up into an high mountain apart by themselves: and he was transfigured before them. And his raiment became shining, exceeding white as snow; so as no fuller on earth can white them. And there appeared unto them Elias with Moses: and they were talking with Jesus. And Peter answered and said to Jesus, Master, it is good for us to be here: and let us make three tabernacles; one for thee, and one for Moses, and one for Elias. For he wist not what to say; for they were sore afraid. And there was a cloud that overshadowed them: and a voice came out of the cloud, saying, This is my beloved Son: hear him. And suddenly, when they had looked round about, they saw no man any more, save Jesus only with themselves.

And as they came down from the mountain, he charged them that they should tell no man what things they had seen, till the Son of man were risen from the dead. And they kept that saying with themselves, questioning one with another what the rising from the dead should mean. . . .

And when he was gone forth into the way [to Jerusalem], there came one running, and kneeling to him, and asked him, Good Master, what shall I do that I may inherit eternal life? And Jesus said unto him, Why callest thou me good? there is none good but one, that is, God. Thou knowest the commandments, Do not commit adultery, Do not kill, Do not steal, Do not bear false witness, Defraud not, Honour thy father and mother. And he answered and said unto him, Master, all these have I observed from my youth. Then Jesus beholding him loved him, and said unto him, One thing thou lackest: go thy way, sell whatsoever thou hast, and give to the poor, and thou shalt have treasure in heaven: and come, take up the cross, and follow me. And he was sad at that saying, and went away grieved: for he had great possessions.

And Jesus looked round about, and saith unto his disciples, How hardly shall they that have riches enter into the kingdom of God! And the disciples were astonished at his words. But

Jesus answereth again, and saith unto them, Children, how hard is it for them that trust in riches to enter into the kingdom of God! It is easier for a camel to go through the eye of a needle, than for a rich man to enter into the kingdom of God. And they were astonished out of measure, saying among themselves, Who then can be saved? And Jesus looking upon them saith, With men it is impossible, but not with God: for with God all things are possible.

Then Peter began to say unto him, Lo, we have left all, and have followed thee. And Jesus answered and said, Verily I say unto you, There is no man that hath left house, or brethren, or sisters, or father, or mother, or wife, or children, or lands, for my sake, and the gospel's, but he shall receive an hundredfold now in this time, houses, and brethren, and sisters, and mothers, and children, and lands, with persecutions; and in the world to come eternal life. But many that are first shall be last; and the last first.

And they were in the way going up to Jerusalem; and Jesus went before them: and they were amazed; and as they followed, they were afraid. And he took again the twelve, and began to tell them what things should happen unto him, saying, Behold, we go up to Jerusalem; and the Son of man shall be delivered unto the chief priests, and unto the scribes; and they shall condemn him to death, and shall deliver him to the Gentiles. And they shall mock him, and shall scourge him, and shall spit upon him, and shall kill him: and the third day he shall rise again. . . .

And when they came nigh to Jerusalem, unto Bethphage and Bethany, at the mount of Olives, he sendeth forth two of his disciples, and saith unto them, Go your way into the village over against you: and as soon as ye be entered into it, ye shall find a colt tied, whereon never man sat; loose him, and bring him. And if any man say unto you, Why do ye this? say ye that the Lord hath need of him; and straightway he will send him hither. And they went their way, and found the colt tied by the door without in a place where two ways met; and they loose him. And certain of them that stood there said unto them, What do ye, loosing the colt? And they said unto them even as Jesus had commanded: and they let them go. And they brought the colt to Jesus, and cast their garments on him; and he sat upon him. And many spread their garments in the way: and others cut down branches off the trees, and strawed them in the way. And they that went before, and they that followed, cried, saying, Hosanna; Blessed is he that cometh in the name of the Lord; blessed be the kingdom of our father David, that cometh in the name of the Lord: Hosanna in the highest.

And Jesus entered into Jerusalem, and into the temple: and when he had looked round about upon all things, and now the eventide was come, he went out unto Bethany with the twelve.

And on the morrow, when they were come from Bethany, he was hungry. And seeing a fig tree afar off having leaves, he came, if haply he might find any thing thereon: and when he came to it, he found nothing but leaves; for the time of figs was not yet. And Jesus answered and said unto it, No man eat fruit of thee hereafter for ever. And his disciples heard it.

And they came to Jerusalem: and Jesus went into the temple, and began to cast out them that sold and bought in the temple, and overthrew the tables of the money-changers, and the seats of them that sold doves; and would not suffer that any man should carry any vessel through the temple. And he taught, saying unto them, Is it not written, My house shall be called of all nations the house of prayer? but ye have made it a den of thieves. And the scribes and chief priests heard it, and sought how they might destroy him: for they feared him, because all the people was astonished at his doctrine. And when even was come, he went out of the city.

And in the morning, as they passed by, they saw the fig tree dried up from the roots. And Peter calling to remembrance saith unto him, Master, behold, the fig tree which thou cursedst is withered away. And Jesus answering saith unto them, Have faith in God. For verily I say unto you, That whosoever shall say unto this mountain, Be thou removed, and be thou cast into the sea; and shall not doubt in his heart, but shall believe that those things which he saith shall come to pass; he shall have whatsoever he saith. Therefore I say unto you, What things soever ye desire, when ye pray, believe that ye receive them, and ye shall have them. And when ye stand praying, forgive, if ye have ought against any: that your Father also which is in heaven may forgive you your trespasses. But if ye do not forgive, neither will your Father which is in heaven forgive your trespasses.

And they come again to Jerusalem. . . .

Certain of the Pharisees and of the Herodians [tried] to catch him in his words. And when they were come, they say unto him, Master, we know that thou art true, and carest for no man: for thou regardest not the person of men, but teachest the way of God in truth: Is it lawful to give tribute to Caesar, or not? Shall we give, or shall we not give? But he, knowing their hypocrisy, said unto them, Why tempt ye me? bring me a penny, that I may see it. And they brought it. And he saith unto them, Whose is this image and superscription? And they said unto him, Caesar's. And Jesus answering said unto them, Render to Caesar the things that are Caesar's, and to God the things that are God's. And they marvelled at him.

Then come unto him the Sadducees, which say there is no resurrection; and they asked him, saying, Master, Moses wrote unto us, If a man's brother die, and leave his wife behind him, and leave no children, that his brother should take his wife, and raise up seed unto his brother. Now there were seven brethren: and the first took a wife, and dying left no seed. And the second took her, and died, neither left he any seed: and the third likewise. And the seven had her, and left no seed: last of all the woman died also. In the resurrection therefore, when they shall rise, whose wife shall she be of them? for the seven had her to wife.

And Jesus answering said unto them, Do ye not therefore err, because ye know not the scriptures, neither the power of God? For when they shall rise from the dead, they neither marry, nor are given in marriage; but are as the angels which are in heaven. And as touching the dead, that they rise: have ye not read in the book of Moses, how in the bush God spake unto him, saying, I am the God of Abraham, and the God of Isaac, and the God of Jacob? He is not the God of the dead, but the God of the living: ye therefore do greatly err.

And one of the scribes came, and having heard them reasoning together, and perceiving that he had answered them well, asked him, Which is the first commandment of all? And Jesus answered him, The first of all the commandments is, Hear, O Israel; The Lord our God is one Lord: And thou shalt love the Lord thy God with all thy heart, and with all thy soul, and with all thy mind, and with all thy strength: this is the first commandment. And the second is like, namely this, Thou shalt love thy neighbour as thyself. There is none other commandment greater than these. And the scribe said unto him, Well, Master, thou hast said the truth: for there is one God; and there is none other but he; and to love him with all the heart, and with all the understanding, and with all the soul, and with all the strength, and to love his neighbour as himself, is more than all whole burnt offerings and sacrifices. And when Jesus saw that he answered discreetly, he said unto him, Thou art not far from the kingdom of God. And no man after that durst ask him any question. . . .

After two days was the feast of the passover, and of unleavened bread: and the chief priests and the scribes sought how they might take him by craft, and put him to death. But they said, Not on the feast day, lest there be an uproar of the people.

And being in Bethany in the house of Simon the leper, as he sat at meat, there came a woman having an alabaster box of ointment of spikenard very precious; and she brake the box, and poured it on his head. And there were some that had indignation within themselves, and said, Why was this waste of the ointment made? For it might have been sold for more than three hundred pence, and have been given to the poor. And they murmured against her. And Jesus said, Let her alone; why trouble ye her? she hath wrought a good work on me. For ye have the poor with you always, and whensoever ye will ye may do them good: but me ye have not always. She hath done what she could: she is come aforehand to anoint my body to the burying. Verily I say unto you, Wheresoever this gospel shall be preached throughout the whole world, this also that she hath done shall be spoken of for a memorial of her.

And Judas Iscariot, one of the twelve, went unto the chief priests, to betray him unto them. And when they heard it, they were glad, and promised to give him money. And he sought how he might conveniently betray him.

And the first day of unleavened bread, when they killed the passover, his disciples said unto him, Where wilt thou that we go and prepare that thou mayest eat the passover? And he sendeth forth two of his disciples, and saith unto them, Go ye into the city, and there shall meet you a man bearing a pitcher of water: follow him. And wheresoever he shall go in, say ye to the goodman of the house, The Master saith, Where is the guest-chamber, where I shall eat the passover with my disciples? And he will shew you a large upper room furnished and pre-pared: there make ready for us. And his disciples went forth, and came into the city, and found as he had said unto them: and they made ready the passover.

And in the evening he cometh with the twelve. And as they sat and did eat, Jesus said, Verily I say unto you, One of you which eateth with me shall betray me. And they began to be sorrowful, and to say unto him one by one, Is it I? and another said, Is it I? And he answered and said unto them, It is one of the twelve, that dippeth with me in the dish. The Son of man indeed goeth, as it is written of him: but woe to that man by whom the Son of man is betrayed! good were it for that man if he had never been born.

And as they did eat, Jesus took bread, and blessed, and brake it, and gave to them, and said, Take, eat: this is my body. And he took the cup, and when he had given thanks, he gave it to them: and they all drank of it. And he said unto them, This is my blood of the new testament, which is shed for many. Verily I say unto you, I will drink no more of the fruit of the vine, until that day that I drink it new in the kingdom of God.

And when they had sung an hymn, they went out into the mount of Olives. And Jesus saith unto them, All ye shall be offended because of me this night: for it is written, I will smite the shepherd, and the sheep shall be scattered. But after that I am risen, I will go before you into Galilee. But Peter said unto him, Although all shall be offended, yet will not I. And Jesus saith unto him, Verily I say unto thee, That this day, even in this night, before the cock crow twice, thou shalt deny me thrice. But he spake the more vehemently, If I should die with thee, I will not deny thee in any wise. Likewise also said they all.

And they came to a place which was named Gethsemane: and he saith to his disciples, Sit ye here, while I shall pray. And he taketh with him Peter and James and John, and began to be sore amazed, and to be very heavy; and saith unto them, My soul is exceeding sorrowful unto death: tarry ye here, and watch. And he went forward a little, and fell on the ground, and prayed that, if it were possible, the hour might pass from him. And he said, Abba, Father, all things are possible unto thee; take away this cup from me: nevertheless not what I will, but what thou wilt. And he cometh, and findeth them sleeping,

and saith unto Peter, Simon, sleepest thou? couldest not thou
watch one hour? Watch ye and pray, lest ye enter into temp-
tation. The spirit truly is ready, but the flesh is weak. And again
he went away, and prayed, and spake the same words. And
when he returned, he found them asleep again (for their eyes
were heavy), neither wist they what to answer him. And he
cometh the third time, and saith unto them, Sleep on now, and
take your rest: it is enough, the hour is come; behold, the Son
of man is betrayed into the hands of sinners. Rise up, let us
go; lo, he that betrayeth me is at hand.

And immediately, while he yet spake, cometh Judas, one of
the twelve, and with him a great multitude with swords and
staves, from the chief priests and the scribes and the elders. And
he that betrayed him had given them a token, saying, Whomsoever I shall kiss, that same is he; take him, and lead him
away safely. And as soon as he was come, he goeth straightway
to him, and saith, Master, master; and kissed him.

And they laid their hands on him, and took him. And one
of them that stood by drew a sword, and smote a servant of
the high priest, and cut off his ear. And Jesus answered and
said unto them, Are ye come out, as against a thief, with swords
and with staves to take me? I was daily with you in the temple
teaching, and ye took me not: but the scriptures must be fulfilled.
And they all forsook him, and fled. And there followed him a
certain young man, having a linen cloth cast about his naked
body; and the young men laid hold on him: and he left the
linen cloth, and fled from them naked.

And they led Jesus away to the high priest: and with him
were assembled all the chief priests and the elders and the scribes.
And Peter followed him afar off, even into the palace of the
high priest: and he sat with the servants, and warmed himself
at the fire. And the chief priests and all the council sought for
witness against Jesus to put him to death: and found none. For
many bare false witness against him, but their witness agreed

not together. And there arose certain, and bare false witness against him, saying, We heard him say, I will destroy this temple that is made with hands, and within three days I will build another made without hands. But neither so did their witness agree together. And the high priest stood up in the midst, and asked Jesus, saying, Answerest thou nothing? what is it which these witness against thee? But he held his peace, and answered nothing. Again the high priest asked him, and said unto him, Art thou the Christ, the Son of the Blessed? And Jesus said, I am: and ye shall see the Son of man sitting on the right hand of power, and coming in the clouds of heaven. Then the high priest rent his clothes, and saith, What need we any further witnesses? Ye have heard the blasphemy: what think ye? And they all condemned him to be guilty of death. And some began to spit on him, and to cover his face, and to buffet him, and to say unto him, Prophesy: and the servants did strike him with the palms of their hands.

And as Peter was beneath in the palace, there cometh one of the maids of the high priest: and when she saw Peter warming himself, she looked upon him, and said, And thou also wast with Jesus of Nazareth. But he denied, saying, I know not, neither understand I what thou sayest. And he went out into the porch; and the cock crew. And a maid saw him again, and began to say to them that stood by, This is one of them. And he denied it again. And a little after, they that stood by said again to Peter, Surely thou art one of them: for thou art a Galilaean, and thy speech agreeth thereto. But he began to curse and to swear, saying, I know not this man of whom ye speak. And the second time the cock crew. And Peter called to mind the word that Jesus said unto him, Before the cock crow twice thou shalt deny me thrice. And when he thought thereon, he wept.

And straightway in the morning the chief priests held a consultation with the elders and scribes and the whole council, and bound Jesus, and carried him away, and delivered him to Pilate. And Pilate asked him, Art thou the King of the Jews? And he answering said unto him, Thou sayest it. And the chief priests accused him of many things: but he answered nothing. And Pilate asked him again, saying, Answerest thou nothing? behold how many things they witness against thee. But Jesus yet answered nothing; so that Pilate marvelled.

Now at that feast he released unto them one prisoner, whomsoever they desired. And there was one named Barabbas, which lay bound with them that had made insurrection with him, who had committed murder in the insurrection. And the multitude crying aloud began to desire him to do as he had ever done unto them. But Pilate answered them, saying, Will ye that I release unto you the King of the Jews? For he knew that the chief priests had delivered him for envy. But the chief priests moved the people, that he should rather release Barabbas unto them. And Pilate answered and said again unto them, What will ye then that I shall do unto him whom ye call the King of the Jews? And they cried out again, Crucify him. Then Pilate said unto them, Why, what evil hath he done? And they cried out the more exceedingly, Crucify him.

And so Pilate, willing to content the people, released Barabbas unto them, and delivered Jesus, when he had scourged him, to be crucified.

And the soldiers led him away into the hall, called Praetorium; and they called together the whole band. And they clothed him with purple, and platted a crown of thorns, and put it about his head, and began to salute him, Hail, King of the Jews! And they smote him on the head with a reed, and did spit upon him, and bowing their knees worshipped him. And when they had mocked him, they took off the purple from him, and put his own clothes on him, and led him out to crucify him.

And they compel one Simon a Cyrenian, who passed by, coming out of the country, the father of Alexander and Rufus, to bear his cross. And they bring him unto the place Golgotha, which is, being interpreted, The place of a skull. And they gave him to drink wine mingled with myrrh: but he received it not. And when they had crucified him, they parted his garments, casting lots upon them, what every man should take. And it was the third hour, and they crucified him. And the superscription of his accusation was written over, THE KING OF THE JEWS. And with him they crucify two thieves; the one on his right hand, and the other on his left. And the scripture was fulfilled, which saith, And he was numbered with the transgressors. And they that passed by railed on him, wagging their heads, and saying, Ah, thou that destroyest the temple, and buildest it in three days, Save thyself, and come down from the cross. Likewise also the chief priests mocking said among themselves with the scribes, He saved others; himself he cannot save. Let Christ the King of Israel descend now from the cross, that we may see and believe. And they that were crucified with him reviled him.

And when the sixth hour was come, there was darkness over the whole land until the ninth hour. And at the ninth hour Jesus cried with a loud voice, saying, Eloi, Eloi, lama sabachthani? which is, being interpreted, My God, my God, why hast thou forsaken me? And some of them that stood by, when they heard it, said, Behold, he calleth Elias. And one ran and filled a spunge full of vinegar, and put it on a reed, and gave him to drink, saying, Let alone; let us see whether Elias will come to take him down. And Jesus cried with a loud voice, and gave up the ghost. And the vail of the temple was rent in twain from the top to the bottom.

And when the centurion, which stood over against him, saw that he so cried out, and gave up the ghost, he said, Truly this man was the Son of God. There were also women looking on afar off: among whom was Mary Magdalene, and Mary the mother of James the less and of Joses, and Salome (who also, when he was in Galilee, followed him, and ministered unto him); and many other women which came up with him unto Jerusalem.

And now when the even was come, because it was the preparation, that is, the day before the sabbath, Joseph of Arimathaea, an honourable counsellor, which also waited for the kingdom of God, came, and went in boldly unto Pilate, and craved the body of Jesus. And Pilate marvelled if he were already dead: and calling unto him the centurion, he asked him whether he had been any while dead. And when he knew it of the centurion, he gave the body to Joseph. And he bought fine linen, and took him down, and wrapped him in the linen, and laid him in a sepulchre which was hewn out of a rock, and rolled a stone unto the door of the sepulchre. And Mary Magdalene and Mary the mother of Joses beheld where he was laid.

And when the sabbath was past, Mary Magdalene, and Mary the mother of James, and Salome, had bought sweet spices, that they might come and anoint him. And very early in the morning the first day of the week, they came unto the sepulchre at the rising of the sun. And they said among themselves, Who shall roll us away the stone from the door of the sepulchre? And when they looked, they saw that the stone was rolled away: for it was very great. And entering into the sepulchre, they saw a young man sitting on the right side, clothed in a long white garment; and they were affrighted. And he saith unto them, Be not affrighted: Ye seek Jesus of Nazareth, which was crucified: he is risen; he is not here: behold the place where they laid him. But go your way, tell his disciples and Peter that he goeth before you into Galilee: there shall ye see him, as he said unto you. And they went out quickly, and fled from the sepulchre; for they trembled and were amazed: neither said they any thing to any man; for they were afraid.

THUCYDIDES was born in about 460 B.C. in Athens, Greece. Knowledge of his life is sketchy. When he was a young man, the Peloponnesian War broke out between Athens and Sparta, and Thucydides began writing a historical account of the conflict. Soon after he had begun, Thucydides became ill with the plague, but regained his health. In 424, he was appointed a general to defend Athenian colonies then under attack by the Spartans. When he failed to save Amphipolis from the enemy, Thucydides went into exile from Athens for twenty years. For part of this time, he probably travelled in Sparta and Sicily. Thucydides died shortly after returning from exile, most likely before he was able to complete his life's work, *The Peloponnesian War*.

A selection from *History of the Peloponnesian War*, translated by Rex Warner. Publisher: Penguin Books, Ltd., 1982. From Book 1, pages 35–49; Book 3, pages 194–223; and Book 5, pages 400–408.

History of the Peloponnesian War

Thucydides the Athenian wrote the history of the war fought between Athens and Sparta,[1] beginning the account at the very outbreak of the war, in the belief that it was going to be a great war and more worth writing about than any of those which had taken place in the past. My belief was based on the fact that the two sides were at the very height of their power and preparedness, and I saw, too, that the rest of the Hellenic world was committed to one side or the other; even those who were not immediately engaged were deliberating on the courses which they were to take later. This was the greatest disturbance in the history of the Hellenes, affecting also a large part of the non-Hellenic world, and indeed, I might almost say, the whole of mankind. For though I have found it impossible, because of its remoteness in time, to acquire a really precise knowledge of the distant past or even of the history preceding our own period, yet, after looking back into it as far as I can, all the evidence leads me to conclude that these periods were not great periods either in warfare or in anything else.

It appears, for example, that the country now called Hellas[2]

---

[1] [431–404 B.C.]

[2] [In the Greek language, ancient as well as modern, the name of the country is "Hellas," of the people "Hellenes." "Hellas" included all Greek communities, wherever they were established, but here Thucydides is referring more narrowly to the Greek peninsula. — TRANS.]

had no settled population in ancient times; instead there was a series of migrations, as the various tribes, being under the constant pressure of invaders who were stronger than they were, were always prepared to abandon their own territory. There was no commerce, and no safe communication either by land or sea; the use they made of their land was limited to the production of necessities; they had no surplus left over for capital, and no regular system of agriculture, since they lacked the protection of fortifications and at any moment an invader might appear and take their land away from them. Thus, in the belief that the day-to-day necessities of life could be secured just as well in one place as in another, they showed no reluctance in moving from their homes, and therefore built no cities of any size or strength, nor acquired any important resources. Where the soil was most fertile there were the most frequent changes of population. . . . For in these fertile districts it was easier for individuals to secure greater powers than their neighbours: this led to disunity, which often caused the collapse of these states, which in any case were more likely than others to attract the attention of foreign invaders.

It is interesting to observe that Attica, which, because of the poverty of her soil, was remarkably free from political disunity, has always been inhabited by the same race of people. Indeed, this is an important example of my theory that it was because of migrations that there was uneven development elsewhere; for when people were driven out from other parts of Greece by war or by disturbances, the most powerful of them took refuge in Athens, as being a stable society; then they became citizens, and soon made the city even more populous than it had been before, with the result that later Attica became too small for her inhabitants and colonies were sent out to Ionia.

Another point which seems to be good evidence for the weakness of the early inhabitants of the country is this: we have no record of any action taken by Hellas as a whole before the Trojan War. Indeed, my view is that at this time the whole country was not even called "Hellas." Before the time of Hellen, the son of Deucalion, the name did not exist at all, and different parts were known by the names of different tribes. . . . The Hellenes were not yet known by one name, and so marked off as something separate from the outside world. By "Hellenic" I mean here both those who took on the name city by city, as the result of a common language, and those who later were all called by the common name. In any case these various Hellenic states, weak in themselves and lacking in communications with one another, took no kind of collective action before the time of the Trojan War. And they could not have united even for the Trojan expedition unless they had previously acquired a greater knowledge of seafaring.

Minos, according to tradition, was the first person to organize a navy. He controlled the greater part of what is now called the Hellenic Sea; he ruled over the Cyclades, in most of which he founded the first colonies, putting his sons in as governors after having driven out the Carians. And it is reasonable to suppose that he did his best to put down piracy in order to secure his own revenues.

For in these early times, as communication by sea became easier, so piracy became a common profession both among the Hellenes and among the barbarians who lived on the coast and in the islands. The leading pirates were powerful men, acting both out of self-interest and in order to support the weak among their own people. They would descend upon cities which were unprotected by walls and indeed consisted only of scattered settlements; and by plundering such places they would gain most of their livelihood. At this time such a profession, so far from being regarded as disgraceful, was considered quite honourable. It is an attitude that can be illustrated even today by some of the inhabitants of the mainland among whom successful piracy is regarded as something to be proud of; and in the old poets, too, we find that the regular question always asked of those who arrive by sea is "Are you pirates?" It is never assumed either that those who were so questioned would shrink from admitting the fact, or that those who were interested in finding out the fact would reproach them with it.

The same system of armed robbery prevailed by land; and even up to the present day much of Hellas still follows the old way of life. . . . Among these people the custom of carrying arms still survives from the old days of robbery; for at one time, since houses were unprotected and communications unsafe, this was a general custom throughout the whole of Hellas and it was the normal thing to carry arms on all occasions, as it is now among foreigners. The fact that the peoples I have mentioned still live in this way is evidence that once this was the general rule among all the Hellenes.

The Athenians were the first to give up the habit of carrying weapons and to adopt a way of living that was more relaxed and more luxurious. In fact the elder men of the rich families who had these luxurious tastes only recently gave up wearing linen undergarments and tying their hair behind their heads in a knot fastened with a clasp of golden grasshoppers; the same fashions spread to their kinsmen in Ionia, and lasted there among the old men for some time. It was the Spartans who first began to dress simply and in accordance with our modern taste, with the rich leading a life that was as much as possible like the life of the ordinary people. They, too, were the first to play games naked, to take off their clothes openly, and to rub themselves down with olive oil after their exercise. In ancient times even at the Olympic Games the athletes used to wear coverings for their loins, and indeed this practice was still in existence not very many years ago. Even today many foreigners, especially in Asia, wear these loincloths for boxing matches and wrestling bouts. Indeed, one could point to a number of other instances where the manners of the ancient Hellenic world are very similar to the manners of foreigners today.

Cities were sited differently in the later periods; for, as seafaring became more general and capital reserves came into existence, new walled cities were built actually on the coasts, and isthmuses were occupied for commercial reasons and for purposes of defence against neighbouring powers. Because of the wide prevalence of piracy, the ancient cities, both in the islands and on the mainland, were built at some distance from the sea, and still remain to this day on their original sites. For the pirates would rob not only each other but everyone else, seafaring or not, who lived along the coasts.

. . . But after Minos had organized a navy, sea communications improved; he sent colonies to most of the islands and drove out the notorious pirates, with the result that those who lived on the seacoasts were now in a position to acquire wealth and live a more settled life. Some of them, on the strength of their new riches, built walls for their cities. The weaker, because of the general desire to make profits, were content to put up with being governed by the stronger, and those who won superior power by acquiring capital resources brought the smaller cities under their control. Hellas had already developed some way along these lines when the expedition to Troy took place.

Agamemnon, it seems to me, must have been the most powerful of the rulers of his day; and it was for this reason that he raised the force against Troy, not because the suitors of Helen were bound to follow him by the oaths which they had sworn to Tyndareus.[3] Pelops, according to the most reliable tradition in the Peloponnese, came there from Asia. He brought great

---

[3] [The tradition was that Helen was wooed by many leading Greek kings and nobles, that she was allowed to make her own choice, and that all the suitors swore on oath to her father Tyndareus to abide by her decision. — TRANS.]

wealth with him, and, settling in a poor country, acquired such power that, though he was a foreigner, the whole land was called after him. His descendants became still more prosperous. . . . It was to this empire that Agamemnon succeeded, and at the same time he had a stronger navy than any other ruler; thus, in my opinion, fear played a greater part than loyalty in the raising of the expedition against Troy. It appears, if we can believe the evidence of Homer, that Agamemnon himself commanded more ships than anyone else and at the same time equipped another fleet for the Arcadians. And in describing the sceptre which Agamemnon had inherited, Homer calls him:

> Of many islands and all Argos King.

As his power was based on the mainland, he could not have ruled over any islands, except the few that are near the coast, unless he had possessed a considerable navy. And from this expedition we can make reasonable conjectures about other expeditions before that time.

Mycenae certainly was a small place, and many of the towns of that period do not seem to us today to be particularly imposing; yet that is not good evidence for rejecting what the poets and what general tradition have to say about the size of the expedition. Suppose, for example, that the city of Sparta were to become deserted and that only the temples and foundations of buildings remained, I think that future generations would, as time passed, find it very difficult to believe that the place had really been as powerful as it was represented to be. Yet the Spartans occupy two-fifths of the Peloponnese and stand at the head not only of the whole Peloponnese itself but also of numerous allies beyond its frontiers. Since, however, the city is not regularly planned and contains no temples or monuments of great magnificence, but is simply a collection of villages, in the ancient Hellenic way, its appearance would not come up to expectation. If, on the other hand, the same thing were to happen to Athens, one would conjecture from what met the eye that the city had been twice as powerful as in fact it is.

We have no right, therefore, to judge cities by their appearances rather than by their actual power, and there is no reason why we should not believe that the Trojan expedition was the greatest that had ever taken place. It is equally true that it was not on the scale of what is done in modern warfare. . . .

The reason for this was not so much shortage of man-power as shortage of money. Lack of supplies made them cut down their numbers to the point at which they expected they would be able to live off the country in which they were fighting. Even after the victory which they won on landing (it is clear that there must have been a victory; otherwise they could not have put up the fortifications round their camp), it does not appear that they brought the whole of their force into action; instead they cultivated the soil of the Chersonese and went on plundering expeditions because of their shortage of supplies. It was because of this dispersal of their forces that the Trojans managed to hold out for ten years of warfare, since they were always strong enough to deal with that fraction of the Greek army which at any one time remained in the field. If, however, Agamemnon had had plenty of supplies with him when he arrived, and if they had used their whole force in making war continuously, without breaking off for plundering expeditions and for cultivating the land, they would have won easily, as is obvious from the fact that they could contain the Trojans when they were not in full force but employing only whatever portion of their army happened to be available. If, therefore, they had all settled down to the siege at once, they would have taken Troy in a shorter time and with less trouble.

As it was, just as lack of money was the reason why previous expeditions were not really considerable, so in the case of this one, which was more famous than any others before it, we shall find, if we look at the evidence of what was actually done, that

it was not so important as it was made out to be and as it is
still, through the influence of the poets, believed to have been.

Even after the Trojan War Hellas was in a state of ferment;
there were constant resettlements, and so no opportunity for
peaceful development. It was long before the army returned
from Troy, and this fact in itself led to many changes. There
was party strife in nearly all the cities, and those who were
driven into exile founded new cities. . . .

Thus many years passed by and many difficulties were encountered before Hellas could enjoy any peace or stability, and
before the period of shifting populations ended. Then came the
period of colonization. Ionia and most of the islands were col-
onized by the Athenians. The Peloponnesians founded most of
the colonies in Italy and Sicily, and some in other parts of Hellas.
All of them were founded after the Trojan War.

The old form of government was hereditary monarchy with
established rights and limitations; but as Hellas became more
powerful and as the importance of acquiring money became
more and more evident, tyrannies were established in nearly all
the cities, revenues increased, shipbuilding flourished, and ambition turned towards sea-power.

The Corinthians are supposed to have been the first to adopt
more or less modern methods in shipbuilding, and it is said
that the first triremes ever built in Hellas were laid down in
Corinth. . . . And the first naval battle on record is the one between the Corinthians and the Corcyraeans: this was about 260
years ago.

Corinth, planted on its isthmus, had been from time im-
memorial an important mercantile centre, though in ancient days
traffic had been by land rather than by sea. The communications
between those who lived inside and those who lived outside the
Peloponnese had to pass through the Corinthian territory. So
Corinth grew to power by her riches, as is shown by the adjective
"wealthy" which is given to her by the ancient poets. And when

the Greeks began to take more to seafaring, the Corinthians acquired a fleet, put down piracy, and, being able to provide trading facilities on both the land and the sea routes, made their city powerful from the revenues which came to it by both these ways.

Later the Ionians were a great naval power. This was in the time of Cyrus, the first King of the Persians, and of his son Cambyses. Indeed, when they were fighting against Cyrus, they were for some time masters of all the sea in their region.

Then Polycrates, the tyrant of Samos, made himself powerful by means of his navy. He conquered a number of the islands, among which was Rhenea, which he dedicated to the Delian Apollo.

The Phocaeans, too, when they were founding Marseilles, defeated the Carthaginians in a naval engagement.

These were the greatest navies of the past, and even these navies, though many generations later than the Trojan War, do not seem to have possessed many triremes, but to have been still composed, as in the old days, of long-boats and boats of fifty oars. . . .

All the same these Hellenic navies, whether in the remote past or in the later periods, although they were as I have described them, were still a great source of strength to the various naval powers. They brought in revenue and they were the foundation of empire. It was by naval action that those powers, and especially those with insufficient land of their own, conquered the islands. There was no warfare on land that resulted in the acquisition of an empire. What wars there were were simply frontier skirmishes; no expedition by land was sent far from the country of its origin with the purpose of conquering some other power. There were no alliances of small states under the leadership of the great powers, nor did the smaller states form leagues for action on a basis of equality among themselves. Wars were simply local affairs between neighbours. . . .

And in the Hellenic states that were governed by tyrants, the tyrant's first thought was always for himself, for his own personal safety, and for the greatness of his own family. Consequently security was the chief political principle in these governments, and no great action ever came out of them—nothing, in fact, that went beyond their immediate local interests, except for the tyrants in Sicily, who rose to great power. So for a long time the state of affairs everywhere in Hellas was such that nothing very remarkable could be done by any combination of powers and that even the individual cities were lacking in enterprise.

Finally, however, the Spartans put down tyranny in the rest of Greece, most of which had been governed by tyrants for much longer than Athens. From the time when the Dorians first settled in Sparta there had been a particularly long period of political disunity; yet the Spartan constitution goes back to a very early date, and the country has never been ruled by tyrants. For rather more than 400 years, dating from the end of the late war, they have had the same system of government, and this has been not only a source of internal strength, but has enabled them to intervene in the affairs of other states.

Not many years after the end of tyrannies in Hellas the battle of Marathon[4] was fought between the Persians and the Athenians. Ten years later the foreign enemy returned with his vast armada for the conquest of Hellas, and at this moment of peril the Spartans, since they were the leading power, were in command of the allied Hellenic forces. In face of the invasion the Athenians decided to abandon their city; they broke up their homes, took to their ships, and became a people of sailors. It was by a common effort that the foreign invasion was repelled; but not long afterwards the Hellenes—both those who had fought in the war together and those who later revolted from the King of Persia—split into two divisions, one group following Athens

---

[4] [490 B.C.]

and the other Sparta. These were clearly the two most powerful states, one being supreme on land, the other on the sea. For a short time the war-time alliance held together, but it was not long before quarrels took place and Athens and Sparta, each with her own allies, were at war with each other, while among the rest of the Hellenes, states that had their own differences now joined one or other of the two sides. So from the end of the Persian War till the beginning of the Peloponnesian War, though there were some intervals of peace, on the whole these two Powers were either fighting with each other or putting down revolts among their allies. They were consequently in a high state of military preparedness and had gained their military experience in the hard school of danger.

The Spartans did not make their allies pay tribute, but saw to it that they were governed by oligarchies who would work in the Spartan interest. Athens, on the other hand, had in the course of time taken over the fleets of her allies (except for those of Chios and Lesbos) and had made them pay contributions of money instead. Thus the forces available to Athens alone for this war were greater than the combined forces had ever been when the alliance was still intact.

In investigating past history, and in forming the conclusions which I have formed, it must be admitted that one cannot rely on every detail which has come down to us by way of tradition. People are inclined to accept all stories of ancient times in an uncritical way—even when these stories concern their own native countries. . . . Most people, in fact, will not take trouble in finding out the truth, but are much more inclined to accept the first story they hear.

However, I do not think that one will be far wrong in accepting the conclusions I have reached from the evidence which I have put forward. It is better evidence than that of the poets, who exaggerate the importance of their themes, or of the prose chroniclers, who are less interested in telling the truth than in catching the attention of their public, whose authorities cannot be checked, and whose subject matter, owing to the passage of time, is mostly lost in the unreliable streams of mythology. We may claim instead to have used only the plainest evidence and to have reached conclusions which are reasonably accurate, considering that we have been dealing with ancient history. As for this present war, even though people are apt to think that the war in which they are fighting is the greatest of all wars and, when it is over, to relapse again into their admiration of the past, nevertheless, if one looks at the facts themselves, one will see that this was the greatest war of all.

In this history I have made use of set speeches some of which were delivered just before and others during the war. I have found it difficult to remember the precise words used in the speeches which I listened to myself and my various informants have experienced the same difficulty; so my method has been, while keeping as closely as possible to the general sense of the words that were actually used, to make the speakers say what, in my opinion, was called for by each situation.

And with regard to my factual reporting of the events of the war I have made it a principle not to write down the first story that came my way, and not even to be guided by my own general impressions; either I was present myself at the events which I have described or else I heard of them from eye-witnesses whose reports I have checked with as much thoroughness as possible. Not that even so the truth was easy to discover: different eye-witnesses give different accounts of the same events, speaking out of partiality for one side or the other or else from imperfect memories. And it may well be that my history will seem less easy to read because of the absence in it of a romantic element. It will be enough for me, however, if these words of mine are judged useful by those who want to understand clearly the events which happened in the past and which (human nature being what it is) will, at some time or other and in much the same ways, be repeated in the future. My work is not a piece of writing designed to meet the taste of an immediate public, but was done to last forever.

The greatest war in the past was the Persian War; yet in this war the decision was reached quickly as a result of two naval battles and two battles on land. The Peloponnesian War, on the other hand, not only lasted for a long time, but throughout its course brought with it unprecedented suffering for Hellas. Never before had so many cities been captured and then devastated, whether by foreign armies or by the Hellenic powers themselves (some of these cities, after capture, were resettled with new inhabitants); never had there been so many exiles; never such loss of life—both in the actual warfare and in internal revolutions. Old stories of past prodigies, which had not found much confirmation in recent experience, now became credible. Wide areas, for instance, were affected by violent earthquakes; there were more frequent eclipses of the sun than had ever been recorded before; in various parts of the country there were extensive droughts followed by famine; and there was the plague which did more harm and destroyed more life than almost any other single factor. All these calamities fell together upon the Hellenes after the outbreak of war.

War began when the Athenians and the Peloponnesians broke the Thirty Years Truce which had been made after the capture of Euboea. As to the reasons why they broke the truce, I propose first to give an account of the causes of complaint which they had against each other and of the specific instances where their interests clashed: this is in order that there should be no doubt in anyone's mind about what led to this great war falling upon the Hellenes. But the real reason for the war is, in my opinion, most likely to be disguised by such an argument. What made war inevitable was the growth of Athenian power and the fear which this caused in Sparta. . . .

MACEDONIA

Potidaea

MT. OLYMPUS ▲

Corcyra

Sciathos

A E

THERMOPYLAE †

ACARNANIA

EUBOEA

Leucas

Naupactus

BOEOTIA

Oeniadae

Thebes
Plataea

Elis

ARCADIA

ATTICA

Athens

Corinth

Olympia

ISTHMUS

Salamis

PELOPONNESE

Aegina

Argos

Pylos

Sparta

Melos

LACONIA

MALAEA

Cythera

Greece and
Western Asia Minor
5th Century, B.C.

C R

REVOLT OF MYTILENE[5]

Next summer, at the time when the corn was ripe, the Peloponnesians and their allies marched into Attica under the command of the Spartan King. . . . They settled down in the country and laid it waste. As on previous occasions, the Athenian cavalry went into action wherever possible and prevented the mass of enemy light troops from leaving the protection of the main body of the army and doing harm in the districts close to the city. The Peloponnesians stayed in Attica for the period for which they had come supplied, and then retired and dispersed to their various cities.

Directly after the invasion of the Peloponnesians the island of Lesbos, except for Methymna, revolted from Athens. Even before the war the Lesbians had wanted to revolt, but the Spartans had not been willing to receive them into their alliance; and now they were compelled to revolt before the time that they had planned. They were waiting until they had narrowed the mouths of their harbours and finished the fortifications and the shipbuilding which they had in hand; also for the arrival of various supplies which were due to come from Pontus—archers, corn, and other things that they had sent for. Meanwhile, however, the Tenedians, who were enemies of theirs, the Methymnians, and a certain group of individuals in the city itself, people who represented Athenian interests in Mytilene, informed the Athenians that the Mytilenians were forcibly making the whole of Lesbos into one state under the control of Mytilene, and that the various activities on which they were so busy were planned in cooperation with the Spartans and with the Boeotians, who were their kinsmen, for the purpose of making a revolt; and

---

[5] [428–427 B.C. In previous chapters, Thucydides has described the outbreak of the war in 431 B.C., its early progress, and a plague in Athens in 430 B.C.]

that unless preventive measures were taken at once, Athens would lose Lesbos.

At this time, however, the Athenians were suffering from the plague and also from the full force of the war which had only just broken out. They thought it would be a very serious thing indeed to have to fight Lesbos as well, with its fleet and with its untapped resources. Thus, rather through a process of wishful thinking, they at first believed that the accusations were untrue. Later, however, when they had sent out representatives and failed to induce the Mytilenians to abandon the idea of the union of Lesbos or to give up their warlike preparations, they became frightened and decided to take action before it was too late. They hurriedly sent out a fleet of forty ships that had been equipped for sailing round the Peloponnese. . . . It had been reported at Athens that there was a feast held in honour of the Malean Apollo outside the city, and that the whole people of Mytilene took part in this feast; so there was a chance, if they acted quickly, of catching them by surprise. If this plan worked, so much the better; if not, they were to order the people of Mytilene to surrender their ships and to demolish their fortifications, and, if they failed to comply with these demands, to make war on them.

So the fleet set sail. The ten triremes of Mytilene which happened to be serving with the fleet according to the provisions of the alliance were kept back by the Athenians and their crews placed under arrest. Nevertheless, news of the expedition reached Mytilene through a man who crossed over from Athens to Euboea, went on foot to Geraestus, found a merchant ship on the point of sailing, and got by sea to Mytilene on the third day after he had left Athens. So the people of Mytilene did not go out to the temple at Malea. Instead they reinforced the unfinished parts of their walls, and their harbours, and stood on guard.

Soon afterwards the Athenian fleet sailed in. When the commanders saw what the situation was they said what they had been instructed to say and, as the Mytilenians refused to obey, they made war upon them. The Mytilenians, suddenly forced into a war for which they were unprepared, did make the gesture of sailing out with their fleet to fight a little way in front of their harbour, but were soon chased back again by the Athenian ships, and immediately began to enter into negotiations with the Athenian commanders, wishing, if they could, to have the Athenian fleet recalled for the time being on any reasonable conditions. The Athenian commanders themselves were doubtful of their ability to deal with the whole of Lesbos, and so they accepted the overtures made to them. An armistice was made, and the Mytilenians sent to Athens a delegation including one of the people who had already informed against them, but had now repented of his action, to try to persuade the Athenians to withdraw their fleet and to make them believe that there was no danger of any revolutions in Mytilene. At the same time they sent ambassadors to Sparta in a trireme which escaped the notice of the Athenian fleet anchored at Malea to the north of the town; for they had little hope that their representatives in Athens would do any good.

The mission to Sparta reached their destination after a difficult voyage across the open sea and started conversations with a view to securing military aid. The mission which had gone to Athens returned without having succeeded in any of its objects, and thus Mytilene and the rest of Lesbos, except for Methymna, went to war with Athens. . . .

The Mytilenians now marched out in full force against the Athenian camp, and in the battle that took place they had rather the better of things, but they lacked confidence in themselves and retired to their city without venturing to camp in the open. Afterwards they kept quiet, not wishing to try their fortune again until they had the support of whatever forces might be coming to them from the Peloponnese. For Meleas, a Laconian, and Hermaeondas, a Theban, now arrived. These two had been sent out to them before the revolt, but had not been able to get to Lesbos before the appearance of the Athenian fleet. Now, after the battle, they managed to steal into the place in a trireme and persuaded the Mytilenians to send another trireme with ambassadors back with them to Sparta. This the Mytilenians did.

The Athenians meanwhile were much encouraged by the inaction of the Mytilenians. They summoned forces from their allies, and these forces arrived all the sooner because they saw so little evidence of vigorous action on the part of the Lesbians. They brought their fleet round to a station south of the city and built two fortified camps, one on each side of the city, blockading both the harbours. They thus deprived the Mytilenians of the use of the sea, though they and the other Lesbians who supported them had control of the land. All that the Athenians held was a small area round their camps. . . .

While the war in Mytilene was going on as I have described it, the Athenians also sent out, at about the same time of the summer, a fleet of thirty ships round the Peloponnese. This fleet was under the command of Phormio's son Asopius, the Acarnanians having requested that the commander sent out to them should be either a son or a relation of Phormio. Various places on the coast were laid waste by this fleet as it sailed off Laconia. Afterwards Asopius sent most of the ships back to Athens and with twelve ships came himself to Naupactus. He then raised an army from the whole country of Acarnania and marched against Oeniadae. The fleet sailed down the Achelous and the army laid waste the land. Oeniadae, however, showed no signs of giving in, and Asopius, after dismissing his army, sailed himself to Leucas and made a landing at Nericus. On his way back he was killed and a large number of his troops destroyed by the people of those parts who had come out against him, supported by a few soldiers of the garrison. Afterwards the Athenians sailed away, having recovered their dead from the Leucadians under an armistice.

Meanwhile the ambassadors from Mytilene who had been
sent out in the first ship had been told by the Spartans to come
to Olympia, so that the other allies also could hear and discuss
what they had to say. They therefore went to Olympia, in the
Olympiad at which Dorieus of Rhodes won his second victory,
and when, after the festival was over, a meeting of the allies
was called, they made the following speech:

"Spartans and allies, we know what the established rule among
the Hellenes is on this subject. When a state revolts in the
middle of a war and deserts its previous allies, those who welcome it into their alliance are just so far pleased with it as they
find it useful to them, but otherwise think the worse of it for
having betrayed its former friends. And this is a perfectly fair
way of looking at things, so long as there is a like-mindedness
in policy and feeling, an equality in power and resources between
the state that revolts and the state from which it revolts, and
so long as there is no reasonable excuse for making the revolt.
These conditions did not apply with regard to us and the Athenians, and no one should think the worse of us for revolting
from them in time of danger, after being honoured by them in
time of peace.

"Justice and honesty are the first subjects with which we shall
deal, especially as we are here to ask for your alliance, and we
know that there can never be a firm friendship between man
and man or a real community between different states unless
there is a conviction of honesty on both sides and a certain like-
mindedness in other respects; for if people think differently they
will act divergently.

"The alliance between us and Athens dates from the end of
the Persian war, when you withdrew from the leadership and
the Athenians stayed to finish what was left to do. But the object
of the alliance was the liberation of the Hellenes from Persia,
not the subjugation of the Hellenes to Athens. So long as the
Athenians in their leadership respected our independence, we

followed them with enthusiasm. But when we saw that they were becoming less and less antagonistic to Persia and more and more interested in enslaving their own allies, then we became frightened. Because of the multiple voting system, the allies were incapable of uniting in self-defence, and so they all became enslaved except for us and for Chios. We, supposed to be independent and nominally free, furnished our own contingents in the allied forces. But with the examples before us of what had already happened, we no longer felt any confidence in Athenian leadership. It seemed very unlikely that, after having brought under their control the states who were fellow members with us, they would refrain from acting towards us, too, in the same way, if ever they felt strong enough to do so.

"If we had all still been independent, we could have had more confidence in their not altering the state of affairs. But with most of their allies subjected to them and us being treated as equals, it was natural for them to object to a situation where the majority had already given in and we alone stood out as independent—all the more so since they were becoming stronger and stronger and we were losing whatever support we had before. And in an alliance the only safe guarantee is an equality of mutual fear; for then the party that wants to break faith is deterred by the thought that the odds will not be on his side.

"In fact the only reason why we were left with our independence was because the Athenians, in building up their empire, thought that they could seize power more easily by having some specious arguments to put forward and by using the methods of policy rather than of brute force. We were useful to them because they could point to us and say that we, who had votes like themselves, could not possibly have joined them unwillingly in their various expeditions and could only be doing so because the people against whom we were being led were in the wrong. By these methods they first led the stronger states against the weaker ones, leaving the strongest to the last in the certainty of finding them, once all the rest had been absorbed, much less formidable to deal with. If, on the other hand, they had started with us, when all the other states still had their strength and had also a centre round which they could stand, they would not have subjugated them so easily. Then also they felt some alarm about our navy, in case it might come together as one force and join you or some other power, and so become a danger to Athens. Another factor in securing our independence was the trouble we took to be on good terms with the Athenian assembly and with their various leading statesmen. Yet, with the examples we had of how they had behaved to others, we never expected to be able to maintain ourselves for long, if this war had not broken out.

"How could we feel any genuine friendship or any confidence in our liberty when we were in a situation like this? The terms on which we accepted each other ran counter to the real feelings of both sides. In wartime they did their best to be on good terms with us because they were frightened of us; we, for the same reason, tried to keep on good terms with them in peacetime. In most cases goodwill is the basis of loyalty, but in our case fear was the bond, and it was more through terror than through friendship that we were held together in alliance. And the alliance was certain to be broken at any moment by the first side that felt confident that this would be a safe move to make. So it is wrong to condemn us for breaking away first simply because Athens had not yet taken action against us, or to say that we ought to have waited until we were quite sure what action they would take. For if we had the same ability as they have for planning action and then putting it off, we should be their equals, and there would be no need for us to be their subjects. As it is, they are always in the position where they can take the initiative in aggression; we should be allowed the initiative in self-defence.

"These, Spartans and allies, are the reasons and the causes for our revolt. They are clear enough to convince our hearers that we have not acted improperly, and they constitute sufficient grounds for us to feel alarmed and to look round for what security we can find. Indeed, we wanted to do so long ago, and when it was still peacetime we sent ambassadors to you on the subject; but we could not get your help, since you refused to accept us. Now we have responded immediately to the invitation of the Boeotians and we have decided to make a double break with the past—a break in our relations both with the Hellenes and with the Athenians. As for the Hellenes, we shall no longer join the Athenians in acts of aggression on them, but shall help in the work of liberation; and as for the Athenians, we shall take the initiative in breaking away from them, instead of waiting to be destroyed by them later.

"However our revolt has taken place earlier than we intended and without adequate preparations. This is all the more reason why you should take us into your alliance and send us help quickly, thus revealing yourselves as people capable of helping those who should be helped and at the same time of hurting your enemies. Never has there been such an opportunity. Owing to the plague and the expenses they have incurred, the Athenians are in a state of exhaustion; part of their fleet is sailing round your coasts, and the rest is engaged in blockading us. It is improbable that they have any ships in reserve, and if you invade for the second time this summer with naval and military forces at the same time, they will either be unable to resist your fleet or will have to withdraw their own from your shores and from ours.

"And do not think that you are endangering your own persons for the sake of a country that has nothing to do with you. You may think that Lesbos is a long way away, but you will find that the good it can do you is very close at hand. It is not in Attica, as some people think, that the war will be won or lost, but in the countries from which Attica draws her strength. Her financial power comes from the tribute paid by her allies, and this will be greater still if we are conquered. For there will be no other revolts, our resources will be added to theirs, and we shall be treated more harshly than those who were enslaved before us. But if you give us your whole-hearted support you will gain for yourselves a state which has a large navy (which is the thing you need most); you will be in a much better position for breaking the power of Athens by detaching her allies from her, since the others will be greatly encouraged to come over to you; and you will clear yourselves of the charge that has been made against you of not giving help to those who revolt. Once you come forward in the role of liberators, you will find that your strength in the war is enormously increased.

"We ask you, therefore, to respect the hopes set on you by the Hellenes, and to respect Olympian Zeus, in whose temple we stand as suppliants. Come to the help of Mytilene. Be our allies, and do not desert us. It is our own lives that we are risking, but we are doing so in a way by which the general good of all will be the result of our success, and an even more general calamity, if you will not listen to us, will follow upon our failure. Be the men, therefore, that the Hellenes think you and that our fears require you to be."

This was the speech of the Mytilenians. When the Spartans and their allies had heard it, they accepted the proposals made and welcomed the Lesbians into their alliance. They decided on the invasion of Attica and instructed their allies, who were present, to gather at the Isthmus as quickly as possible with two-thirds of their total forces. They themselves were the first to arrive there, and they got ready machines for hauling the ships across from Corinth to the sea on the side of Athens, so that they could attack simultaneously by land and sea. In all this they showed great energy, but the other allies were slow in coming in, since they were busy in harvesting their corn and tired of military service.

The Athenians were aware that these preparations were being made on the theory that they themselves were weak, and wished to make it clear that the theory was a mistaken one and that they could easily beat off any attack from the Peloponnesian fleet without recalling their own fleet from Lesbos. They therefore manned 100 ships with their own citizens . . . and with their resident aliens, sailed out to the Isthmus, where they made a demonstration of their power and carried out landings just as they pleased on the Peloponnesian coast. The Spartans, finding that matters were not at all what they had expected, came to the conclusion that what the Lesbians had said was untrue; other difficulties faced them in the non-appearance of their allies and the news that the thirty Athenian ships round the Peloponnese were now laying waste the country near Sparta itself. They therefore returned home, but later they got ready a fleet to send to Lesbos. A total of forty ships was ordered from their various allies, and Alcidas was appointed as admiral to sail with the fleet. The Athenians also went back to Athens with their hundred ships when they saw that the Spartans had gone.

At the time when this fleet was at sea, Athens seems to have had almost the largest number of ships in action at the same time that she ever had, and beautifully equipped too. Yet the numbers were as great or greater at the beginning of the war. Then a hundred ships were guarding Attica, Euboea, and Salamis; another hundred were sailing round the Peloponnese, and there were other ships at Potidaea and in various other stations, making a grand total of 250 on active service in one summer. It was this, together with the campaign at Potidaea, which was the chief drain on the revenue. For the hoplites in the garrison at Potidaea were paid two drachmae a day (one for the soldier and one for his servant). From the beginning there were 3,000 hoplites, and the number was not reduced till the siege was over. Then, too, there were 1,600 men with Phormio who left before the end of the siege. The crews of the ships were all paid at the same rate. This was the expenditure of money at first, at a time when Athens had the very largest number of ships in service.

At the time when the Spartans were at the Isthmus, the Mytilenians, supported by a force of mercenaries, marched by land against Methymna in the belief that they would have the place betrayed to them. They made an assault on the city, but nothing went as they had expected and they withdrew to Antissa, Pyrrha, and Eresus. They made arrangements for the internal security of these places, strengthened their walls, and then quickly marched home again.

After the Mytilenians had retired, the people of Methymna marched out against Antissa, but they were defeated by the Antissians and their mercenaries, who came outside the walls to fight. Many of the Methymnians were killed and the rest retreated as fast as they could. When the Athenians were informed of this and realized that the Mytilenians were masters of the whole country and that their own soldiers were too few to keep them in check, they sent out at the beginning of the autumn Paches, the son of Epicurus, with 1,000 citizen hoplites under his command. The hoplites rowed the ships themselves, and when they arrived at Mytilene they built a single wall completely surrounding the place, with forts, garrisoned by soldiers, placed at various strong points. Thus Mytilene was now firmly blockaded both from the land and from the sea, and winter was approaching.

The Athenians still needed more money for the siege, though they had for the first time raised from their own citizens a contribution of 200 talents. They now sent out twelve ships to collect money from their allies, with Lysicles and four others in command. After sailing to various places and collecting contributions, Lysicles . . . was set upon by the Carians and by the people of Anaia; he himself and a great part of his army were killed.

In the same winter the Plataeans, who were still being besieged by the Peloponnesians and the Boeotians,[6] finding them-

---

[6] [Thucydides has spoken earlier of this encounter.]

selves in distress as their provisions ran out, and seeing no hope of help coming to them from Athens or any chance of survival by any other means, made a plan with the Athenians who were besieged with them by which they were to leave the city and do their best to force their way over the enemy's surrounding wall. . . . The original intention was that they should all join in the attempt, but later half of them shrank back from being involved in what seemed to them too risky a venture. There remained about 220 volunteers who persisted in the idea of breaking out. Their method was as follows: they constructed ladders to reach to the top of the enemy's wall, and they did this by calculating the height of the wall from the number of the layers of bricks at a point which was facing in their direction and had not been plastered. The layers were counted by a lot of people at the same time, and though some were likely to get the figure wrong, the majority would get it right, especially as they counted the layers frequently and were not so far away from the wall that they could not see it well enough for their purpose. Thus, guessing what the thickness of a single brick was, they calculated how long their ladders would have to be.

The wall of the Peloponnesians was constructed in the following way. There were in fact two walls, each forming a circle, one directed against Plataea, and one facing outwards to guard against any attack that might be made from Athens. Between the two walls was a space of about sixteen feet, and inside this space were built the huts where the men on guard were quartered. The building was continuous, so that the impression made was that of one thick wall with battlements on either side of it. Every ten battlements there were towers of some size and of the same breadth as the wall, reaching right across from its inner to its outer face, and built so that there was no way past the towers, the only way being through the middle of them. On nights when it was wet and stormy they did not man the battlements, but kept guard from the towers, which were roofed in above and were not far away from each other.

This was the structure of the wall inside which the Plataeans were penned. And now, when everything was ready, they waited for a stormy night with wind and rain and no moon, and then they slipped out of the city, led by the men who had been the originators of the plan. First they crossed the ditch that surrounded the town, and then they came up to the enemy's wall without being detected by the men on guard, who could not see them in the darkness or hear the noise they made as they approached, because it was drowned by the blustering of the wind. They also kept a good distance away from each other, to prevent the risk of their weapons clashing together and giving them away. They were lightly armed and only wore shoes on the left foot, to stop them slipping in the mud. They reached the battlements at a place halfway between two towers which they knew to be unguarded. The ones who carried the ladders went first and set them in position; next twelve light-armed men, with daggers and breast-plates, climbed up, led by Ammias, the son of Coroebus, who was the first to ascend. His men followed him, and six went to each of the two towers. After them came more light-armed soldiers with spears; their shields were carried by others who came behind them, and they were to give them their shields when they came in contact with the enemy. It was not until most of them had ascended the wall that they were discovered by the sentries in the towers. One of the Plataeans had knocked down a tile from the battlements as he was getting a grip of it, and it made a noise as it fell. The alarm was given immediately, and the troops rushed out to the wall. In the darkness and the storm they had no notion of what the danger was, and at the same moment the Plataeans who were left behind in the city made a sortie and attacked the wall at a point opposite to the place where their comrades were climbing up, so as to distract attention from them as far as possible. So the besieging troops stood still in a state of confusion, no one daring to leave his own sector to reinforce any other point, and unable to guess what was happening. The 300 troops, however, who were specially detailed for service in an emergency, went outside the wall and marched in the direction of the alarm. Fire signals of an enemy attack were made to Thebes; but the Plataeans in the town also displayed a number of fire signals from their own walls, having them all ready made for this very purpose, so as to make the enemy's signals unintelligible, to stop help coming from Thebes, and to prevent the Thebans from having a true idea of what was happening, until their own men who had gone out had escaped and got into safety.

Meanwhile the Plataeans were climbing up onto the wall. The first who ascended had captured the two towers and killed the sentries. They then took up their stand in the passages through the towers to prevent any reinforcements coming through against them. They also set up ladders from the wall and sent a number of men up to the tops of the towers; so, by hurling their missiles both from above and from below, they kept back the enemy from approaching. Meanwhile the main body planted a number of ladders against the outer wall, knocked down the battlements, and kept passing over between the towers. As each man got across he formed up with the others at the edge of the ditch, and from there they shot their arrows and hurled their javelins at all who came up along the wall to prevent their comrades crossing over. When the rest had got across, last of all, and with some difficulty, the men on the towers came down and ran to the ditch, and at that very moment the enemy force of 300 came up, carrying torches. The Plataeans, standing in the darkness at the edge of the ditch, could see them better than they could be seen themselves, and shot their arrows and hurled javelins at the parts of their bodies which were unprotected with armour. The light of the torches made it even more difficult for them to be seen in the darkness, so that even the last of them managed to get across the ditch, though it was a hard business and difficult going. Ice had formed on the surface, not hard enough to walk on, but of the watery kind which comes when the wind is more in the east than in the north, and the snow which fell in the night, with the great wind which was blowing, had raised the level of the water in the ditch so much that they could only just get across with their heads out of the water. Nevertheless, it was chiefly because the storm was so violent that they managed to escape at all.

The Plataeans then set out from the ditch in one body and took the road to Thebes, with the shrine of the hero Androcrates on their right. They imagined that this road, leading into their enemies' country, would be the very last one that they would be suspected of having taken, and, in fact, when they were on it they saw the Peloponnesians with torches trying to find them on the road to Athens in the direction of Cithaeron and Druos-Kephalae. The Plataeans went for rather more than half a mile on the road to Thebes, and then turned off it and took the road leading to the mountains in the direction of Erythrae and Hysiae. On reaching the mountains they made their way safely to Athens, 212 of them all told. Some of them had turned back to the city before crossing the wall, and one archer had been taken prisoner at the outer ditch.

Finally the Peloponnesians gave up the pursuit and returned to their positions. The Plataeans in the city knew nothing of what had taken place, and were informed by the men who turned back that the whole of the escaping party had been destroyed. So as soon as it was day they sent out a herald to ask for a truce so that they could recover their dead; but they abandoned the idea when they learned the truth. In this way the Plataeans who made the attempt got across the wall and reached safety.

At the end of this same winter the Spartan Salaethus was sent from Sparta to Mytilene in a trireme. He went by sea to Pyrrha, and from there went on foot along the bed of a watercourse to a place where it was possible to get through the surrounding wall, and so slipped into Mytilene unobserved. There he told the magistrates that Attica was going to be invaded, that the forty ships which were to help them were coming, and that he himself had been sent in advance to tell them the news and to take charge of things generally. The Mytilenians were encouraged by this and became less inclined to try to make terms with Athens. So ended this winter, and so ended the fourth year of this war recorded by Thucydides.

Next summer the Peloponnesians sent out to Mytilene the forty-two ships under the command of their admiral Alcidas. They themselves and their allies invaded Attica, so that the Athenians would have trouble on two fronts at once and would find it more difficult to take action against the fleet going to Mytilene. . . . The invading forces destroyed everything that had started to grow up again in the districts which they had laid waste previously, and they went on to destroy such property as had been left untouched in earlier invasions. Thus, this was the worst invasion of all except the second. The enemy prolonged their stay in Attica and overran most of the country, since they were constantly waiting to hear news of what their fleet, which they thought must have arrived by now, had done in Lesbos. Finally, however, when none of their expectations was realized and their provisions had begun to run out, they retired and dispersed to their various cities.

Meanwhile the Mytilenians were forced to come to terms with the Athenians. Their supplies of food had run out, and the ships from the Peloponnese, so far from putting in an appearance, continued to waste time on the way. The surrender took place under the following circumstances. Salaethus himself had given up hope of the arrival of the ships, and he now issued heavy armour to the people (who previously had been only equipped as light troops), with the intention of leading them out to battle with the Athenians. But as soon as the people found themselves properly armed, they refused any longer to obey the government.

They held meetings among themselves and demanded that the authorities should openly produce all the food there was and distribute it among them all; otherwise, they said, they themselves would come to terms with the Athenians and surrender the city to them.

The government realized that they were quite incapable of preventing this and also that they would be in danger themselves if an agreement was concluded without them. They therefore joined in coming to terms with Paches and the Athenian army. The terms were as follows: Athens was to have the right to act as she saw fit with regard to the people of Mytilene, and the army was allowed to enter the city; the Mytilenians were to send representatives to Athens to put their case, and until these representatives returned, Paches was to undertake not to imprison or enslave or kill any of the population.

Though these were the terms of the surrender, the party among the Mytilenians who had been most active in the Spartan interest were still terrified—so much so indeed that, when the army entered the city, they felt it necessary to go and take refuge at the altars. Paches raised them up from their suppliant position, promising that he would do them no harm, and put them in custody on Tenedos until he learned what decision the Athenians would come to about them. He also sent triremes to Antissa and occupied the place, and took various other military measures which seemed desirable.

Meanwhile the Peloponnesians in the forty ships, who should have hurried to the relief of Mytilene, wasted a lot of time in their voyage round the Peloponnese itself, and then proceeded on their way in a leisurely manner, finally arriving at Delos without being observed by the Athenians at Athens.

From Delos they went on to Icarus and Myconus, and there first heard the news that Mytilene had fallen. Wishing to obtain more precise information, they sailed on to Embatum in Erythraea, arriving there about seven days after the surrender of

Mytilene. Here they got the information they required, and begin to discuss what they should do in view of what had happened. Teutiaplus, a man from Elis, made a speech giving them the following advice:

"Alcidas and fellow commanders from the Peloponnese, I propose that we should sail to Mytilene just as we are and before they know that we are here. In all probability, since they have only just taken the city, we shall find that their precautions have been greatly relaxed; and this will certainly be so by sea, where they have no idea of having to face any possible attack, and where, in fact, our main strength happens to lie. It is likely, too, that their land forces, after their victory, will be dispersed about the houses in the city and not properly organized. So that if we were to attack suddenly and by night, I think that, with the help of those inside the town who are still on our side, we ought to be able to gain control of the place. Let us not be afraid of the danger, but let us remember that this is an example of the unknown factor in warfare, and that the good general is the one who guards against such unknown factors in his own case, but exploits them for attack in the case of the enemy."

Alcidas, however, was unconvinced by this advice. It was then suggested to him by some of the Ionian exiles and by the Lesbians who were in his fleet that, if this risk seemed too great to him, he should seize one of the Ionian cities or Cumae in Aeolia, and use it as a base for organizing revolt in Ionia. This, they claimed, was a distinct possibility, since they would be welcomed everywhere. Their aim would be to cut Athens off from this, the greatest of her sources of revenue, and at the same time to involve her in more expense if she decided to maintain a fleet against them. They said, too, that they thought they could persuade Pissuthnes to come in on their side.

Not even this plan commended itself to Alcidas, whose main idea was, since he had been too late for Mytilene, to get back to the Peloponnese as soon as possible. He therefore put out from Embatum and sailed along the coast to the Teian town of Myonnesus. There he put to death most of the prisoners whom he had taken on the voyage. Later, when he was at anchor at Ephesus, a deputation of Samians from Anaia came to him and told him that it was not the right way to set about the liberation of Hellas by massacring people who had never raised a hand against him, who were not his enemies, but only allies of Athens under compulsion, and that unless he stopped, so far from turning any enemies into friends, he would turn most of his friends into enemies.

Alcidas saw the force of this argument and released all the prisoners from Chios whom he still had and a few others from other places. For when his fleet was sighted the people made no effort to run away; instead they came to meet the ships, under the impression that they must be Athenian, since they never even imagined that, with Athens in control of the sea, a Peloponnesian fleet would come across to Ionia.

From Ephesus Alcidas set sail in a hurry and fled. While he was still at anchor off Clarus he had been sighted by the Athenian ships, the *Salaminia* and the *Paralus,* which happened to be sailing from Athens. So, in fear of a pursuit, he set out across the open sea with the firm intention of not putting in to land anywhere at all, if he could help it, until he reached the Peloponnese.

Meanwhile news of his presence had reached Paches and the Athenians from Erythraea—in fact from all directions. For, since the cities of Ionia were not fortified, the inhabitants were greatly afraid that the Peloponnesians, even if they had no intention of remaining, might, as they sailed along, make landings and lay waste the towns. And now the *Paralus* and the *Salaminia* arrived with the news that they had seen the enemy fleet at Clarus. Paches, therefore, immediately set out in pursuit and went after them as far as the island of Patmos. From here he turned back again, since it appeared that Alcidas had got away out of reach.

In fact, since he had not managed to overtake the Peloponnesian on the open sea, he thought it a lucky thing that they had not been discovered anywhere else where they would have been compelled to build a fortified camp, and so have given the Athenians the trouble of organizing a regular blockade by sea and land.

As he sailed back along the coast he put in, among other places, at Notium, the harbour of Colophon, where the Colophonians had settled after the upper city had been captured, at about the time of the second Peloponnesian invasion of Attica, by Itamenes and his foreign troops who had been called in as a result of the political ambition of individuals. However, the exiles who had settled at Notium again split up into two hostile parties. One of these called in Arcadian and foreign mercenaries from Pissuthnes, quartered them in a part of the town which they cut off from the rest by a wall, and so formed a separate state with the help of the pro-Persian party among the Colophonians from the upper city. The other party at Notium had fled into exile and now called in Paches. Paches invited Hippias, the general of the Arcadian mercenaries inside the fortification, to meet him for a discussion, promising that, if no agreement was reached, he would see that he got back again safe and sound to the fortification. Hippias therefore came out to meet Paches, who put him under arrest, though not into chains. He then made a sudden attack and took the fortification by surprise. He put to death all the Arcadian and foreign troops who were inside, and, later, as he had promised, he brought Hippias back there, and, as soon as he was inside, he had him seized and shot down with arrows. He handed over Notium to the Colophonians, excluding the pro-Persian party among them. Later the Athenians sent out settlers and made a colony of the place under Athenian laws, after having collected together all the Colophonians who could be found in other cities.

Paches then returned to Mytilene and reduced Pyrrha and Eresus. He found the Spartan Salaethus in hiding in the city and sent him to Athens, together with the Mytilenians whom he had placed in Tenedos and others whom he considered implicated in the organization of the revolt. He also sent back the greater part of his army. He himself stayed behind with the remainder of his forces and settled matters in Mytilene and the rest of Lesbos as he thought fit.

THE MYTILENIAN DEBATE

When Salaethus and the other prisoners reached Athens, the Athenians immediately put Salaethus to death in spite of the fact that he undertook, among other things, to have the Peloponnesians withdrawn from Plataea, which was still being besieged. They then discussed what was to be done with the other prisoners and, in their angry mood, decided to put to death not only those now in their hands but also the entire adult male population of Mytilene, and to make slaves of the women and children. What they held against Mytilene was the fact that it had revolted even though it was not a subject state, like the others, and the bitterness of their feelings was considerably increased by the fact that the Peloponnesian fleet had actually dared to cross over to Ionia to support the revolt. This, it was thought, could never have happened unless the revolt had been long premeditated. So they sent a trireme to Paches to inform him of what had been decided, with orders to put the Mytilenians to death immediately.

Next day, however, there was a sudden change of feeling and people began to think how cruel and how unprecedented such a decision was—to destroy not only the guilty, but the entire population of a state. Observing this, the deputation from Mytilene which was in Athens and the Athenians who were supporting them approached the authorities with a view to having the question debated again. They won their point the more easily because the authorities themselves saw clearly that most of the citizens were wanting someone to give them a chance of reconsidering the matter. So an assembly was called at once. Various opinions were expressed on both sides, and Cleon, the son of Cleaenetus, spoke again. It was he who had been responsible for passing the original motion for putting the Mytilenians to death. He was remarkable among the Athenians for the violence of his character, and at this time he exercised by far the greatest influence over the people. He spoke as follows:

"Personally I have had occasion often enough already to observe that a democracy is incapable of governing others, and I am all the more convinced of this when I see how you are now changing your minds about the Mytilenians. Because fear and conspiracy play no part in your daily relations with each other, you imagine that the same thing is true of your allies, and you fail to see that when you allow them to persuade you to make a mistaken decision and when you give way to your own feelings of compassion you are being guilty of a kind of weakness which is dangerous to you and which will not make them love you any more. What you do not realize is that your empire is a tyranny exercised over subjects who do not like it and who are always plotting against you; you will not make them obey you by injuring your own interests in order to do them a favour; your leadership depends on superior strength and not on any goodwill of theirs. And this is the very worst thing—to pass measures and then not to abide by them. We should realize that a city is better off with bad laws, so long as they remain fixed, than with good laws that are constantly being altered, that lack of learning combined with sound common sense is more helpful than the kind of cleverness that gets out of hand, and that as a general rule states are better governed by the man in the street than by intellectuals. These are the sort of people who want to appear wiser than the laws, who want to get their own way in every general discussion, because they feel that they cannot show off their intelligence in matters of greater importance, and who, as a result, very often bring ruin on their country. But the other kind—the people who are not so confident in their own intelligence—are prepared to admit that the laws are wiser than they are and that they lack the ability to pull to pieces a speech made by a good speaker; they are unbiased judges, and not people taking part in some kind of a competition; so things usually go well when they are in control. We statesmen, too, should try to be like them, instead of being carried away by mere cleverness and a desire to show off our intelligence and so giving you, the people, advice which we do not really believe in ourselves.

"As for me, I have not altered my opinion, and I am amazed at those who have proposed a reconsideration of the question of Mytilene, thus causing a delay which is all to the advantage of the guilty party. After a lapse of time the injured party will lose the edge of his anger when he comes to act against those who have wronged him; whereas the best punishment and the one most fitted to the crime is when reprisals follow immediately. I shall be amazed, too, if anyone contradicts me and attempts to prove that the harm done to us by Mytilene is really a good thing for us, or that when we suffer ourselves we are somehow doing harm to our allies. It is obvious that anyone who is going to say this must either have such confidence in his powers as an orator that he will struggle to persuade you that what has been finally settled was, on the contrary, not decided at all, or else he must have been bribed to put together some elaborate speech with which he will try to lead you out of the right track. But in competitions of this sort the prizes go to others and the state takes all the danger for herself. The blame is yours, for stupidly instituting these competitive displays. You have become regular speech-goers, and as for action, you merely listen to accounts of it; if something is to be done in the future you estimate the possibilities by hearing a good speech on the subject, and as for the past you rely not so much on the facts which you have seen with your own eyes as on what you have heard about them in some clever piece of verbal criticism. Any novelty in an argument deceives you at once, but when the argument is tried and proved you become unwilling to follow it; you look with suspicion on what is normal and are the slaves of every paradox that comes your way. The chief wish of each one of you is to be able to make a speech himself, and, if you cannot do that, the next best thing is to compete with those who can make this sort of speech by not looking as though you were at all out of your depth while you listen to the views put forward, by applauding a good point even before it is made, and by being as quick at seeing how an argument is going to be developed as you are slow at understanding what in the end it will lead to. What you are looking for all the time is something that is, I should say, outside the range of ordinary experience, and yet you cannot even think straight about the facts of life that are before you. You are simply victims of your own pleasure in listening, and are more like an audience sitting at the feet of a professional lecturer than a parliament discussing matters of state.

"I am trying to stop you behaving like this, and I say that no single city has ever done you the harm that Mytilene has done. Personally I can make allowances for those who revolt because they find your rule intolerable or because they have been forced into it by enemy action. Here, however, we have the case of people living on an island, behind their own fortifications, with nothing to fear from our enemies except an attack by sea against which they were adequately protected by their own force of triremes; they had their own independent government and they were treated by us with the greatest consideration. Now, to act as they acted is not what I should call a revolt (for people only revolt when they have been badly treated); it is a case of calculated aggression, of deliberately taking sides with our bitterest enemies in order to destroy us. And this is far worse than if they had made war against us simply to increase their own power. They learned nothing from the fate of those of their neighbours who had already revolted and been subdued; the prosperity which they enjoyed did not make them hesitate before running into danger; confident in the future, they declared war on us, with hopes that indeed extended beyond their means, though still fell short of their desires. They made up their minds to put might first and right second, choosing the moment when they thought they would win, and then making their unprovoked attack upon us.

"The fact is that when great prosperity comes suddenly and unexpectedly to a state, it usually breeds arrogance; in most cases it is safer for people to enjoy an average amount of success rather than something which is out of all proportion; and it is easier, I should say, to ward off hardship than to maintain happiness. What we should have done long ago with the Mytilenians was to treat them in exactly the same way as all the rest; then they would never have grown so arrogant; for it is a general rule of human nature that people despise those who treat them well and look up to those who make no concessions. Let them now therefore have the punishment which their crime deserves. Do not put the blame on the aristocracy and say that the people were innocent. The fact is that the whole lot of them attacked you together, although the people might have come over to us and, if they had, would now be back again in control of their city. Yet, instead of doing this, they thought it safer to share the dangers, and join in the revolt of the aristocracy.

"Now think of your allies. If you are going to give the same punishment to those who are forced to revolt by your enemies and those who do so of their own accord, can you not see that they will all revolt upon the slightest pretext, when success means freedom and failure brings no very dreadful consequences? Meanwhile we shall have to spend our money and risk our lives against state after state; if our efforts are successful, we shall recover a city that is in ruins, and so lose the future revenue from it, on which our strength is based; and if we fail to subdue it, we shall have more enemies to deal with in addition to those we have already, and we shall spend the time which ought to be used in resisting our present foes in making war on our own allies.

"Let there be no hope, therefore, held out to the Mytilenians that we, either as a result of a good speech or a large bribe, are likely to forgive them on the grounds that it is only human to make mistakes. There was nothing involuntary about the harm they did us; they knew what they were about and they planned it all beforehand; and one only forgives actions that were not deliberate. As for me, just as I was at first, so I am now, and I shall continue to impress on you the importance of not altering your previous decisions. To feel pity, to be carried away by the pleasure of hearing a clever argument, to listen to the claims of decency are three things that are entirely against the interests of an imperial power. Do not be guilty of them. As for compassion, it is proper to feel it in the case of people who are like ourselves and who will pity us in their turn, not in the case of those who, so far from having the same feelings towards us, must always and inevitably be our enemies. As for the speech-makers who give such pleasure by their arguments, they should hold their competitions on subjects which are less important, and not on a question where the state may have to pay a heavy penalty for its light pleasure, while the speakers themselves will no doubt be enjoying splendid rewards for their splendid arguments. And a sense of decency is only felt towards those who are going to be our friends in future, not towards those who remain just as they were and as much our enemies as they ever have been.

"Let me sum the whole thing up. I say that, if you follow my advice, you will be doing the right thing as far as Mytilene is concerned and at the same time will be acting in your own interests; if you decide differently, you will not win them over, but you will be passing judgment on yourselves. For if they were justified in revolting, you must be wrong in holding power. If, however, whatever the rights or wrongs of it may be, you propose to hold power all the same, then your interest demands that these too, rightly or wrongly, must be punished. The only alternative is to surrender your empire, so that you can afford to go in for philanthropy. Make up your minds, therefore, to pay them back in their own coin, and do not make it look as though you who escaped their machinations are less quick to react than they who started them. Remember how they would have been likely to have treated you, if they had won, especially as they were the aggressors. Those who do wrong to a neighbour when there is no reason to do so are the ones who persevere to the point of destroying him, since they see the danger involved in allowing their enemy to survive. For he who has suffered for no good reason is a more dangerous enemy, if he escapes, than the one who has both done and suffered injury.

"I urge you, therefore, not to be traitors to your own selves. Place yourselves in imagination at the moment when you first suffered and remember how then you would have given anything to have them in your power. Now pay them back for it, and do not grow soft just at this present moment, forgetting meanwhile the danger that hung over your heads then. Punish them as they deserve, and make an example of them to your other allies, plainly showing that revolt will be punished by death. Once they realize this, you will not have so often to neglect the war with your enemies because you are fighting with your own allies."

So Cleon spoke. After him Diodotus, the son of Eucrates, who in the previous assembly also had vigorously opposed the motion to put the Mytilenians to death, came forward again on this occasion and spoke as follows:

"I do not blame those who have proposed a new debate on the subject of Mytilene, and I do not share the view which we have heard expressed, that it is a bad thing to have frequent discussions on matters of importance. Haste and anger are, to my mind, the two greatest obstacles to wise counsel—haste, that usually goes with folly, anger, that is the mark of primitive and narrow minds. And anyone who maintains that words cannot be a guide to action must be either a fool or one with some personal interest at stake; he is a fool, if he imagines that it is possible to deal with the uncertainties of the future by any other medium, and he is personally interested if his aim is to persuade you into some disgraceful action, and, knowing that he cannot make a good speech in a bad cause, he tries to frighten his opponents and his hearers by some good-sized pieces of misrepresentation. Then still more intolerable are those who go further and accuse a speaker of making a kind of exhibition of himself, because he is paid for it. If it was only ignorance with which he was being charged, a speaker who failed to win his case could retire from the debate and still be thought an honest man, if not a very intelligent one. But when corruption is imputed, he will be suspect if he wins his case, and if he loses it, will be regarded as dishonest and stupid at the same time. This sort of thing does the city no good; her counsellors will be afraid to speak and she will be deprived of their services. Though certainly it would be the best possible thing for the city if these gentlemen whom I have been describing lacked the power to express themselves; we should not then be persuaded into making so many mistakes.

"The good citizen, instead of trying to terrify the opposition, ought to prove his case in fair argument; and a wise state, without giving special honours to its best counsellors, will certainly not deprive them of the honour they already enjoy; and when a man's advice is not taken, he should not even be disgraced, far less penalized. In this way successful speakers will be less likely to pursue further honours by speaking against their own convictions in order to make themselves popular, and unsuccessful speakers, too, will not struggle to win over the people by the same acts of flattery. What we do here, however, is exactly the opposite. Then, too, if a man gives the best possible advice but is under the slightest suspicion of being influenced by his own private profit, we are so embittered by the idea (a wholly unproved one) of this profit of his, that we do not allow the state to receive the certain benefit of his good advice. So a state of affairs has been reached where a good proposal honestly put forward is just as suspect as something thoroughly bad, and the result is that just as the speaker who advocates some monstrous measure has to win over the people by deceiving them, so also a man with good advice to give has to tell lies if he expects to be believed. And because of this refinement in intellectuality, the state is put into a unique position; it is only she to whom no one can ever do a good turn openly and without deception. For if one openly performs a patriotic action, the reward for one's pains is to be thought to have made something oneself on the side. Yet in spite of all this we are discussing matters of the greatest importance, and we who give you our advice ought to be resolved to look rather further into things than you whose attention is occupied only with the surface—especially as we can be held to account for the advice we give, while you are not accountable for the way in which you receive it. For indeed you would take rather more care over your decisions, if the proposer of a motion and those who voted for it were all subject to the same penalties. As it is, on the occasions when some emotional impulse on your part has led you into disaster, you turn upon the one man who made the original proposal and you let yourself off, in spite of the fact that you are many and in spite of the fact that you were just as wrong as he was.

"However, I have not come forward to speak about Mytilene in any spirit of contradiction or with any wish to accuse anyone. If we are sensible people, we shall see that the question is not so much whether they are guilty as whether we are making the right decision for ourselves. I might prove that they are the most guilty people in the world, but it does not follow that I shall propose the death penalty, unless that is in your interests; I might argue that they deserve to be forgiven, but should not recommend forgiveness unless that seemed to me the best thing for the state.

"In my view our discussion concerns the future rather than the present. One of Cleon's chief points is that to inflict the death penalty will be useful to us in the future as a means for deterring other cities from revolt; but I, who am just as concerned as he is with the future, am quite convinced that this is not so. And I ask you not to reject what is useful in my speech for the sake of what is specious in his. You may well find his speech attractive, because it fits in better with your present angry feelings about the Mytilenians; but this is not a law-court, where we have to consider what is fit and just; it is a political assembly, and the question is how Mytilene can be most useful to Athens.

"Now, in human societies the death penalty has been laid down for many offences less serious than this one. Yet people still take risks when they feel sufficiently confident. No one has ever yet risked committing a crime which he thought he could not carry out successfully. The same is true of states. None has ever yet rebelled in the belief that it had insufficient resources, either in itself or from its allies, to make the attempt. Cities and individuals alike, all are by nature disposed to do wrong, and there is no law that will prevent it, as is shown by the fact that men have tried every kind of punishment, constantly adding to the list, in the attempt to find greater security from criminals. It is likely that in early times the punishments even for the greatest crimes were not as severe as they are now, but the laws were still broken, and in the course of time the death penalty became generally introduced. Yet even with this, the laws are still broken. Either, therefore, we must discover some fear more

potent than the fear of death, or we must admit that here
certainly we have not got an adequate deterrent. So long as
poverty forces men to be bold, so long as the insolence and pride
of wealth nourish their ambitions, and in the other accidents of
life they are continually dominated by some incurable master
passion or another, so long will their impulses continue to drive
them into danger. Hope and desire persist throughout and cause
the greatest calamities—one leading and the other following,
one conceiving the enterprise, and the other suggesting that it
will be successful—invisible factors, but more powerful than the
terrors that are obvious to our eyes. Then too, the idea that
fortune will be on one's side plays as big a part as anything else
in creating a mood of over-confidence; for sometimes she does
come unexpectedly to one's aid, and so she tempts men to run
risks for which they are inadequately prepared. And this is
particularly true in the case of whole peoples, because they are
playing for the highest stakes—either for their own freedom or
for the power to control others—and each individual, when
acting as part of a community, has the irrational opinion that
his own powers are greater than in fact they are. In a word it
is impossible (and only the most simple-minded will deny this)
for human nature, when once seriously set upon a certain course,
to be prevented from following that course by the force of law
or by any other means of intimidation whatever.

"We must not, therefore, come to the wrong conclusions
through having too much confidence in the effectiveness of capital punishment, and we must not make the condition of rebels
desperate by depriving them of the possibility of repentance and
of a chance of atoning as quickly as they can for what they did.
Consider this now: at the moment, if a city has revolted and
realizes that the revolt cannot succeed, it will come to terms
while it is still capable of paying an indemnity and continuing
to pay tribute afterwards. But if Cleon's method is adopted,
can you not see that every city will not only make much more

careful preparations for revolt, but will also hold out against siege to the very end, since to surrender early or late means just the same thing? This is, unquestionably, against our interests— to spend money on a siege because of the impossibility of coming to terms, and, if we capture the place, to take over a city that is in ruins so that we lose the future revenue from it. And it is just on this revenue that our strength in war depends.

"Our business, therefore, is not to injure ourselves by acting like a judge who strictly examines a criminal; instead we should be looking for a method by which, employing moderation in our punishments, we can in future secure for ourselves the full use of those cities which bring us important contributions. And we should recognize that the proper basis of our security is in good administration rather than in the fear of legal penalties. As it is, we do just the opposite: when we subdue a free city, which was held down by force and has, as we might have expected, tried to assert its independence by revolting, we think that we ought to punish it with the utmost severity. But the right way to deal with free people is this—not to inflict tremendous punishments on them after they have revolted, but to take tremendous care of them before this point is reached, to prevent them even contemplating the idea of revolt, and, if we do have to use force with them, to hold as few as possible of them responsible for this.

"Consider what a mistake you would be making on this very point, if you took Cleon's advice. As things are now, in all the cities the democracy is friendly to you; either it does not join in with the oligarchies in revolting, or, if it is forced to do so, it remains all the time hostile to the rebels, so that when you go to war with them, you have the people on your side. But if you destroy the democratic party at Mytilene, who never took any hand in the revolt and who, as soon as they got arms, voluntarily gave the city up to you, you will first of all be guilty of killing those who have helped you, and, secondly, you will be doing exactly what the reactionary classes want most. For now, when they start a revolt, they will have the people on their side from the beginning, because you have already made it clear that the same punishment is laid down both for the guilty and the innocent. In fact, however, even if they were guilty, you should pretend that they were not, in order to keep on your side the one element that is still not opposed to you. It is far more useful to us, I think, in preserving our empire, that we should voluntarily put up with injustice than that we should justly put to death the wrong people. As for Cleon's point—that in this act of vengeance both justice and self-interest are combined—this is not a case where such a combination is at all possible.

"I call upon you, therefore, to accept my proposal as the better one. Do not be swayed too much by pity or by ordinary decent feelings. I, no more than Cleon, wish you to be influenced by such emotions. It is simply on the basis of the argument which you have heard that I ask you to be guided by me, to try at your leisure the men whom Paches has considered guilty and sent to Athens, and to allow the rest to live in their own city. In following this course you will be acting wisely for the future and will be doing something which will make your enemies fear you now. For those who make wise decisions are more formidable to their enemies than those who rush madly into strong action."

This was the speech of Diodotus. And now, when these two motions, each so opposed to each, had been put forward, the Athenians, in spite of the recent change of feeling, still held conflicting opinions, and at the show of hands the votes were nearly equal. However, the motion of Diodotus was passed.

Immediately another trireme was sent out in all haste, since they feared that, unless it overtook the first trireme, they would find on their arrival that the city had been destroyed. The first trireme had a start of about twenty-four hours. The ambassadors from Mytilene provided wine and barley for the crew and promised great rewards if they arrived in time, and so the men made such speed on the voyage that they kept on rowing while they took their food (which was barley mixed with oil and wine) and rowed continually, taking it in turn to sleep. Luckily they had no wind against them, and as the first ship was not hurrying on its distasteful mission, while they were pressing on with such speed, what happened was that the first ship arrived so little ahead of them that Paches had just had time to read the decree and to prepare to put it into force, when the second ship put into the harbour and prevented the massacre. So narrow had been the escape of Mytilene.

The other Mytilenians whom Paches had sent to Athens as being the ones chiefly responsible for the revolt were, on the motion of Cleon, put to death by the Athenians. There were rather more than 1,000 of them. The Athenians also destroyed the fortifications of Mytilene and took over their navy. Afterwards, instead of imposing a tribute on Lesbos, they divided all the land, except that belonging to the Methymnians, into 3,000 holdings, 300 of which were set apart as sacred for the gods, while the remainder was distributed by lot to Athenian shareholders, who were sent out to Lesbos. The Lesbians agreed with these shareholders to pay a yearly rent of two minae for each holding, and cultivated the land themselves. The Athenians also took over all the towns on the mainland that had been under the control of Mytilene. So for the future the Mytilenians became subjects of Athens. This completes the account of what took place in Lesbos.

THE MELIAN DIALOGUE[7]

Next summer Alcibiades sailed to Argos with twenty ships and seized 300 Argive citizens who were still suspected of being

---

[7] [416–415 B.C. Since the Revolt of Mytilene, the war has continued on a variety of fronts.]

pro-Spartan. These were put by the Athenians into the nearby islands under Athenian control.

The Athenians also made an expedition against the island of Melos. They had thirty of their own ships, six from Chios, and two from Lesbos; 1,200 hoplites, 300 archers, and twenty mounted archers, all from Athens; and about 1,500 hoplites from the allies and the islanders.

The Melians are a colony from Sparta. They had refused to join the Athenian empire like the other islanders, and at first had remained neutral without helping either side; but afterwards, when the Athenians had brought force to bear on them by laying waste their land, they had become open enemies of Athens.

Now the generals Cleomedes, the son of Lycomedes, and Tisias, the son of Tisimachus, encamped with the above force in Melian territory and, before doing any harm to the land, first of all sent representatives to negotiate. The Melians did not invite these representatives to speak before the people, but asked them to make the statement for which they had come in front of the governing body and the few. The Athenian representatives then spoke as follows:

"So we are not to speak before the people, no doubt in case the mass of the people should hear once and for all and without interruption an argument from us which is both persuasive and incontrovertible, and should so be led astray. This, we realize, is your motive in bringing us here to speak before the few. Now suppose that you who sit here should make assurance doubly sure. Suppose that you, too, should refrain from dealing with every point in detail in a set speech, and should instead interrupt us whenever we say something controversial and deal with that before going on to the next point? Tell us first whether you approve of this suggestion of ours."

The Council of the Melians replied as follows:

"No one can object to each of us putting forward our own views in a calm atmosphere. That is perfectly reasonable. What is scarcely consistent with such a proposal is the present threat, indeed the certainty, of your making war on us. We see that you have come prepared to judge the argument yourselves, and that the likely end of it all will be either war, if we prove that we are in the right, and so refuse to surrender, or else slavery."

ATHENIANS: If you are going to spend the time in enumerating your suspicions about the future, or if you have met here for any other reason except to look the facts in the face and on the basis of these facts to consider how you can save your city from destruction, there is no point in our going on with this discussion. If, however, you will do as we suggest, then we will speak on.

MELIANS: It is natural and understandable that people who are placed as we are should have recourse to all kinds of arguments and different points of view. However, you are right in saying that we are met together here to discuss the safety of our country and, if you will have it so, the discussion shall proceed on the lines that you have laid down.

ATHENIANS: Then we on our side will use no fine phrases saying, for example, that we have a right to our empire because we defeated the Persians, or that we have come against you now because of the injuries you have done us—a great mass of words that nobody would believe. And we ask you on your side not to imagine that you will influence us by saying that you, though a colony of Sparta, have not joined Sparta in the war, or that you have never done us any harm. Instead we recommend that you should try to get what it is possible for you to get, taking into consideration what we both really do think; since you know as well as we do that, when these matters are discussed by practical people, the standard of justice depends on the equality of power to compel and that in fact the strong do what they have the power to do and the weak accept what they have to accept.

MELIANS: Then in our view (since you force us to leave justice out of account and to confine ourselves to self-interest)—in our view it is at any rate useful that you should not destroy a principle that is to the general good of all men—namely, that in the case of all who fall into danger there should be such a thing as fair play and just dealing, and that such people should be allowed to use and to profit by arguments that fall short of a mathematical accuracy. And this is a principle which affects you as much as anybody, since your own fall would be visited by the most terrible vengeance and would be an example to the world.

ATHENIANS: As for us, even assuming that our empire does come to an end, we are not despondent about what would happen next. One is not so much frightened of being conquered by a power which rules over others, as Sparta does (not that we are concerned with Sparta now), as of what would happen if a ruling power is attacked and defeated by its own subjects. So far as this point is concerned, you can leave it to us to face the risks involved. What we shall do now is to show you that it is for the good of our own empire that we are here and that it is for the preservation of your city that we shall say what we are going to say. We do not want any trouble in bringing you into our empire, and we want you to be spared for the good both of yourselves and of ourselves.

MELIANS: And how could it be just as good for us to be the slaves as for you to be the masters?

ATHENIANS: You, by giving in, would save yourselves from disaster; we, by not destroying you, would be able to profit from you.

MELIANS: So you would not agree to our being neutral, friends instead of enemies, but allies of neither side?

ATHENIANS: No, because it is not so much your hostility that injures us; it is rather the case that, if we were on friendly terms with you, our subjects would regard that as a sign of weakness in us, whereas your hatred is evidence of our power.

MELIANS: Is that your subjects' idea of fair play—that no distinction should be made between people who are quite unconnected with you and people who are mostly your own colonists or else rebels whom you have conquered?

ATHENIANS: So far as right and wrong are concerned they think that there is no difference between the two, that those who still preserve their independence do so because they are strong, and that if we fail to attack them it is because we are afraid. So that by conquering you we shall increase not only the size but the security of our empire. We rule the sea and you are islanders, and weaker islanders too than the others; it is therefore particularly important that you should not escape.

MELIANS: But do you think there is no security for you in what we suggest? For here again, since you will not let us mention justice, but tell us to give in to your interests, we, too, must tell you what our interests are and, if yours and ours happen to coincide, we must try to persuade you of the fact. Is it not certain that you will make enemies of all states who are at present neutral, when they see what is happening here and naturally conclude that in course of time you will attack them too? Does not this mean that you are strengthening the enemies you have already and are forcing others to become your enemies even against their intentions and their inclinations?

ATHENIANS: As a matter of fact we are not so much frightened of states on the continent. They have their liberty, and this means that it will be a long time before they begin to take precautions against us. We are more concerned about islanders like yourselves, who are still unsubdued, or subjects who have already become embittered by the constraint which our empire imposes on them. These are the people who are most likely to act in a reckless manner and to bring themselves and us, too, into the most obvious danger.

MELIANS: Then surely, if such hazards are taken by you to keep your empire and by your subjects to escape from it, we who are still free would show ourselves great cowards and weaklings if we failed to face everything that comes rather than submit to slavery.

ATHENIANS: No, not if you are sensible. This is no fair fight, with honour on one side and shame on the other. It is rather a question of saving your lives and not resisting those who are far too strong for you.

MELIANS: Yet we know that in war fortune sometimes makes the odds more level than could be expected from the difference in numbers of the two sides. And if we surrender, then all our hope is lost at once, whereas, so long as we remain in action, there is still a hope that we may yet stand upright.

ATHENIANS: Hope, that comforter in danger! If one already has solid advantages to fall back upon, one can indulge in hope. It may do harm, but will not destroy one. But hope is by nature an expensive commodity, and those who are risking their all on one cast find out what it means only when they are already ruined; it never fails them in the period when such a knowledge would enable them to take precautions. Do not let this happen to you, you who are weak and whose fate depends on a single movement of the scale. And do not be like those people who, as so commonly happens, miss the chance of saving themselves in a human and practical way, and when every clear and distinct hope has left them in their adversity, turn to what is blind and vague, to prophecies and oracles and such things which by encouraging hope lead men to ruin.

MELIANS: It is difficult, and you may be sure that we know it, for us to oppose your power and fortune, unless the terms be equal. Nevertheless we trust that the gods will give us fortune as good as yours, because we are standing for what is right against what is wrong; and as for what we lack in power, we trust that it will be made up for by our alliance with the Spartans, who are bound, if for no other reason, then for honour's sake, and because we are their kinsmen, to come to our help. Our confidence, therefore, is not so entirely irrational as you think.

ATHENIANS: So far as the favour of the gods is concerned, we think we have as much right to that as you have. Our aims and our actions are perfectly consistent with the beliefs men hold about the gods and with the principles which govern their own conduct. Our opinion of the gods and our knowledge of men lead us to conclude that it is a general and necessary law of nature to rule whatever one can. This is not a law that we made ourselves, nor were we the first to act upon it when it was made. We found it already in existence, and we shall leave it to exist forever among those who come after us. We are merely acting in accordance with it, and we know that you or anybody else with the same power as ours would be acting in precisely the same way. And therefore, so far as the gods are concerned, we see no good reason why we should fear to be at a disadvantage. But with regard to your views about Sparta and your confidence that she, out of a sense of honour, will come to your aid, we must say that we congratulate you on your simplicity but do not envy you your folly. In matters that concern themselves or their own constitution the Spartans are quite remarkably good; as for their relations with others, that is a long story, but it can be expressed shortly and clearly by saying that of all people we know, the Spartans are most conspicuous for believing that what they like doing is honourable and what suits their interests is just. And this kind of attitude is not going to be of much help to you in your absurd quest for safety at the moment.

MELIANS: But this is the very point where we can feel most sure. Their own self-interest will make them refuse to betray their own colonists, the Melians, for that would mean losing the confidence of their friends among the Hellenes and doing good to their enemies.

ATHENIANS: You seem to forget that if one follows one's self-interest one wants to be safe, whereas the path of justice and honour involves one in danger. And, where danger is concerned, the Spartans are not, as a rule, very venturesome.

MELIANS: But we think that they would even endanger themselves for our sake and count the risk more worth taking than in the case of others, because we are so close to the Peloponnese that they could operate more easily, and because they can depend on us more than on others, since we are of the same race and share the same feelings.

ATHENIANS: Goodwill shown by the party that is asking for help does not mean security for the prospective ally. What is looked for is a positive preponderance of power in action. And the Spartans pay attention to this point even more than others do. Certainly they distrust their own native resources so much that when they attack a neighbour they bring a great army of allies with them. It is hardly likely therefore that, while we are in control of the sea, they will cross over to an island.

MELIANS: But they still might send others. The Cretan sea is a wide one, and it is harder for those who control it to intercept others than for those who want to slip through to do so safely. And even if they were to fail in this, they would turn against your own land and against those of your allies left unvisited by Brasidas. So, instead of troubling about a country which has nothing to do with you, you will find trouble nearer home, among your allies, and in your own country.

ATHENIANS: It is a possibility, something that has in fact happened before. It may happen in your case, but you are well aware that the Athenians have never yet relinquished a single siege operation through fear of others. But we are somewhat shocked to find that, though you announced your intention of discussing how you could preserve yourselves, in all this talk you have said absolutely nothing which could justify a man in thinking that he could be preserved. Your chief points are concerned with what you hope may happen in the future, while your actual resources are too scanty to give you a chance of survival against the forces that are opposed to you at this moment. You will therefore be showing an extraordinary lack of common sense if, after you have asked us to retire from this meeting, you still fail to reach a conclusion wiser than anything you have mentioned so far. Do not be led astray by a false sense of honour—a thing which often brings men to ruin when they are faced with an obvious danger that somehow affects their pride. For in many cases men have still been able to see the dangers ahead of them, but this thing called dishonour, this word, by its own force of seduction, has drawn them into a state where they have surrendered to an idea, while in fact they have fallen voluntarily into irrevocable disaster, in dishonour that is all the more dishonourable because it has come to them from their own folly rather than their misfortune. You, if you take the right view, will be careful to avoid this. You will see that there is nothing disgraceful in giving way to the greatest city in Hellas when she is offering you such reasonable terms—alliance on a tribute-paying basis and liberty to enjoy your own property. And, when you are allowed to choose between war and safety, you will not be so insensitively arrogant as to make the wrong choice. This is the safe rule—to stand up to one's equals, to behave with deference towards one's superiors, and to treat one's inferiors with moderation. Think it over again, then, when we have withdrawn from the meeting, and let this be a point that constantly recurs to your minds—that you are discussing the fate of your country, that you have only one country, and that its future for good or ill depends on this one single decision which you are going to make.

The Athenians then withdrew from the discussion. The Melians, left to themselves, reached a conclusion which was much the same as they had indicated in their previous replies. Their answer was as follows:

"Our decision, Athenians, is just the same as it was at first. We are not prepared to give up in a short moment the liberty which our city has enjoyed from its foundation for 700 years. We put our trust in the fortune that the gods will send and which has saved us up to now, and in the help of men—that is, of the Spartans; and so we shall try to save ourselves. But we invite you to allow us to be friends of yours and enemies to neither side, to make a treaty which shall be agreeable to both you and us, and so to leave our country."

The Melians made this reply, and the Athenians, just as they were breaking off the discussion, said:

"Well, at any rate, judging from this decision of yours, you seem to us quite unique in your ability to consider the future as something more certain than what is before your eyes, and to see uncertainties as realities, simply because you would like them to be so. As you have staked most on and trusted most in Spartans, luck, and hopes, so in all these you will find yourselves most completely deluded."

The Athenian representatives then went back to the army, and the Athenian generals, finding that the Melians would not submit, immediately commenced hostilities and built a wall completely round the city of Melos, dividing the work out among the various states. Later they left behind a garrison of some of their own and some allied troops to blockade the place by land and sea, and with the greater part of their army returned home. The force left behind stayed on and continued with the siege.

About the same time the Argives invaded Phliasia and were ambushed by the Phliasians and the exiles from Argos, losing about eighty men.

Then, too, the Athenians at Pylos captured a great quantity of plunder from Spartan territory. Not even after this did the Spartans renounce the treaty and make war, but they issued a proclamation saying that any of their people who wished to do so were free to make raids on the Athenians. The Corinthians also made some attacks on the Athenians because of private quarrels of their own, but the rest of the Peloponnesians stayed quiet.

Meanwhile the Melians made a night attack and captured the part of the Athenian lines opposite the marketplace. They killed some of the troops, and then, after bringing in corn and everything else useful that they could lay their hands on, retired again and made no further move, while the Athenians took measures to make their blockade more efficient in future. So the summer came to an end.

In the following winter the Spartans planned to invade the territory of Argos, but when the sacrifices for crossing the frontier turned out unfavourably, they gave up the expedition. The fact that they had intended to invade made the Argives suspect certain people in their city, some of whom they arrested, though others succeeded in escaping.

About this same time the Melians again captured another part of the Athenian lines where there were only a few of the garrison on guard. As a result of this, another force came out afterwards from Athens under the command of Philocrates, the son of Demeas. Siege operations were now carried on vigorously and, as there was also some treachery from inside, the Melians surrendered unconditionally to the Athenians, who put to death all the men of military age whom they took, and sold the women and children as slaves. Melos itself they took over for themselves, sending out later a colony of 500 men.